WEAPONS, CULTURE, AND SELF-INTEREST

WEAPONS, CULTURE, AND SELF-INTEREST

Soviet Defense Managers in the New Russia

Kimberly Marten Zisk

COLUMBIA UNIVERSITY PRESS   NEW YORK

Columbia University Press
Publishers Since 1893
New York   Chichester, West Sussex

Library of Congress Cataloging-in-Publication Data
Zisk, Kimberly Marten
    Weapons, culture, and self-interest : Soviet defense managers in
the new Russia / Kimberly Marten Zisk.
        p.   cm.
    Includes bibliographical references (p.   ) and index.
    ISBN 0–231–11078–2 (cloth : alk. paper). — ISBN 0–231–11079–0 (pbk.)
    1. Defense industries—Russia (Federation)—Management.   2. Executives—
Russia (Federation)—Attitudes.   3. Crisis management—Russia (Federation)—
case studies.   4. Social change—Russia (Federation)   I. Title.
HD9743.R92Z57   1998
338.4'76233'0947—dc21   97–26199

Casebound editions of Columbia University Press books are printed on permanent
and durable acid-free paper.
Printed in the United States of America
c 10 9 8 7 6 5 4 3 2 1
p 10 9 8 7 6 5 4 3 2 1

To Mom and Dad

Contents

Acknowledgments

A great many organizations and individuals helped make the research and writing of this book possible, and many people gave me helpful criticism and advice along the way.

I am grateful beyond measure for a two-year fellowship from the Social Science Research Council/MacArthur Foundation Program in International Peace and Security, which played a crucial role in getting this project off the ground. It gave me both time away from other responsibilities and the chance to spend an inspiring year at Harvard University attending seminars, auditing classes, reading the political economy literature, and making research contacts. Two workshops for SSRC/MacArthur fellows also introduced me to a supportive scholarly community whose suggestions and ideas helped to shape my research agenda.

Special thanks go to Samuel P. Huntington, director of Harvard's John M. Olin Institute for Strategic Studies, who provided me with a vibrant academic home during the first year of my project and went out of his way to include me in various Olin activities. I benefited from my interaction with all the members of the Olin Institute community and especially from Olin's joint project with the Diplomatic Academy of the Russian Foreign Ministry, which issued the official invitation for my research trip to Russia and allowed me to present my work in progress to a lively audience of Russian diplomatic students and professionals. Bruce Porter and David Rivera were especially helpful in Moscow.

I am grateful to Timothy Colton, who as director of Harvard's Russian Research Center made me feel welcome even though I was not an official member of that community, and to Celeste Wallander, who included me in her Olin Foundation–sponsored project on Russian foreign policy after the cold war and was (as always) a supportive colleague and good friend.

A generous grant from the National Council for Soviet and East European Research provided me with graduate research assistants for a year, allowed me to spend three months in Russia doing field research, and also paid for research visits to Stanford University, the University of Birmingham, and the Library of Congress.

I owe an immense debt to the Stanford University Center for International Security and Arms Control (CISAC) and especially to David Holloway, who as its codirector gave me office space for a month, access to a large library of files on current events in the Russian defense industry, and, perhaps most important, the opportunity to accompany a CISAC team on visits to four defense enterprises in the Moscow region in September 1994. I am grateful for the encouragement and assistance provided by all the members of the CISAC defense conversion project, including (among others) David Bernstein, Susan Gates, Michael McFaul, Elaine Naugle, and Tova Perlmutter.

I wrote this book while a faculty member at the Ohio State University. I am thankful for the research support I received during the years I was there from the Graduate School, the College of Social and Behavioral Sciences (and its dean, Randall Ripley), and the Political Science Department (and its chair, Paul Allen Beck), the Mershon Center, and the Slavic Center. The Mershon Center, first under the direction of Charles F. Hermann and later under Richard K. Herrmann and then R. Ned Lebow, provided me with a quiet office and the resources necessary for completion of the manuscript. Several members of the Political Science faculty gave me useful criticism on my work in progress, and my thanks go to Rick Herrmann, Kevin O'Brien, and the members of the Junior Faculty Seminar. Tanya Charlick-Paley, Ted Lehmann, Sharon Shible, and Courtney Smith provided able research assistance, and I owe an additional note of thanks to Sharon for being my courageous and steadfast research companion in Russia. I especially appreciate Margaret G. Hermann's kindness during my OSU years.

I am grateful to Julian Cooper, who allowed me to use the resources of the Centre for Russian and East European Studies library at the University of Birmingham, and to Jared Ingersoll-Casey, who as the Slavic librarian at Ohio State helped me get access to the sources I needed. A special note of appreciation goes to Helen Sullivan, Slavic librarian at the University of Illinois at Urbana-Champaign, who kindly faxed me articles from newspaper issues unavailable elsewhere. I am also grateful to all those Russians who remain off the record, who helped me to arrange meetings or find sources or agreed to be interviewed by me.

Along the way I received advice and criticism from a wide variety of scholars, and in addition to all those mentioned above, I am particularly grateful to Marianne Afanasieva, Eva Busza, Jeff Checkel, Elena Denezhkina, Matthew Evangelista, Clifford Gaddy, Ethan Kapstein, Peter Katzenstein, Jeffrey Knopf, James Richter, Randall Stone, and Kathryn Stoner-Weiss for their input on pieces of the project in progress. Special thanks go to those who read and critiqued the entire manuscript as various drafts became available, especially Eileen Crumm, Peter Almquist, and David Holloway.

Kate Wittenberg has been a marvelous editor, and I greatly appreciate the encouragement, advice, and enthusiasm she has provided for this project at Columbia University Press. I am also grateful to Jack Snyder for his advice and vote of confidence and to Sarah St. Onge for copyediting.

I am thankful to my brother-in-law Stephen Zisk and his wife, Veronica McClure, who showed their incredible generosity by giving me a roof over my head during the year I was in Boston. As always, I am indebted to my husband, Matt, who has encouraged my independence and perseverance with love and understanding. This book is dedicated to my parents, Lynette and Gordon Marten, whose love and generosity started me on my way and have helped me ever since.

1　Soviet Defense Managers and Economic Upheaval

Imagine for a moment that the world as you know it has been turned suddenly upside down, like a game board being upended. One day the rules you had been playing by all your life were crystal clear, and you knew exactly who was on your team. The next day the rules were anybody's guess, the players changed by the minute, and you began to suspect that some of your long-time team members were cheating you. What would you do?

This was the situation Soviet defense enterprise managers faced during the transition to the new Russia. In Soviet times, these managers lived comfortable lives inside a closed network where everybody knew everybody else. To move up in the world, they pleased their patrons at the top, who took care of them in return. Managers were likewise expected to take care of the employees they supervised. Everyone's basic needs were met through a system of mutual help that prevented anyone from having to make many independent decisions. Then suddenly the framework crumbled. People stopped sheltering those who had been their responsibility, and resources dried up. A persistent rumor began to circulate that a more exciting game was now afoot, but the rules were complicated and alien, and information was scarce. Some old friends became untrustworthy. Meanwhile, those lower down in the network continued to cry out for help, constantly reminding managers of their traditional obligations.

While the players in this game happened to be Soviet defense enterprise managers, a parallel set of circumstances could easily befall other people, including ourselves. The rules of the old and new games might be different—perhaps the old game favored self-help, while the new game would force people into dependence on others—but the shock would be the same. History has repeatedly overturned existing economic systems. Whether it was seventeenth-century Native Americans first encountering European claims to private property, Polish landowners confronting the imposition of Soviet-style collectivism following World War II, or freed slaves in the Reconstruction-era South first facing economic independence, well-established social groups have often been challenged to react and adapt as best they can to upheaval in their economic environments. Even today's United States has encountered dramatic change, though it may happen more slowly: people are confronting a new economic reality. U.S. companies are challenged to compete in the differing business cultures of the new global marketplace; successful corporate executives are looking at the threat of unemployment because of downsizing; and the country may face the end of the welfare system as we know it.

This book aims to contribute to our understanding of how social groups react to systemic economic shock. It does this by examining one very important group: Soviet (now Russian) defense enterprise managers. In 1992 Russian defense enterprise managers faced two simultaneous economic upheavals: (1) the sudden restructuring of the state budget away from huge, subsidized, and guaranteed military purchases,[1] and (2) the increasingly likely prospect of enterprise privatization, with an end to state planning and ministerial control over directors' economic decisions. In their struggle to make it in the new Russia under the presidency of Boris Yeltsin, these managers confronted unimagined economic freedom and unimagined economic constraints, both of which were potentially terrifying. The military-industrial complex was plunged into crisis, and managers had to figure out for themselves how best to survive.

This crisis serves as a kind of natural experiment, allowing us to gain new insights about how people, especially powerful people, react to revolutionary circumstances. When those who are members of the political and economic elite of a well-established social system are confronted with radical change, how do they navigate? How quickly and how well do they adapt to (or even shape) the requirements of the new system?

These questions are particularly interesting to political scientists when they are framed in terms of a debate that splits the discipline from top to bottom today, namely, how best to describe people's underlying economic and political preferences and interests. Should we assume that virtually all people everywhere in the world act primarily to further their own economic self-interest, as many economists would have us believe? Or should we assume instead that people's motives and behavior are shaped by different cultural mindsets and diverse social habits, requiring deep study by anthropologists? Both of these approaches are reflected in the broad academic literature on political economy, which comes from two competing traditions (discussed more below): positive political economy, on the one hand, and economic sociology, on the other. These traditions reflect a profound divide among social scientists more generally about what drives economic and political behavior.[2]

To answer the question of how members of political and economic elites deal with radical change, why should we study Russian defense managers in particular? The truth is that we could look at many different instances across countries and across history where groups of people have reacted to revolutionary economic circumstances and find similarly interesting answers to the questions raised by this debate. But I have chosen to study this particular case in depth because it has vital implications for tomorrow's real-world problems of international security. If we understand why Russian defense enterprise managers have done what they have in the new economy, we can make better predictions about what will happen next.

This book focuses on three key institutions that structured the Russian defense manager's working life in the 1992–95 transition era and endure today. These are: (1) the large defense enterprises dating from the Soviet era (including industrial factories, design bureaus, and scientific institutes), where most managers continue to make their professional homes; (2) the web of official political authorities at both the local and the national ministry levels, with whom all defense managers must negotiate on a regular basis; and (3) the market-oriented spin-off firms that emerged from most Soviet defense enterprises, where many managers make most of their personal income. Once we understand the combination of material incentives and cultural ties that defines the typical manager's relationship to these institutions, we can gain new insights into how the managers and institutions interact with each other to influence important aspects of Russia's future. The political economy of the Russian defense sector is having an impact on everything from the cohesion of the vast Russian state to the likelihood that advanced Russian weapons or mass destruction technology will proliferate throughout the third world. How this particular social group reacts to crisis matters to all of us, not merely to theoreticians.

This book is in fact intended to be a bridge between political economy and international security studies, two areas of research that scholars have kept artificially separated for too long.[3] While many detailed and excellent studies of Russian defense industrial reform exist,[4] none is designed to speak to people from both traditions. In the following pages, I will discuss the relevant theoretical social science issues in more depth, and in the final section of this chapter, I will briefly foreshadow the factual findings and predictions of chapters 2 through 4, suggesting why and how these results may be useful to those interested more in policy than in theory.

Culture and Self-Interest

The question of how Soviet defense industrial managers reacted to systemic shock is tailor-made for a test of whether rational self-interest or cultural socialization better explains political and economic behavior. This is because the system these managers came from was filled with rules for social interaction that are markedly different from those that define successful behavior in a free-market economy. The system placed overwhelming importance on the need to meet or exceed the production targets set by the state plan every year. To accomplish this, managers needed to concentrate on two basic skills. First, they had to be able to bargain with state authorities to ensure that the plan they were given was one they were actually able to meet. The plan was not merely sent down from above as an unchanging directive. Instead, it was the result of negotiation and bargaining. Managers who were willing to work with state authorities got better deals than did those who went their own way. Second, managers needed to be able to cooperate with the groups of employees and colleagues who surrounded them, because success in fulfilling the plan depended on group performance, not individual initiative or productivity. Fundamentally, the Soviet system rewarded group effort and group cohesion, not individual achievement. Groups who exceeded plan targets were rewarded with bonuses and special access to scarce consumer goods. Managers needed to create group solidarity and a sense of group morale in order to get these benefits.

Now that system has evaporated. As the conspicuous consumption of the Moscow nouveaux riches and the prevalence of what one Russian observer has called "the siren call of predatory capitalism" show,[5] the new Russian business world of the early 1990s rewarded those who sacrificed group well-being and pursued individual wealth opportunistically and even violently. Following the social behavior patterns encouraged by Soviet society could have left one at a real material disadvantage in post–Soviet Russia.

Economic revolutions, such as the one Russia has undergone in recent years, give us a unique opportunity to assess how durable economic culture really is and how much socialization influences the choices people make.[6] In stable societies, it is hard to determine which goals motivate people. When the economic system does not undergo drastic change, it is often impossible to disentangle people's material self-interest from their emotional identification with societal norms of propriety and morality. This is because most societies reward their adult members materially for doing those things that they learned to do through socialization and education. For example, U.S. society has traditionally encouraged individual competitiveness in school, sports, and work. In turn, the U.S. political economy rewards individual achievement through such things as high salary differentials, career stratification, and (one could even argue) the use of a presidential, not parliamentary, political system, where the achievements and character of an individual candidate often outweigh the importance of party platforms. Japanese society presents a clear contrast to this. The Japanese school system encourages children to be oriented toward the group, and powerful political-economic networks in Japan ostracize those who as adults fail to practice group loyalty.[7] In both cases, an individual's material self-interest is best met by following behavior patterns inculcated by society since childhood.

Economic revolutions provide us with a before-and-after contrast that most stable societies cannot offer. In revolutionary circumstances, following old social norms is no longer the best way to get ahead, because the underlying economic incentive structures have changed. What effect, then, do economic revolutions have on the social behavior patterns established over lifetimes in previously stable societies? The existing literature's answers to this question fall into two categories.

The first category is made up of those who call themselves positive political economists. These scholars have tended to explain away culture and its attendant values and habits, viewing them either as window dressing or as tools to be used by those following the universal human pattern of self-interested materialism.[8] This school, which operates under the label of *rational self-interest*, argues that the most useful assumption to make about the behavior of people everywhere in the world, and especially about those among the economic and political elite, is that they act primarily to protect and expand their own individual wealth, property rights, and power over the distribution of resources.[9] By uncovering actors' underlying economic motives, this perspective claims to be able to explain most political behavior. Neither cultural attributes nor past socialization patterns should cause individuals to falter in their pursuit of material well-being.[10] Because Russian defense managers were powerful and well-connected actors in the Soviet system, they should have used the advantages they had (especially in terms of information) to seize opportunities during the transition era to enrich themselves as individuals. They should have made every attempt to adapt quickly to the demands of the largely unregulated market. Along the way, they should have discarded any old social obligations or ethical norms that no longer served their individual interests in the new system.[11]

In contrast, those labeling themselves practitioners of socioeconomics or historical institutionalism have argued that both the interests people pursue and the means they use to achieve them are influenced and changed by the social environments in which they live. Political and economic behavior is not limited to the search for wealth and power but includes such things as the upholding of social codes and societal values for their own sake and responsiveness to the demands of informal social networks.[12] Members of this *socialization* school argue that people's behavior is influenced and constrained not merely by objective economic, political, and legal structures but by informal behavioral norms and social customs that vary across cultures and societies. People are motivated to follow patterns of action that they learn are proper and socially acceptable through both the upbringing and education they receive as children and the experiences and rewards they gain as members of social networks throughout life. Hence the goals that individuals pursue are constructed by the social environment surrounding them,[13] and it would be a mistake to think that some kind of universal and objective notion of material self-interest can accurately capture their motivations.[14]

From this perspective, social norms are "sticky," because they tend to condition people's identities and values and are thus likely to continue to influence people's behavior even as rapid environmental change occurs.[15] Over time, the culture changes, but in the short term, people should turn to their past experiences and socialization for advice about how to proceed.[16] Because Russian defense managers were socialized into Soviet-era behavior patterns that stressed group welfare and the maintenance of collective well-being over the achievement of individual goals and individual wealth, these patterns should have been maintained even as managers made efforts to adapt and survive in a changed environment. Other Russian economic groups who were not well socialized into Soviet-era norms, such as the old black marketeers who sought profits even under communism or the young who came to maturity in the late 1980s when copying Western-style commercialism was the social fashion, would be the ones to thrive in a system that encourages individuals to be materialistic and self-regarding.[17]

The major point of contention between the two perspectives described above is the degree to which past socialization colors present behavior. From the rational self-interest perspective, the institutions surrounding people's lives merely *constrain* the means individuals can use to achieve their given ends in the here and now, without changing their goals and preferences.

Soviet defense managers were forced to follow the rules of the old game in order to get ahead when that was the dominant game in society. Now they should adapt in order to follow the rules of the new game of the market, following the siren call of capitalism and ignoring old obligations when they no longer further self-advancement. Under both systems, managers wanted to get ahead; it was merely the means for doing this that changed. From the socialization perspective, in contrast, institutions actually help to *condition* individuals' identities, thereby changing the goals and preferences they hold.[18] Soviet defense managers would be expected to have different goals and preferences from those of their counterparts in the West and as a result should not have made the same kinds of individual profit-maximizing choices that the average U.S. corporate executive might make in similar circumstances. Instead, Russian managers should have maintained the social norms and networks with which they were familiar and comfortable, even if that meant sacrificing opportunities for self-enrichment.

It is these two perspectives, then, that this study is designed to compare and test. While proponents of the two perspectives often argue against each other, they tend to portray their opposites in what we might call "straw man" terms, focusing their critiques on older or narrower scholarship that is easy to dismiss rather than on more subtle, nuanced, and hence convincing arguments.[19] This book tries to avoid that tendency and does not begin by taking a single perspective as its base. Instead it is designed to allow each perspective its own best say over the available evidence. By giving each perspective its due, a theoretical contribution can be made that adherents of both schools should take seriously.

My findings are based on evidence collected from sources reflecting a wide variety of geographic locales and military technologies throughout Russia. This variety means that these sources are likely to provide a good basis for understanding what has happened inside the "typical" Russian defense enterprise in the transition period. Indeed, the similarity of problems faced by defense enterprises across Russia has been striking, as I shall show in the chapters that follow. The sources I used include several Russian newspapers at the national level that frequently cover defense sector issues[20] and (what turned out to be more significant) a number of Russian newspapers published at the local level, in cities with a heavy concentration of defense enterprises.[21] Included in this second group are papers from St. Petersburg (known especially for military shipbuilding), Zelenograd (which was created as a closed military electronics city and only recently opened to outsiders), and Arzamas-16 (the still-closed flagship city of nuclear warhead research and construction) and, to a lesser extent, those from the region of Nizhnii Novgorod (which houses a wide variety of defense enterprises) and the city of Zhukovskii (famous for its aviation institute and test facilities). Local newspapers tend to go into much more depth about the political and economic situations faced by particular defense factories and institutes than does the central Russian press. Beyond press analysis, this book reflects the results of interviews I conducted at the Nizhnii Novgorod Arms Fair in September 1994, as well as during visits to four defense enterprises in the Moscow region at that time[22] and at meetings with defense industrial representatives in Moscow and St. Petersburg during several visits between 1991 and 1994. Where examples from studies conducted by other researchers fill crucial gaps in the available information or provide additional support or challenge to these findings, I cite them, too.

In the next two sections, I will draw out the arguments made by the two schools described above, so that the value of each can be compared against the other. In the final section, I will return to the question of how our theories allow us to understand better the real-world consequences of Russian defense enterprise reform.

Rational Self-Interest: Structure and Goals

The rational self-interest school of positive political economy assumes that the goal of maximizing individual wealth and power is inherent in human nature. Ulterior motives are sought for any behavior that appears on the surface not to be self-serving. While different societies provide individuals with different paths for achieving wealth and control over resources, cultural attributes do not give people fundamentally different motives. A nineteenth-century clan leader from Kenya may have gained wealth and social power differently from the way a late-twentieth-century U.S. corporate executive does, but in both societies the end goals of the two people remain basically the same (even though they are couched in terms of different religious beliefs and social mores).[23] Individuals want wealth and power, and those whose resource bases are the strongest will get the most of both. Actors in post–Soviet Russia, as everywhere else, are limited in their attempts to gain wealth only by the initial assets (such as wealth and information) that they bring to the game and by the formal constraints on behavior (such as enforced laws or their absence) that are found in the new system.[24]

This leads directly and easily to the first argument of the rational self-interest paradigm: *Most individuals most of the time (and especially those who are among a society's elite, such as Russian defense enterprise managers) will act primarily to maximize their individual wealth and/or personal control over resource allocations. Self-serving explanations should be discoverable for the vast majority of economic and political actions taken by the vast majority of people.* This means that rational self-interest arguments can be disconfirmed if instances are found where the desire to protect and expand wealth and property rights cannot provide a satisfactory explanation for the choices people make. If most people in a given social group give up wealth and material resources to pursue other goals, positive political economy cannot explain their political and economic actions.

In revolutionary circumstances, we should expect that those who held the most resources at the start of the game (in the case at hand, at the end of the Soviet era) will take advantage of new opportunities for wealth and power as they arise. The winners in any situation act to create the political, economic, and legal institutions that they believe will benefit them most in the future.[25] What has been called *"nomenklatura* capitalism," where the old Soviet Communist Party elite captured the property rights that permitted the acquisition of new wealth in the new system, comes as no surprise to the members of this school. Because reform originated at the top under both Mikhail Gorbachev and Boris Yeltsin, it was the people who were connected to the top who had the most political savvy and the best information networks to take advantage of fast-changing events.[26] Because defense managers in the USSR were well represented in high-ranking positions (controlling nine state ministries and occupying prestigious positions in local and regional Communist Party organizations), they should have been well placed to take advantage of the reform processes. This is especially the case because managers already had partial ownership rights over state-owned capital resources in Soviet times; they had the power to make day-to-day decisions about how the property of the state enterprises should be used.[27] During the transition period they should have used their existing access to capital to provide themselves with new paths to individual wealth and resource control.

This single argument alone is not specific enough to provide tests of some key questions. Two more issues in particular have to be addressed. First, when rational self-interested individuals face a trade-off between short-term and long-term material gains, how do they choose one over the other? What are the underlying conditions that (in economic terms) determine how heavily potential future gains are discounted, or, in other words, whether people would rather have access to cash now or a larger saved investment in years to come? The answer to this question will tell us what combination of the two self-interested material goals (immediate wealth and long-term resource control) the average person is supposed to pursue in particular circumstances. (It is essentially the same question that economists ask when they wonder why younger Americans spend more and save less of their income than older Americans do, or why the United States has a lower overall personal savings rate than Japan does.)

The question as positive political economists would frame it, is how does the incentive structure of the situation affect the degree to which the future is discounted? When people look at the economic and political environment surrounding them, how do they decide whether to put their efforts into getting short-term gains or instead into building long-term resources? The literature tells us that under conditions of great institutional uncertainty (a description that certainly fits the legal, political, and economic climate of Russia through 1995), rational self-interested actors should be oriented toward short-term gains, because there is little likelihood that delaying profits by making long-term investments will pay off.[28] Defense enterprise managers in post–Soviet Russia should have maximized their immediate income, even at the cost of possible long-term economic benefits, because the future consequences of current behavior were unpredictable (and thus lacked what economists call "present value"). Contracts were not easily enforceable, nationalization of profitable industry was a distinct possibility, the taxation structure changed from week to week (often retroactively), and even the borders of the Russian state were contested.[29] Opportunistic Russian actors in the 1992–95 period should have focused on getting while the getting was good, either spending their profits on immediate gratification or investing them in stable foreign countries.

Indeed, this appears to be largely what happened. The Russian Central Bank reported in mid-1995 that there had been $30 billion of untaxed capital flight abroad since 1990; although this exodus peaked in 1992–93, by August 1995, capital was still estimated to be leaving at a rate of $400 million per month.[30] Russians without the means to send earnings abroad "invested" them in under-the-mattress dollar-currency stashes; the Ministry of Economics estimated in August 1995 that this untapped source of potential capital investment measured $20 billion.[31] Direct foreign investment in Russia remained relatively low during this period, and in the first quarter of 1995 actually fell 25 percent from the level achieved in the last quarter of 1994.[32] Some large U.S. companies were willing to take the risk and have in fact invested significantly in the conversion of the Russian defense industry.[33] Yet a 1995 conference of U.S. corporate leaders in Moscow revealed "uneasiness" about Russian investments, citing "the lack of a connection between the taxation and economic policies of the government; the problems of certification, standardization, and licensing . . . ; the absence of [mechanisms for] defense of intellectual property; and all-encompassing corruption." Said one anonymous conference participant, "Given all that has been said here, only a lunatic would invest more than two dollars in Russia."[34] This assessment was largely confirmed by an early 1996 report from the American Chamber of Commerce in Russia.[35] According to the rational self-interest perspective, while particularly risk-acceptant individuals may be willing to invest in Russia's long-term business future, the average investor should not be willing to bear that risk and should instead be playing a game where what political economists call the "shadow of the future" is faint to nonexistent. And most major foreign investors in Russia are in fact big, diversified corporations; while the dollar amounts they have devoted to Russian businesses may seem large, they are probably a small fraction of the corporations' overall investment and planning portfolios.

This conclusion, that rational people should apply short-term thinking in their approaches to business at times of societal upheaval, is important theoretically because it tells us something unexpected. It says that in these circumstances, one's reputation in the wider community doesn't count for much. Building a reputation for honesty and quality workmanship can be seen as a kind of investment in the future, made at the expense of the higher immediate profits available to those who cheat people or cut corners. If people are interested only in gaining material wealth for themselves and not in doing what they believe is moral or "right," then when the future is heavily discounted, they will take advantage of each other to get ahead.

Intuitively, this might seem to go against the common wisdom of capitalist business practice. After all, anyone who wants to get ahead in U.S. business today knows that word-of-mouth advertising is often the best kind and that building customer loyalty is important. I argue, however, that this practice is rational only in a stable society. In an unstable society where the future is unpredictable and the rules are undefined, rational self-interested individuals will take whatever they can while they can and will even cheat if necessary. Consider, for example, what capitalism in the United States looked like during the era of cut-throat robber barons, or among patent medicine salesmen before consumer protection laws were implemented, or during Prohibition when competition commonly resulted in gangland warfare, or today, for that matter, when drug wars are fought on urban streets.

This insight provides us with a means for distinguishing between two explanations for why individuals choose behavior that is socially correct but costly. On the one hand, such behavior may reflect people's desire to follow appropriate social norms for their intrinsic emotional value (i.e., it may fit the theories put forward by the socialization approach). On the other hand, it may be seen as a long-term investment in the person's own reputation and thus in his or her own material future (i.e., it may fit the theories put forward by the rational self-interest approach). An example of where this matters is the well-known phenomenon of Japanese reciprocal gift giving between coworkers and supervisors. If such gift giving is expected by others in the business world, there are two possibilities for the persistence of this practice: Perhaps participants see it as the appropriate "way things are done," where the networks and actions involved bring intrinsic emotional rewards, such as enjoyment of tradition and the warmth of community, regardless of economic costs. Or perhaps each self-interested participant is caught involuntarily in this tradition's catch-22 net. Each individual might believe that breaking the tradition would leave him or her with more disposable income and might prefer that result but at the same time recognizes that anyone violating the rule would be ostracized from the Japanese business world and thus doomed to economic ruin.

In a stable society where rational self-interested people are concerned about the future economic payoffs of their current social behavior, there is no real means for distinguishing between behavior based on expected material gains and behavior based on the embeddedness of a tradition that everyone agrees is appropriate. But in an unstable society, such delayed reputational payoffs should have a minimal impact on self-interested calculations and maybe no impact at all. Social conventions should only be followed by rational self-interested people if the resulting social networks provide them with immediate, short-term access to resources. Long-term concern about future reputation appears unrealistic. Given the cataclysmic swings of Russian economic history (recall that the successful businessman of the Soviet 1920s, in the era of the New Economic Policy, was likely to be shot in the Stalinist 1930s if he had failed to emigrate) and the evident regime instability of the immediate era (including the attempted coup of 1991, the bloody parliamentary crisis of 1993, the Chechen civil war that began in 1994, and constant rumors that the government is shaky), the self-interested Russian had plenty of reason not to expend resources on an investment in future reputation.

As a result of short-term thinking, predatory behavior should have been dominant in society during the early reform period, including within the society of Russian defense enterprise managers. No one should have been able to place much trust in anyone else, even in old partners. At every oppor-

tunity, the temptation to cheat should have outweighed the perceived benefits of cooperation for the common good, given that the shadow of the future
(in other words, concern about maintaining relationships tomorrow) was
short.[36] Each actor in any business relationship had to make a move in a
competitive game where play was unlikely to be repeated over the long haul.
Since economic instability might convince anyone at any time to cut his or
her losses and run (going abroad or into the arms of the mafia, for example),
no one should be trustworthy. It is in everyone's interest to take advantage of
everyone else, unless such behavior threatens one's own immediate gain.
(And in fact news reports from Russia by 1995 make clear that everything
from pyramid schemes and hit killings to government graft and the betrayal
of political allies was so common as to be ho-hum.)

There are only two exceptions to the rule that in times of economic turmoil everyone should cheat everyone else. The first exception is that people
have to cooperate with those who can give them either immediate favors or
immediate punishment. If a person's own future directly depends on someone else's actions, it makes sense to treat that second individual well. For
example, managers might have to make a good impression on authorities who
impose taxes or provide credits, on monopoly suppliers or monopsonistic buyers of their factories' outputs, or on those who control access to advertising.

Using this logic, economists have argued that when individuals trading in
the market have reason to suspect that their partners may take advantage of
their weaknesses and vulnerability, it is in their interests to institute a set of
internal controls over this interaction by forming a single firm.[37] By merging
the economic interests of partners, the temptation of each to take advantage
of the other is overcome. Hence rational self-interested actors in the uncertain situation of reformist Russia should be able to trust one particular kind
of partner: those whose economic lot is tied inexorably to their own.

The second exception is that reputation did continue to matter in one
area: the world market outside of Russia. Those operating businesses in Russia
who have an important interest in maintaining their reputations in other,
non-Russian contexts—for example, large Western conglomerates—need to
be concerned about how their reputations follow them outside Russian borders. Short-term, rapacious gains in Russia would not serve the long-term
interests of these corporations in other markets. Similarly, a Russian manager
engaged in a business relationship with representatives of stable foreign countries may have an interest in building a good reputation abroad. Foreign business representatives might offer the manager the hope of future employment
in a better environment should Russia fall to pieces. The manager's future

prospects may depend on that contact. Pleasing a business partner from abroad might thus reasonably be viewed by a self-interested individual much as investing cash in a Swiss bank account would be: as a sensible and stable long-term investment.

It is only toward those Russian partners who can promise no acceptable counterincentive that predatory behavior should be common. This logic, then, provides the rational self-interest school with its second major argument: *Reputation, the upholding of social norms, and the preservation of preexisting social networks should be decidedly secondary considerations for Russian defense industrial managers during this period, if they are considerations at all. Immediate personal wealth should not be sacrificed in order to uphold old customs or friendships. Reputation and friendship matter only matter when they involve those who have immediate power over the manager's future.*

This argument provides an important means for distinguishing between the theories of the rational self-interest and socialization schools, because the socialization school argues that existing social networks cement trust between actors.[38] If reputation mattered, then self-interested managers could use their past experiences with other people to gauge their trustworthiness. Rational self-interest scholars do argue that in the absence of developed legal institutions, personal trust can substitute for contracts as a means of establishing long-term business relationships without fear of predation, because experience provides information about the other players' likely strategy.[39] But the underlying assumption of this argument is that people's strategies will remain constant, and this in turn requires a stable business climate that will endure for the foreseeable future. Trust depends on the likelihood of repeat dealings. If actors are oriented toward the short term, then trust should not be a primary basis for building long-term relationships, since everyone has the incentive to cheat in a context where the long term may never come to pass.

The second question yet to be answered from this perspective is, what does rational self-interest mean for group-oriented behavior? Do groups of like-minded individuals tend to cooperate for mutual gain, or instead do they compete against each other? Certainly an argument could be made that the survival and health of a particular group can benefit individual members in the long run. Yet most positive political economists in fact argue that the individual pursuit of self-interest often undercuts group interests.[40] Self-interested individuals will recognize that they are acting within the confines of a strategic game involving competition against other self-interested people. This fact should make interest groups in Russia, as anywhere else, difficult to maintain because of what positive political economists call the "collective action problem."[41]

Individuals face a collective action problem when they have to decide whether or not to make a sacrifice that contributes to the welfare of a large group. Each individual's contribution alone is by nature insignificant; it takes lots of individuals acting together to make a difference. But it is easier for each individual to sit back and let someone else make the sacrifice. Everyone in the group benefits from the efforts made by those who are generous, and those who don't make the effort can get the same advantages for free. The end result is that few people bother to make the necessary sacrifices, and the group ends up failing to get the result that would lead to a joint benefit. For example, it is not logical for a businessperson to spend his or her own time and money in political lobbying activity that benefits other businesses in a large industry, because the individual firm does not get any relative profit from this activity. And in any case free riders who contribute nothing to the group can still take advantage of the benefits supplied by those who commit resources to lobbying, thereby gaining a competitive economic advantage over the active participant by spending less but getting the same result.

According to this logic, most individuals join large-scale interest groups, or at least are active in supporting them, only when doing so is rewarded (or when not doing so is punished) by selective incentives. Selective incentives are benefits that accrue only to those who expend resources to join or costs that accrue only to those who do not. Such incentives must be provided by those whose interests in the success of the joint endeavor are much higher than that of the typical participant. There are many examples of this logic operating in everyday experience. For example, environmental lobbying groups in the United States issue glossy nature magazines to those who pay their membership fees and thereby provide them with a selective incentive for joining the group, a benefit received only by those who are members. Similarly, political parties provide special opportunities to meet their candidates at fee-per-plate dinners, and big campaign contributors are rewarded with political appointments. The same logic, used this time from the perspective of punishment rather than benefit, explains why striking coal-mine workers in West Virginia have sometimes posted the names and addresses of strikebreakers on telephone poles with the notation "Death to Scabs."[42] Those who continue to be loyal to the striking coal workers' group won't suffer, but those who don't stick by the group had better watch out. Only those who pay the costs involved in staying on strike (namely, lost wages) will get the selective incentive—protection—that is offered to those who remain true to the cause.

In each of these cases, group-aiding action is encouraged by the provision of selective costs or benefits. And while, of course, some individuals always exhibit altruism, the rational self-interest school sees these individuals as rare exceptions. Getting back to our case, defense enterprise managers as a large[43] interest group (standard estimates indicate that there were somewhere between 500 and 2,500 defense enterprises in Russia in 1992) should not be a powerful lobby because few should bother to participate in lobbying activity, unless organizers of the lobby (possibly, government authorities themselves)[44] could provide selective incentives to those who joined. What should matter most to the rational self-interested manager is profit opportunities and control over resources at his or her own enterprise, not the well-being of the sector as a whole.

This leads to the third major argument of the rational self-interest school: *Given that Russian defense enterprises are very numerous and are competing against each other for access to scarce resources (such as state subsidies and contracts), the collective action problem should make a unified lobby hard to maintain. Cohesive lobbies should only be active when outside organizers can provide valuable selective incentives to encourage participation.*

Socialization: Structure and Goals

Analysts from the socialization school tend to see post-Soviet actors as products of their own past environment. What these actors want, and what these actors do, is a reflection of the set of values inculcated in Soviet times. These values leave many actors unsuited for individual success under new conditions. Instead, old social networks and informal cultural institutions are maintained for their own sake, as group success is still sought.[45] Those individuals who were most strongly acculturated into the old system are the ones who have had the hardest time adapting to change.

This school turns to the set of long-standing societal expectations or norms that surrounds each individual to explain the sources of economic and political action. These expectations are internalized by individuals who have been socialized into the society in question. Of course, following such norms can certainly have material benefits. For example, a good job and the prospects for promotion depend on following behavior patterns that do not disgust or offend one's peers and supervisors. However, the socialization perspective sees the primary motive for such behavior as being not an underlying desire to gain material wealth but instead as the desire to do what is appropriate and expected.[46] Notions of appropriateness vary by society and continue to operate on the individual consciousness because of education and background history, regardless of where the individual finds him- or herself at the moment.

Most socialization scholars see change in these norms and habits occurring slowly and incrementally.[47] A shock to the system can, of course, result in a disruption to this path of incremental evolution.[48] Nevertheless, those who were socialized best into the old system should be the ones who have the hardest time adapting to that shock. One socialization scholar who has applied this perspective to the postsocialist economies argues that new, small entrepreneurial organizations unrelated to the old Soviet enterprises have the best chance for survival under capitalism, while the old Soviet-era dinosaurs will flail about, searching for a means to stay alive by referring back to the behavioral norms that they already know and understand.[49]

The socialization school bases its expectations on the continuation of well-established, Soviet-era behavior patterns, which should still have been operating throughout the transition era among those who had thrived under the old system, such as Russian defense managers. Anyone who had been among the managerial corps in Soviet times would have internalized the social norms that were taught in the previous era. And in fact, at least through 1995, most Russian defense directors, even those who were newly elected or appointed to the director's chair, had worked in their enterprises for several decades and had previously held some sort of upper-management positions there.

In order to determine what the old patterns of social expectations are, we need to turn to specific historical analysis. The socialization school's hypotheses, while based on a set of general principles, cannot be applied across nations and cultures as easily as those of the rational self-interest school. Yet once the cultural and institutional history surrounding a particular set of actors is known, the socialization school can make clear predictions about how that history will affect current action: old networks, old values, and old norms of proper social behavior will be maintained regardless of system change, at least in the short run. (And certainly the four-year period from early 1992, when the double shock of defense budget slashing and expected privatization occurred, and late 1995 would reasonably constitute a short run.)

To formulate the socialization perspective's arguments, I will foreshadow the institutional history of Soviet defense enterprises, which I will detail in the following chapters. A number of in-depth studies of the institutions surrounding Soviet enterprises in general and Soviet defense enterprises in particular have been completed over the years, giving us a solid basis from which to work.[50] From the work of other analysts, we also know that the key pattern of social relations followed both inside factories and between various enterprises and governmental authorities is well described by the notion of paternalism.[51] In a paternalistic system, interactions are hierarchical and take place inside a basically noncash economy. Business relationships are based on the exchange and barter of emotional attention, favors, and concrete material benefits rather than on monetary payments. Within the enterprise, bartered items might include scarce consumer goods and services as well as job promotion; among enterprises and in interactions with government officials, bartered items might also include production equipment, raw materials and components, and policy favors. Each individual has a clear rank within the system, and personal mutual obligations connect each level of the hierarchy to the levels above and below it. The pattern of the hierarchy and its accompanying obligations guide decisions about which types of behavior are appropriate and expected at which times.

Four basic social networks undergirded the Soviet defense enterprise. Each of these was based on a similar combination of mutual dependency and paternalism. As noted above, everyone's primary goal was to pull together to meet or exceed the targets of the state plan. The first network, and the most clearly paternalistic, linked the director to his or her "collective" (the Soviet word used to describe all those employed by the enterprise). This was the bedrock of the Soviet economic endeavor, and it was to this network that the director owed primary attention. The director of a large enterprise was like the mayor of a small, close-knit, traditional village and was similarly obligated to oversee and contribute to his or her society's material well-being. In return, enterprise employees were expected to pull together to meet the plan, so that everyone got the resulting rewards.

The second network connected the enterprise subdivision manager with the employees in his or her subdivision. This was the network that seemed to have the strongest emotional pull for most workers. (Many of these subdivisions would later become the basis for privatized spin-offs from Soviet defense enterprises.) The subdivision manager was obligated to create a sense of cohesion and camaraderie within the subdivision collective. If such an atmosphere were created, the subdivision would work well together and would likely succeed in reaping the bonuses offered to those who overfulfilled state planning norms. Subdivisions competed against each other for those bonuses.

At the level connecting enterprises to outside bodies, there were two additional networks of obligation. While these may have had only an indirect influence on most employees, managers probably spent most of their time nurturing them. The first connected actors across a particular subsectoral ministry.

(As already noted, defense enterprises were divided into nine sectoral ministries at the close of Soviet history. An example here would be the Ministry of Aviation Industry.) It comprised links between enterprise managers and ministry administrators, as well as those among managers of related enterprises. As I shall show in chapter 3, enterprise directors would have had reason not to be overly trusting of the intentions of their former ministerial supervisors once planning was abolished. Yet managers whose enterprises interacted because of ministerial connections would have had reason to turn to each other for mutual support as they entered the market. They would have formed linked supply and production chains and in Soviet times would have helped each other to meet or to bargain over the state plan.

The final network connected enterprises to municipal and regional bodies. It included ties between managers and the local authorities (an example here might be the Communist Party administration of Leningrad), as well as those among managers of nearby defense enterprises.[52] Enterprises and authorities within these local networks helped each other by lending out their resources when the need arose, once again so that everyone could meet or exceed the plan sufficiently. Large enterprises often helped to construct the surrounding cities where they were located.

Each of the four networks described above reflected a shared interest in joint economic success: fulfillment of the plan set by the state. If managers failed to mobilize whatever resources were necessary to meet the plan, then collectives, subdivisions, ministries, and regions all suffered. If the collective, the subdivision, the ministry, or the region blamed the manager for their suffering, then the manager would be less able to meet the plan in the future (and hence less able to gain bonuses), because the willingness of every level to share resources was necessary for the plan to be met. Furthermore, the manager's ability to get special access to consumer goods for both personal use and the collective as a whole depended on the cooperation of others in the circle. Each actor was connected to the others by ties of mutual dependence; the well-being of each depended on the others.

This interdependence led to the development of strong bonds of trust. For example, illegal market transactions were routinely carried out between sets of managers from different enterprises over long time periods. These transactions made it easier to meet and surpass plan goals and so allowed managers to achieve both private wealth and access to the bonuses that were handed out to factories that overfulfilled the state plan.[53] The success of such schemes depended on collusion in lawbreaking: if anyone turned the group in to the authorities, then everyone lost. The operation was thus based on what was called the "circular guarantee" (*krugovaia poruka*), which demanded that everyone participating knew and trusted the other participants.[54]

In the stable system that constituted the Soviet economy from about 1945 through about 1991, social interaction followed behavior patterns that may have been maintained both because they were considered appropriate and had intrinsic emotional value and because they served wealth-maximizing individual interests. The Soviet example of mutual dependence parallels the Japanese example of reciprocal gift exchange, cited above.

It was impossible in Soviet times to determine whether people acted as they did because doing so brought them individual material benefit or because it brought them the emotional and psychic rewards of fellowship and shared purpose. But the advent of the unregulated market, where predatory behavior is dominant and future rewards are uncertain, provides a means for testing whether or not the socialization school is right. Socialization scholars would argue that the habits based on old social networks should largely have continued through 1995 regardless of external economic and political circumstances. This perspective would hypothesize that, because people turn to the patterns they know for an understanding of how to react to new circumstances, defense managers in the new Russia should have acted to maintain trust and goodwill among these old in-groups and to continue paternalistic behavior patterns and existing social roles. Because it was the proper thing to do and because of the intrinsic value associated with them, old patterns of behavior should have been followed even if managers lost greater immediate individual profit as a result. Soviet defense managers' actions in the new Russia should have differed from those of, say, U.S. corporate executives in similar circumstances.

Arguments originating from the socialization school thus can be matched to those of the rational self-interest school concept for concept:

> *Managers act to maintain the health and well-being of their enterprise collectives, of the subdivisions they oversee, and of their ministerial and local networks, because all these are seen as important continuing obligations, part and parcel of the paternalistic social role managers were allotted. Managers will sacrifice personal wealth when necessary in order to help retain jobs, benefits, business orders, and other resources for those inside the* krugovaia poruka. *The closer the social circle is to the manager, the more it should matter.*
>
> *Managers care a great deal about maintaining their reputations for trustworthiness inside these networks, as well as the reputation of their*

work in society. They will turn to trusted colleagues for mutual support when they face uncertain market conditions. It is important that they be seen as playing by the rules, so that their old social groups do not ostracize them.

Managers turn to their long-time colleagues to find mutually beneficial solutions to problems created by market pressures. No collective action problem prevents the formation of strong, voluntary lobbying groups and cooperative commercial structures, because trust-based networks are maintained for their own sake.

Table 1.1 summarizes the arguments to be tested in the chapters that follow:

TABLE 1.1   COMPARISON OF ARGUMENTS TO BE TESTED

Rational Self-Interest	*Socialization*
Defense enterprise managers are self-interested individuals who act to maximize their own wealth and control over resources.	Defense enterprise managers value network maintenance and the fulfillment of established social obligations over individual enrichment.
Defense enterprise managers are unconcerned about societal reputation and thus focus on gaining short-term income in any way possible.	Defense enterprise managers are concerned about their reputations for caring for their employees, as well as about the glory of their work to society.
Collective action among directors is possible only with selective incentives; lobbies and cooperative business activity will be hard to maintain.	Cooperative trust-based relationships are upheld by directors for their intrinsic value; voluntary lobbies and joint business activity are common.

In some instances, the available evidence may not favor the arguments of one perspective over the other. It may turn out, for example, that managers could best meet their material self-interests by maintaining group loyalty, as in modern Japan, where economic incentive structures accurately reflect long-term socialization patterns. In this instance, then, the natural experiment of Russian reforms will not have had the shattering impact on people's economic lives that was originally predicted. Such a result would nevertheless be interesting in and of itself, even though neither of the two perspectives would be disconfirmed by the test, because the evidence would at least demonstrate that history is path-dependent.[55] In other words, it would reveal that revolutions need not disrupt established social institutions as much as one might expect. This would support the literature claiming that national culture leads to variation in objective market structure,[56] even though it would not indicate whether rational self-interest or socialization is the primary source of people's motives. Whether cultures ever matter at all is in fact a contentious issue in the political economy literature, because some scholars believe that all societies facing similar distributions of land, labor, and the natural resources necessary for the creation of capital should look alike.[57] If unique Soviet patterns of economic interaction continue to allow individuals to maximize wealth in the new Russia, then even though those patterns may be based on underlying self-interest, understanding the impact of cultural institutions will be necessary for a complete explanation of outcomes.

The Real-World Value of Theory

Sometimes Western observers are tempted to conclude that with the collapse of the Soviet Union and the end of the cold war, Russian defense industry no longer matters. After all, the argument goes, Russia cannot possibly afford to rebuild a threatening military machine, and by all accounts Russian technology was the loser in the U.S.-Soviet arms race. Such a view is dangerously short-sighted, however. While it is true that a Russian juggernaut no longer threatens the outside world, this book argues that the possibility of Russian anarchy does, and that the struggle of defense managers to find a role for themselves in the new society may be one important determinant of the direction that the Russian polity takes in the future.

What does all the political economy discussed above have to do with international security? Why does it matter what motivates managers? Why not merely collect descriptive material about what is happening in the defense complex, without turning to theory? As I shall show in the chapters that follow, the theory matters because the arguments arising from the two theoretical perspectives I have described cause us to look at the situation faced by managers in new ways. By determining what self-interested people are likely to do in a given set of circumstances and by establishing how people socialized into a particular mindset look at the world, we can discern important behavioral trends whose existence and significance might otherwise be missed.

As I shall show, each of the three institutions described and analyzed in this book has vital implications for the choices managers make. As detailed in chapter 2, rational self-interest leads both managers and many workers to want to keep their enterprises open at all costs. Yet managers have made culturally induced choices about enterprise restructuring that have actually made it harder for those enterprises to stay in business. This means that state support continues to be necessary for enterprise survival, even as budgetary resources evaporate. This in turn can lead to violent protests at enterprises as workers express their frustration and attempt to attract state attention. It can also cause managers to search aggressively for outside buyers of enterprise products, leaving them with less reason to exclude criminals or rogue foreign states from their pool of customers. Yet the very fact that managers and workers are attached to their own individual enterprises also provides a lever for political influence by stable Western countries: enterprises vulnerable to a cutoff of Western trade and investment have an interest in maintaining Russia's cooperation with the Western world economy.

Chapter 3 argues that most managers identify more with local and regional interests and authorities than with those at the national level. Cooperating with provincial-level administrations maximizes managers' own self-interests while simultaneously reflecting long-standing cultural patterns of economic interaction. This gives the identification a double whammy, making it likely to endure for a long time in the future. Given the growth of regional autonomy in Russia, this has important ramifications for the Russian state's ability to control the space it occupies. In particular, it increasingly places in doubt the ability of the Russian state to direct its own foreign, economic, and security policies, as local authorities help their defense plants gain new customers.

In chapter 4, I describe how self-interested conflicts between market-oriented spin-off firms and workers at the enterprises they have left behind have challenged the traditional rules of social cohesion, integrity, and responsibility to authorities that were inculcated into defense complex employees. This situation presents ripe opportunities for organized criminals and terrorists to obtain unauthorized access to Russian weapons and technology. It may also cause the workers left behind to view Western investment in these high-tech spin-offs as exploitative, thereby fueling nationalist or communist political sentiment.

Understanding the combination of rational and cultural motives surrounding managerial behavior thus has important implications for the future of both the Russian state and international security. These findings should give Western policy makers cause for caution and concern. In fact at present a happy ending to the story of Russian defense enterprise reform does not seem possible. Decades of international experience indicate that the idealistic vision of Russian defense industry converting en masse to civilian production is extremely unlikely to be realized. The skills, equipment, and organizational structure necessary for successful market competition are simply too different from the skills, equipment, and structure that characterized Soviet defense enterprises.[58] While it is likely that certain individuals or groups from within Soviet defense enterprises can (at least in theory) become successful long-term market competitors, they will only have the opportunity to do so if they are supported by state institutions and structures—favorable tax codes, enforceable intellectual property rights, fair rental markets, and a supportive environment for foreign investment—that Russia had not yet established when this book went to press. Establishing such institutions requires both economic resources and a great deal of policy maneuvering space, neither of which Russia appears likely to gain any time soon. In fact recent world experience (for example, with such Newly Industrializing Countries as Taiwan, Singapore, South Korea, and Brazil) indicates that such free-market entrepreneur-supporting institutions are most effectively created from scratch by relatively authoritarian states that can put down the political protest bound to arise in response to changes in resource distribution and as a result of economic nationalism.

Foreign arms sales may seem to provide an alternative arena for successful market adaptation by Russian defense enterprises. Yet the global arms market has been shrinking for the past several years, and countries that have established successful client relationships with stable weapons-producing states are unlikely to switch partners wholly or permanently.[59] In the past, the USSR heavily subsidized its arms clients with low-interest loans and deals for barter rather than hard currency. While Russian arms exports apparently have increased substantially in recent years,[60] a large fraction of those exports has been to states such as India and China who hope soon to replace many of their Russian arms imports with domestic production of Russian-licensed weapons technology.[61] Short-term arms export success thus may not translate into long-term orders for Russian enterprises.

The greatest number of potential long-term clients for Russian weapons exports may in fact be pariah or semipariah states that cannot buy their weapons elsewhere. But while by 1994 there were rumblings throughout various Russian governmental structures about the desirability of encouraging arms sales to countries such as Iraq and Libya,[62] the dangling carrot of Western financial aid has thus far prevented the official Russian acceptance of such alternatives.

Of course, the Russian state could always choose to let unproductive defense enterprises die. However, this option carries enormous political costs. Many large Russian metropolises are dominated by defense industrial sites, and dozens of isolated smaller cities are essentially defense company towns. In many of these areas, alternative jobs (outside of such basic home-based services as baby-sitting, clothes tailoring, or car repair) simply do not exist. Because most of the growth in the Russian economy has been based on foreign consumer good imports and domestic natural resource exports, the opportunities for attractive new employment tend also to be geographically limited, clustered around international borders and large mineral deposits. While the city of Moscow, a doorway to international trade and tourism, may be protected from the threat of instability that accompanies defense enterprise bankruptcy and mass layoffs, Siberia, the Volga regions, and the Urals are not. As I show in chapter 3, even Westward-leaning St. Petersburg appears to have felt the political lash of defense industrial decline.

Subsidies to unproductive enterprises cannot continue forever; they are likely to contribute to hyperinflation and economic instability, in turn hindering political stabilization. The fact that none of the alternatives is ideal and all of them carry the risk of either international or domestic upheaval and possible violence makes the future of Russian defense enterprises a pressing concern for all of us. The choices made by Russian defense managers and the political interaction of defense managers, workers, and local and national political authorities has enormous significance for the future tranquillity of a key region of the globe. A Russia pockmarked with regional political protest and economic instability, which would create a political and legal vacuum over a potentially huge swath of territory, arguably constitutes as much a threat to world peace as a Russia that consciously supplies advanced weaponry to pariah states on its periphery. Furthermore, Russian defense industrial enterprises contain the materials necessary for either legal or illegal conventional and nuclear weapons proliferation throughout the third world.

This situation results from strong institutional factors that no one in the outside world can control. Russia will have to reach its own solutions to these problems. But as I show in chapter 5, the actions of Western governments can help to make the underlying situation either better or worse. For this reason, an understanding of how both economic incentives and cultural norms affect the actions taken by defense managers will lead the West to make better policy choices.

2   The Endurance of Soviet Enterprises

One of the striking features of Russian reform has been the obvious reluctance of managers, workers, and the state to let the old Soviet-era defense enterprises die. These large entities, often employing thousands of workers, have remained in existence even when they have no obvious market for their products and when bankruptcy would have seemed logical. Managers seem to continue to hope that the old Soviet-era collectives can find something new to produce, and this is how they look at the notion of defense industry conversion.[1]

This strategy flies in the face of the advice usually given to Russian policy makers by U.S. experts. The consensus in the West has been that the conversion of existing plant floorspace to a new product line, even a line closely related to its existing defense counterpart, is rarely profitable or efficient. The costs of redesigning existing assembly lines and other pieces of infrastructure to engage in flexible, market-oriented production are simply too high.[2] Instead, the preferred strategies for U.S. defense firms facing declining military orders have been either downsizing or diversification, where diversification means acquiring other, existing, nondefense businesses. These diversification efforts are most successful when they are managed by individuals with good track records in the commercial market. U.S. defense industrial managers are thought to be insufficiently innovative and risk-acceptant to be good commercial market managers.[3] Responsiveness to the market often means that the diversified firm must relocate to another city or region, one with an infrastructure base or tax regime that is more appropriate for the new kind of production undertaken. U.S. defense industry experts therefore tend to advise the Russians to raze inefficient plants and "bulldoze the managers."[4] Research or production teams from the old enterprises should restructure themselves into decentralized, high-technology spin-off companies, occupying new spaces under new management principles.[5]

As will be discussed in chapter 4, spin-off and start-up companies from Soviet defense enterprises have indeed become important actors in the Russian economy. But rather than replacing the old Soviet enterprises, these spin-offs have coexisted *alongside* them. Russians often call the Soviet-era enterprises the "mother enterprises" and the spin-off firms the "daughter companies." The mother enterprises tend to become holding companies for the daughter firms. Almost all spin-offs and start-ups continue to occupy the same floorspace they were assigned back when they were subdivisions of the Soviet defense enterprise. Il'ia Klebanov, general director of the Leningrad Optical Mechanical Association (LOMO) in St. Petersburg, made a comment typical of defense managers when he said that his ability to form a holding company for his enterprise's newly independent subdivisions meant that he could keep his Soviet-era enterprise "whole."[6]

Of course, in some cases, maintaining existing Soviet defense enterprises became an economically viable option in the new Russia. Especially in the areas of shipbuilding, space technology, and aircraft manufacture, some large enterprises have found new customers for large-scale projects that resemble their Soviet-era products. With modifications of their former product lines, such as technical upgrades or the addition of Western parts, these enterprises have proved that they can engage in what appears to be profitable business.[7]

Yet there are dozens of examples of enterprises that have been unable to find significant new contracts, unable to pay their bills or workers on time, and unable to keep their main assembly lines operating, often for a year or more, that nonetheless have stubbornly refused to dissolve themselves. Given tight Russian federal budgets and the shrinking international demand for weapons exports,[8] these enterprises have been unlikely to find large new orders. Nevertheless, they endured. Although at least 226 defense enterprises had been labeled bankrupt by federal authorities by April 1995, only 10 of these had actually been examined by the relevant courts, and in four of those cases, the creditors withdrew from the procedure.[9] Enterprises occasionally chose to declare themselves bankrupt,[10] but this was done merely to give them time, under a new director (usually, someone already in the company or closely connected to it), to continue to attempt to survive in the same market, with the same basic organizational building blocks as before.[11] Reports indicate that even if the labor force had to be sent on a forced leave because of a lack of orders, the director and his or her immediate staff usually continued to come in to the factory on a regular basis to try to work out plans for keeping the plant open.[12] An occasional director resigned in protest over the lack of state orders.[13] Yet the vast majority of managers of Russian defense industrial plants have seemed determined to hold on to their positions for as long as possible. As I discuss below, a significant fraction of Soviet-era workers have also remained at the mother enterprises, despite low salaries, late wages, shortened work weeks, and poor working conditions.

In this chapter, I match the arguments from the two contrasting theoretical perspectives outlined in chapter 1 against the available evidence, to see which does the best job of explaining why both managers and workers continue to cling to enterprises that have lost their economic purpose. Does the fact that enterprises continued to exist and employ large numbers of workers in the absence of profitable orders indicate that managers have an abiding social attachment to the collective and its glory, despite the fact that they would have done better to leave or disband the enterprise? Or instead was it in the best material self-interest of workers and managers to use and support these obsolete enterprises to maximize their own advantages as individuals?

The Pattern to Be Explained: Maintenance of the Old Enterprises

Before turning to the arguments about *why* managers and workers have remained at Soviet-era enterprises, let us examine the evidence indicating that remaining at the old workplace was in fact a common behavioral pattern.

Managers

The general directors of the old Soviet defense enterprises have done everything in their power to keep their jobs in the new Russia. For example, in the large number of state defense enterprises that were privatized by 1995,[14] directors have tried to buy a significant percentage of the available enterprise stock. Under Russian law, this allowed them to ensure their own job stability. Control of a significant share of stock meant that they could appoint themselves to the new board of directors and therefore exert influence over the choice of management appointees.[15] They did not have to worry about outsiders coming on to the board and cleaning house.

In order to set the stage for this to happen, directors (from both inside and outside the defense complex) had to take strong political action to affect the progress of Russia's policies for privatizing state enterprises.[16] The original plan of Russian prime minister Yegor Gaidar had been to enact a single variant of mass privatization, whereby all privatizing enterprises would have been sold at auction, primarily in exchange for the free voucher coupons given to every Russian citizen. This would have made small shareholders the controllers of state defense companies. Managers and workers inside those companies would have been granted potential access (through a combination of free shares and purchases) to only 40 percent of their enterprises' stock. Banding together with Russian labor interests in 1992 and 1993, company directors lobbied federal authorities to create a new variant of this state privatization law, the so-called Option Two. This option permitted enterprise insiders (i.e., workers and managers) to buy 51 percent of their own enterprise's shares at the start of the privatization process. In the words of Anders Aslund, a Western economic adviser to the Russian government, "the government was compelled to accommodate the managers."[17] The collectives of the enterprises undergoing privatization were given the right to choose which version of privatization they wanted to adopt, and most chose Option Two.

Pressure on this issue emanated from the directors' faction within the Russian Congress of People's Deputies and the Supreme Soviet, the national legislative bodies that had been freely and popularly elected in 1990.[18] During the early years of Russian reform, the legislature had the legal power to unseat government ministers. They exercised this power against Prime Minister Yegor Gaidar, the man most associated with Yeltsin's original radical reform strategy, by ousting him in December 1992. Yeltsin's economic policy was thus forcibly bent to the will of a powerful congressional faction, the Russian Union of Industrialists and Entrepreneurs (RUIE), led by a man who championed the interests of defense industrialists, Arkady Vol'skii.[19] Managers as a group found themselves well placed at the time of the Soviet collapse to grant themselves the legal right to seize control of a significant percentage of the stock of their own privatizing enterprises.

Managers have furthermore been clever in using privatization laws to their individual advantage. By law, the labor collective as a whole, not managers alone, had responsibility for selecting the privatization option preferred by the enterprise, and under Option Two, it was the collective as a whole that was given the right to buy the majority insider shares. But as time went on, managers were often able to take over the shares originally sold to the workers, thus gaining an even bigger say in how the enterprises were run. There have been many cases of defense enterprise workers being persuaded or coerced to sell their shares to the managers who supervised them.[20]

Defense managers further worked with the Russian State Committee on Defense Industry to ensure that outside investors were largely excluded from the opportunity to buy enterprise shares at auction.[21] Even in those cases where Option Two was not selected by the collective (often because the collective in question lacked the cash to buy a majority of the shares), managers have sometimes arranged matters so that they might eventually buy back control over the stock. An example of this is the strategy followed by the director of the Impuls' Scientific Production Association in Moscow.[22] The labor collective there chose a different state-sanctioned privatization plan, called Option One. Workers received 25 percent of the company's stock for free without voting privileges and were allowed to buy 10 percent of the stock with voting privileges at a discounted rate. Managers were allowed to buy only 5 percent of the voting stock. Of the remaining 60 percent, the Russian State Property Committee (*Gosudarstvennyi Komitet Imushchestva*, or GKI) retained 31 percent for future sale at auction; the final 29 percent of the stock was sold at auction in exchange for the free privatization vouchers given to every Russian citizen in 1992. This would seem to imply that managers lost control of the stock. But it turns out that private citizens did not buy many of those auctioned shares independently. Of the last 29 percent, approximately one-third of the stock was purchased by the employees or other "friends" of Impuls' with their own vouchers, and one-third was purchased by major Russian investment funds. The general director of Impuls', Aleksandr V. Grigor'ev, saw this as a good sign: the investment funds bought the shares as a commercial venture, hoping for quick speculative gain, and this meant that insiders would be able to buy them back easily (if at a higher price).[23] At the conclusion of the privatization process, Grigor'ev hoped that insiders would own 59 percent of the stock (the 40 percent originally designated, plus two-thirds of the 29 percent sold at market), even though the collective had chosen a privatization variant apparently calculated to keep insiders as minority owners. If Impuls' followed the common pattern, all the insider stocks would be likely to end up eventually in the hands of the managers, as workers could be persuaded to sell their shares to them.

Even those directors who have lost control of enterprise stock have not always been willing to step down when the new owners have voted them out of their jobs. At least one case has been reported of a director snatching a document listing the purported stockholders of a privatized company, declaring it fraudulent, and holding it under armed guard so that he might continue to direct the company against the wishes of its trade union.[24] Despite promises that the state would develop a national stock registry, during this period privatized enterprises in Russia often kept the only official list of stockholders locked in a safe in the director's office, and thus, as one analyst noted, "investors risk being deleted from the registry with little evidence of ownership."[25]

Nevertheless, there have been cases where directors were let go against their will. According to one report, one-tenth of all privatized Russian enterprises had their old directors replaced following a stockholders' meeting.[26] In addition, at defense enterprises that are not allowed to privatize for state security reasons (reportedly numbering somewhere in the hundreds)[27] or have not yet completed the privatization process, the employees' Labor Collective Council (Sovet Trudovogo Kollektiva, or STK) has the legal right to hold a referendum and register a no-confidence vote in the director. This has happened frequently when the STK believes that the director has violated the wage or benefit rights of the workers or failed to find a workable conversion plan for the enterprise. After such a vote, the STK communicates the result to the responsible state authorities, who may ask the director to step down and then hold a new employee election for the post. There are numerous cases where Soviet-era defense enterprise directors have been voted out and replaced by this method.[28]

Yet newspapers regularly report on efforts made by directors to stay in power even after STKs have lobbied the appropriate authorities to get them to leave. The state authorities have a great deal of discretion, and directors' efforts to hang on at all costs have sometimes succeeded.[29] Even when they have clear evidence that they are unwanted by their employees, then, directors have often done all they could to retain their jobs.

Workers' Views of Managers

Workers, for the most part, also prefer that management be controlled by insiders. When either the STK or a group of insider shareholders has managed to unseat the old director successfully, the employees almost always elect to the vacant position another, lower-level manager from within the enterprise.[30] According to the deputy director for personnel at the Mashinostroenie enterprise in Reutov, each manager at every level in the company has his or her own corps of "reserves," people who are being trained as possible replacements for the manager in the future.[31] The new contenders for the general director's post usually come from this pool. This system is a holdover from Soviet times, when supervisors trained members of a narrow internal applicant pool for managerial posts.[32] (In Soviet times, there were no business schools in the Western understanding of that term, so future managers had to be trained on the job, from within.) Workers often say that only insiders have sufficient understanding of the plant to be able to manage it successfully.

This system for replacement in the event of conflict with the manager is different from the one in place in large corporations in the United States. U.S. managers who retire in the normal course of things are most often replaced by members of their inside management teams (which ensures stability if good management is in place), but according to one recent study of management turnover in top U.S. companies, in the majority of cases where the chief executive officer (CEO) of a company was forced to resign by the board of directors because of poor performance, the board chose as a replacement either an outside member of the board or someone who was not previously associated with the firm in any capacity.[33] In contrast, even those Russian defense enterprises undergoing crisis prefer insiders to continue as directors.

The preference for inside management in Russian defense industry in fact means that the Soviet-era general director often remains the employees' favorite candidate for the post when elections are held. Well-publicized conflicts between some directors and STKs should not be taken to indicate that most STKs disapprove of their general directors. For example, at the Mashinostroenie plant in Reutov, three candidates, all internal, ran for the general director's post during the last election. The man who had been general director in the 1980s, Gerbert A. Yefremov, is said to have easily won the race, since, as one of his deputies said, "only Yefremov had sufficient upper management experience" to do the job correctly.[34] Even in enterprises facing difficult situations, the workforce often loyally turns to the same general director for guidance.

Workers and the Enterprise

It is not only managers who exhibit a strong desire to remain in their positions and keep their plants open despite a lack of customers. A large number of employees also remain, even after many of the youngest and most talented workers have left. It is difficult to determine the overall outflow of employees from Russian defense industry, because no relevant category appears in official state employment statistics and managers have incentives (including those related to taxation and subsidization) to hide the real level of factory employment. According to one definitive interpretation of official records from the USSR State Committee for Statistics, the Russian Republic of the USSR employed somewhere around 5.5 million people in the military-industrial sector in 1985.[35] (This total may not have included workers in the defense nuclear sector, which may have numbered several million.) By early 1993 Russian defense industrial factories were reported to have lost 600,000 employees, while scientific research institutes in the defense complex were reported to have lost 200,000 (1992 was the year when the drastic cutting of the military procurement and research-and-development budgets began).[36] From mid-1993 to mid-1994, 1 million additional employees apparently left defense industrial production jobs, and another 600,000 left defense scientific enterprises.[37] If the reports are correct, and if their databases are comparable, this would indicate that over 46 percent of the overall workforce left Russian defense enterprises voluntarily between 1992 and the end of 1994.[38]

Clearly, this exodus is massive, and Western analysts have usually focused on it as the key point for analysis, since they see it as evidence of either the market restructuring or the weakness of those enterprises. But these figures also indicate that around 50 percent of the employees *remained* in defense enterprises, despite the objectively poor prospects for continuing long-term employment there. Given how large these enterprises were, at least as of late 1993, this would have meant that the average defense plant still retained more than a thousand workers.[39] Based on reports of individual factories in Moscow, St. Petersburg, Nizhnii Novgorod, Barnaul, and other defense-heavy cities and regions, it seems that a high fraction of these employees were at plants that faced hard times. Managers in turn have avoided mass layoffs whenever possible, preferring to rely on attrition alone to shrink swollen workforces.

The employees who remained faced dismal conditions and low pay. In 1994 and into 1995 the average wage in Russian defense industry was only 60 to 70 percent of the average wage in civilian industry,[40] and often workers did not even receive their full pay. As of October 1994, 400 defense enterprises in Russia had fully stopped work, sending their employees on forced leave at minimal pay (by law, those on forced leave must receive two-thirds of the pay they are entitled to in their employment contracts,[41] although this law is not always enforced).[42] An additional 1,500 enterprises were operating with shortened workdays or workweeks, proportionately lowering the amount of take-home pay.[43] Even when full wages were paid, they were often paid late. A relatively successful enterprise, the Central Aerohydrodynamics Institute (TsAGI) in Zhukovskii (just outside Moscow), regularly paid wages two weeks late throughout 1994 because it received late payments from the Ministry of Defense.[44] Elsewhere in defense industry, payments delayed by several months have been common. When inflation levels in Russia averaged 10 percent per month or more, such delays significantly decreased the value of the pay received.

It is of course likely that many of these employees took on second jobs. The Russian Labor Ministry claimed in late 1994 that 4 million Russians worked in the underground economy, paying no taxes.[45] Presumably, some of these underground workers were people from defense enterprises who were on forced leave or partial workweeks. Yet in many cases such workers have been denied the opportunity for regular full-time work elsewhere, as they were expected to sign in at the defense factory and stay a minimal amount of time there to indicate their continuing employment, even if no actual work was performed. Furthermore, private automobiles are uncommon among those earning average wages in Russia, and most public transportation systems are heavily overburdened, limiting the ability of part-time workers to commute to distant locations for secondary employment.

Defense industry workers may be getting by on multiple employment arrangements, but there is no evidence that they are doing well. As analyst Jerry Hough remarks on reports about the expansion of the underground service economy, "the women selling newspapers on the subway or caring for their friends' children at home are earning peanuts."[46] Many workers spend their forced leaves tending small garden plots at their dachas.[47] While this provides them with food for the winter, and perhaps extra produce to sell in city marketplaces, it likely does not come close to matching the high standard of living they maintained in the past as employees of favored state enterprises. Even those laid-off workers who find work outside the defense sector are often in jobs that do not utilize their advanced skills. A nuclear engineer with a Ph.D. who works as a bank guard and chauffeur while on forced leave may be earning adequate wages,[48] but the expert skills gained through years of work are likely to degrade with nonuse, leaving such experts unemployable in high-technology fields in the future.[49] By hanging on to their jobs at the old enterprises, then, employees appear to be allowing their labor market advantages to atrophy.

The question of why workers hang on to their defense sector jobs through such economic hardship, rather than cutting their ties and looking for permanent work elsewhere, becomes even more puzzling when we add the fact that working conditions at Russian defense industrial sites are often dangerous and unpleasant. Although the Russian press does not often report on such issues, we know from occasional stories that a combination of old habits and funding cuts has meant that factory safety conditions are often poor.[50] Workers remain at jobs that not only pay them poorly but endanger their health. The Russian State Statistics Committee has argued that one of the major reasons for the decline in male life expectancy in Russia in recent years is an increase in industrial accidents.[51]

Why do both managers and workers cling so resolutely to positions that seem objectively undesirable and unlikely to continue for long? One response was provided by the man who was head of Russia's Federal Unemployment Service, Fedor Prokopov, in July 1995. He claimed that it was due to a "tradition of collectivism."[52] Does the evidence in fact support the notion that it is socialization into this tradition that keeps people at the enterprises?

The Soviet Cultural Background: Ingrained Paternalism

Managers and workers in the transition era may have remained bound to the Soviet enterprises because of ingrained social networks and emotional and moral attachment to the system underlying those networks. The Soviet enterprise was a community that surrounded every social aspect of its members' lives. It is not surprising that those whose lives were spent in such a community would come to identify with it. For employees, leaving the enterprise would mean not merely leaving behind coworkers but stepping away from family, friends, neighbors, and teachers, all the people who shape and affirm the individual's identity. For managers, leaving the enterprise in a time of hardship would be akin to a captain deserting a sinking ship.

Many Soviet defense industrial enterprises, particularly those outside Russia's older metropolitan areas, built the apartments in which their employees lived and developed "microcities"[53] (often within existing cities), complete with their own power and heating facilities, for factory employees. Enterprise employees thus lived next door to (and above or below) their coworkers. As anyone who has lived in an apartment building knows, sound travels through walls; this is especially common in Soviet-constructed apartment buildings.[54] Having coworkers as neighbors must have meant that there was virtually no separation between home life and work life. In fact, the factory trade unions established housing committees that delved even further into employees' private lives. Parents' committees were formed within housing blocks to oversee the raising of children; a sanitation subcommittee would inspect individual living quarters on an annual basis to verify that proper standards of cleanliness and fire safety were being followed; and the housing committee wall newspaper often listed the names of those residents not following the rules of polite socialist communal living.[55] People would have grown up in an atmosphere where the enterprise oversaw virtually every aspect of its employees' lives and where such an all-encompassing paternalism was considered normal.

Many enterprises also provided nursery schools and daycare for the children of enterprise employees, reinforcing the pattern of the common workplace surrounding family life. Enterprises owned medical clinics, health spas, vacation rental homes, children's summer camps, dachas, collective farms, sports complexes, musical and theater performance centers, and movie theaters. All the services provided were designated primarily for enterprise employees and were either free or heavily subsidized. These services were known to be of relatively high quality by Soviet standards (for example, Andrei Sakharov wrote that employees of the nuclear installation in the closed defense city of Arzamas-16 received better health care than other residents of the city).[56] It is clear from both observations on the street and conversations with those who lived there that defense enterprises and defense-heavy regions, ranging from Zelenograd and St. Petersburg to Nizhnii Novgorod, were materially favored by the Soviet state. They are reported to have received preferred access to consumer goods such as meat, for example, and lightened restrictions on such things as the ability to buy Western jazz records when the state officially repressed such "decadent" music. While work at Soviet defense enterprises from the Stalin era onward had its disadvantages (including the need to maintain excessive secrecy and the lack of opportunity for innovative experimentation by scientists),[57] and while the lifestyle those enterprises supported may not have been luxurious by Western standards, those choosing to take and keep defense industry jobs in Soviet times lived at a relatively comfortable material level.

The collective farms provided food for workday meals, as well as subsidized baskets of groceries and carloads of cheap winter potatoes.[58] According to a 1959 history of the Krasnoe Sormovo military shipbuilding plant in Nizhnii Novgorod (then known as Gor'kii), "housewives may order meals to take home" from the factory cafeteria.[59] The trade union helped employees plan their vacations, often at enterprise-funded dachas, spas, or campgrounds. The sports complexes provided subsidized ballet and soccer lessons for employees' children.[60] Each large factory had its own sports teams (usually soccer and sometimes hockey as well), and the general director was expected to attend every game.[61] In the evenings, employees and their families participated in musical and drama clubs sponsored by the enterprise, and the internal enterprise newspaper would typically send a reporter to cover their activities.[62] Teenage and young adult children of employees joined the enterprise's Communist Youth League (Komsomol) organization, which, among other things, sponsored field trips to other workplaces, so that the young people could learn about a variety of employment opportunities.[63]

Many enterprises maintained adjunct faculty links to university and higher technical school science and engineering departments and acted as funnels to gather the brightest local children into these programs from an early age. For example, the Mashinostroenie enterprise in Reutov sent representatives to the local elementary schools to advertise their enterprise's technical achieve-

ments and sponsored a Young Pioneers camp to give training through technical games to children they wanted to tap for the future. About half of those
brought into this program were the children of Mashinostroenie employees.[64]
Many enterprises ran vocational-technical training programs for high-school-
age students, giving them four to five years of standard secondary education
along with on-the-job training.[65]

These training programs encouraged multiple generations of the same families to work in the same enterprise. A 1976 history of the Admiralteiskii shipbuilding association in St. Petersburg, which produced both icebreakers and
nuclear attack submarines, proudly noted that one family had worked there for
150 years. It also recounted the job history of the Kuz'mich family: one
brother, Boris, was the night manager in the general director's office; another,
Konstantin, was the head of a berth; Boris's wife, Antonina, also worked at the
shipyard in an unnamed capacity, and their son Yurii and his wife, Galina,
were both technicians there; their other son, Georgii, was a metalworker at the
enterprise.[66] While countrywide statistics on where family members worked
are not available, such situations do not seem to have been unusual.[67]

A position at a Soviet defense enterprise was thus not merely a job: It
meant receipt of one's own apartment, in a country where communal housing was (and is still) common (indeed, given the defense industry's privileged
status in the economy and the importance attached to hiring qualified workers, defense factory housing was probably better than other factory housing).
It meant access to relatively high quality, free medical care, in a country
where publicly available medical care (for example, at open-access municipal clinics) was often poor. It meant home delivery of low-cost fresh food, in
a country of relative scarcity. It meant access to education, entertainment,
moral training, and job prospects for the children, in a country where parents' social and political status significantly determined children's opportunities. Above all, it meant that an all-encompassing community surrounded
one's everyday activities: friends, neighbors, and family tended all to be coworkers, who probably knew each other's private business much more inti-
mately than is common in an individualistic country such as the United
States. Such were the norms of everyday life in many Soviet defense industrial enterprises, norms that were suddenly interrupted by the explosion of
the market economy.

What about the directors of these enterprises? Many analysts, including
some general directors themselves, have referred to the managers of large
Soviet defense enterprises as "mayors."[68] Directors were expected to set aside
time from their regular workdays in order to hear petitions from their employ-

ees,[69] who would ask for their advice or intervention on everything from their children's schooling to meat delivery in local shops.[70] In the dozens of closed military-industrial cities throughout Russia, some of which retain tight control over entrance and exit today, the enterprise literally was the city. For example, in the closed nuclear city of Arzamas-16 (now Sarov), there was no municipal soviet or council until 1990. All the functions normally performed by a city administration were instead performed under the aegis of the Ministry of Atomic Energy (earlier known as the Ministry of Medium Machine-building), and the city was merely a "branch of the enterprise."[71]

Economist Clifford Gaddy notes that even in the defense-heavy city of Saratov, which had more than one large defense enterprise, the multiple enterprises each created their own self-enclosed subcities; he concludes, "There was no 'downtown' Saratov, only a series of 'micro-company towns.' "[72] Journalist Bill Keller discovered that in Sverdlovsk (now Yekaterinburg), a consortium of large enterprises and not the municipal government was responsible for local police protection. He quotes the deputy general director of Uralmash, one of the Sverdlovsk defense factories, as dismissing the need for a city government: "Why do we need them? We have our own city— 180,000 people. Isn't that a city? It's all on our budget."[73]

Managers undoubtedly developed abiding, paternalistic interest in the well-being of their employees and the microregions that they built, almost akin to that of a feudal lord. It would be natural for them to see it as their responsibility to provide jobs and social services for their employees in a time of economic upheaval. From the socialization perspective, it would make sense that to keep the enterprise functioning for the sake of employee well-being would thus be an overriding goal in the manager's life. Directors socialized into feelings of paternalistic responsibility for their employees could not, in good conscience, have sacrificed those duties for the sake of individual gain.

From the socialization perspective, the individuals who had earlier found themselves most frustrated by the bonds of such a community would be the most likely to leave the enterprise when new opportunities arose. If the prospect of continuing to abide by the old system was intolerable to them, they might leave even if the risks of the market threatened their material well-being. Conversely, those most accustomed to the existing order, and especially those most content within it, would fight the most strongly to preserve the community, because the community would legitimate the rules under which they operated. They would not consider the idea of leaving the community to be a viable alternative, even if exit would provide them with better economic opportunities. This would explain, then, the tendency of managers and older workers to remain most closely tied to the enterprise, while the youngest, best educated (and presumably most worldly) employees left.

While an explanation based on historically socialized norms fits the situation outlined above, where enterprises are kept alive at all costs, the fit alone does not demonstrate the power of those norms. New patterns could be consistent with old patterns by coincidence. In fact, as the following section will demonstrate, keeping the existing factories alive served the material interests of managers and workers so strongly that their survival in many cases depended on the old enterprises.

The Rational Self-Interest Explanation: The Lack of Alternatives

The economic system of transitional Russia provided a set of strong material reasons for individuals to choose to remain at the enterprises where they were employed in Soviet times. In particular, most risk-averse individuals, both managers and many workers, had a number of clear economic incentives for trying to hold on to their Soviet-era positions. Given the limited opportunities for employment and economic gain that both managers and workers faced if they chose to leave their enterprises, it was in fact economically rational for them to stay.

Managers

At first glance, it would seem that Soviet-era managers were ideally suited to become successful, independent entrepreneurs in the new Russian market. Directors of large enterprises in particular were high-ranking members of the Communist Party elite *nomenklatura*. Most of them were prominent actors in local and regional politics,[74] as will be discussed more in the next chapter. Most of the senior officials in the nine Soviet ministries overseeing defense industrial-plan implementation were appointed from the ranks of plant managers and chief engineers.[75] Given the widespread perception that the old Soviet *nomenklatura* was very well placed both to enter the market and to shape the laws regulating the market economy,[76] one might have expected Soviet-era defense managers to lead the pack of new millionaires.

Defense managers certainly had a long history of learning how to bargain with authorities to get exceptions made to rules.[77] They also had a long history of cleverly interpreting any available loopholes in Soviet enterprise law and of sweeping laws under the carpet when they could get away with it. They needed to do this to ensure that their factories could meet or surpass

the plan imposed by central authorities, even when it was technically impossible to fulfill.[78] Beginning in the Gorbachev era, this potent mix of capabilities was strengthened by managers' ability to gain control over privatizing
firms and to use Soviet state property to line their own pockets. Evidence
abounds that they in fact did make themselves wealthy this way; stories circulate about managers' fleets of expensive cars and children in the best private schools in the West.

Why, then, haven't managers departed en masse from their old jobs? Why
not devote their contacts, skills, and capital to running booming real estate
firms or brokerage houses in Moscow or St. Petersburg or at least to working
full-time in independent high-technology spin-off firms, instead of staying at
hapless tank plants in Siberia? The fact is that the capital enterprise managers controlled in this transition era, including both the "human capital" of
their skills and the investment capital they garnered during the privatization
process, was anchored in the mother enterprise and would lose most of its
value if moved.

Soviet defense managers did not go to business schools. For the most part,
they spent their entire lives inside a single enterprise, working their way up to
management positions after having joined the factory as an engineer or
designer. When appointed to the post of general director, a manager would
usually remain in that position for a decade or more.[79] This means that managers knew their factories inside and out. They had hands-on knowledge of
the panoply of technical issues involved in production. They had long experience in dealing with both the workplace and home-life concerns of their
employees and probably knew most of their employees by name. They understood who the real powers were behind the trade union and STK. They knew
where to turn for supplies, for bank loans, and for the transport of finished
goods, in a country that lacked a developed market infrastructure. And they
established personal ties and information channels that connected them to
local and regional politicians and leaders, to ministerial officials in Moscow,
and to other directors in their subsector. They were ideally positioned to run
their enterprises smoothly across the potholes of the transition era.

But all these skills would lose meaning outside the context of each manager's specific enterprise. Knowing all one's employees by name, and understanding the subtleties of the power base underlying the factory trade union,
does not mean that one has generalizable personnel management skills.
Grasping the technical bases of a specific set of production outputs does not
make one able to modify a consumer product to keep up with changing market demand, whether for washing machines or for airplane engines. The sup-

ply, funding, and transport relationships established over decades often worked because the providers got something for barter in return for their efforts, not pure cash (this was especially true outside Moscow and certain other big cities, where the variety of consumer goods for sale was and remains more limited because of transportation and other infrastructure costs). At another firm in a different location, those relationships would have to be built again from scratch.

Probably most importantly, access to information—about changing tax and business laws, government credit opportunities and upcoming state orders, visits of foreign delegations, etc.—is the key to survival in a country governed by decree, where public disclosure is haphazard at best. For example, it has been reported that managers of large St. Petersburg enterprises have used their long-standing personal connections for information-gathering operations ranging from background investigations of new business partners to locating new suppliers after their contracts with non-Russian enterprises were severed following the breakup of the USSR.[80] Yet the channels managers have used are specific to their enterprise's location and output profile: the director of a tank factory in Altaiskii Krai would probably find his information channels fairly useless even for running a rocket factory in Moscow Oblast, much less a real estate brokerage in St. Petersburg. There are no business-friendly local public libraries, and few companies advertise on the Internet. Yellow pages are rare, better business bureaus are nonexistent, behavior that would be considered stock fraud in the United States is common, and, from all reports, organized crime is rampant.

But if outside the home enterprise, the manager's human capital skills do not carry much currency, inside the enterprise, those skills are absolutely essential. There are good economic reasons why labor collectives would prefer to have an insider with decades of experience running their factories, rather than an outsider fresh from business school in the West. These reasons go beyond the threat that outsiders pose to employees' jobs. The outsider has not spent years keeping personalities from the local, regional, and central authorities in delicate balance or kept supplies flowing in and laden trucks flowing out in the absence of a developed market. When workers say that only the current general director has sufficient upper-management experience to do the job right, they may be correct, given the absence of a strong, enforceable legal climate for Russian business and the continuing necessity for trade to be cemented by personal ties and mutual backscratching.

There was no guarantee in this era that even experienced directors could succeed in their business efforts. Seven of the nine former ministries were absorbed into one federal committee, Goskomoboronprom (Gosudarstvennyi Komitet na Oboronnuiu Promyshlennost', the State Committee for Defense Industry),[81] and it is has not been clear for quite some time which of the many arms of the state bureaucracy actually controls the purse strings in Moscow (complaints have abounded, for example, about the tendency of the Ministry of Defense to place orders for weapons without first ensuring the funding for them from the Ministry of Finance). Old political contacts may no longer be as useful as they once were. Furthermore, following the demise of the ministries, monopoly Russian suppliers of specialized inputs have forced defense industrial managers to accept unfavorable contracts for incoming goods. Even winning a court case leaves managers unable to collect damages, if the defendant is a monopoly supplier required for the plaintiff's continuing operation.[82] Meanwhile, power configurations at the local and regional levels have also shifted, often repeatedly, in response to the advent of democratization as well as to frequent rule changes governing elections and legislative procedures.[83] Yet even though the personalistic system where defense industrial managers thrived is in such upheaval, the striking endurance of the old party *nomenklatura*'s influence in Russia's new political arenas means that managers with decades of experience in the particular situations of their factories are likely to remain more savvy than generalist outsiders in their responses to an uncertain political and economic environment. Human capital, then, has tied managers to enterprises, as well as tying enterprises to their old managers.

This is not the only capital tie that managers have to their old enterprises, however. They have also been tied to the enterprise through the small private companies established out of the enterprise's subdivisions. Chapter 4 discusses these subdivisions in detail, but I will briefly sketch out here how they have kept defense managers tied to their mother enterprises.

While the ownership arrangements of these privatized divisions differ, in many cases managers from the mother enterprise own a significant share of the daughter company stocks or derive other financial benefit from their operations.[84] If Russia had a normal developed market economy, this alone would not tie managers to their mother enterprise jobs. They could continue to work or own stock in the divisions (which are separate legal entities) without being directly employed by the holding company, or they could sell their division stocks to an outside buyer and transfer their capital investment elsewhere. Throughout Russian defense industry, however, these privatized divisions seem to have survived and often profited precisely because of their links to the managers of the mother enterprises. Given the lack of available rental property in most prime locations in Russia, the privatized divisions could not move out of the mother company's floorspace. In most cases, they therefore had to swallow whatever rent, water and power usage rates, and security service arrangements that the mother enterprise set for them. When mother enterprise managers have had a significant ownership stake in the privatized divisions, the divisions have tended to be given very favorable arrangements on these points. For example, in the closed nuclear city of Arzamas-16, it was reported in January 1994 that VNIIEF, one of the major defense nuclear scientific institutes in Russia, was charging rent at rates ranging from 0.76 to 2.07 rubles per square meter per *year*[85] (at a time when the exchange rate was approximately 2,000 rubles to the dollar). In cases where managers have not had ownership stakes in privatized spin-off companies, the daughter companies have often found themselves in bitter disputes with the mother enterprise.

The dual-ownership and dual-employment interests of managers have thus usually not been transferable at a profitable rate. If a manager resigns from his position at the mother enterprise with the idea of running a daughter company independently, he is likely to find himself punished by the remaining managers of the mother company for the "theft" of the mother company's intellectual property. If he tries to sell his stock in the daughter company to an outsider, that outsider, too, is likely to be punished, because the enterprise has an interest in keeping control over the assets of profitable privatized divisions. Thus the only buyer of a departing manager's stake is likely to be another manager from the mother enterprise. This keeps mother enterprises and their spin-offs closely connected and ensures that the mother enterprises control the costs of inputs for the daughter companies. In most cases, then, those who have an ownership stake in privatized former divisions of the enterprise have every incentive to maintain good relations with mother enterprise managers. (Of course, in situations where the mother enterprise is still the primary owner of the privatized division, the ties bind even more closely.)

Both the human and financial capital of managers has remained institutionally tied to the old Soviet mother enterprises. Leaving those enterprises behind would entail enormous risks, unless managers had made themselves so wealthy during the few years of reform that they could permanently live off their accumulated capital. The absence of other opportunities probably explains why managers have fought so hard to retain their positions, even in cases where STKs have appealed to higher authorities to have them removed (which must leave managers feeling persecuted by their employees).

Employees

If managers need a functioning factory in order to maintain their own wealth, it is perfectly understandable that they would find the voluntary departure of employees threatening. It is also understandable that they would perpetuate a culture centered on the enterprise, so that employees would continue to view the enterprise as the basis for economic life. In fact, there are widespread rumors that when trade unions have engaged in national protest marches and pickets throughout Russia in recent years, agitating for payment of back wages and increased budgetary funding of enterprises, employees have actually been paid by their managers to participate in those activities.[86]

But why would employees choose to stay? It turns out that because of the way the social benefits system was structured in Russia through 1995, most employees and their families remained dependent on positions in the enterprise for social welfare. This has been particularly true in the areas of housing and health care. This means that even those who could find adequate wages in jobs elsewhere did not have the incentive to move. In Russia in the early 1990s, cash did not provide many workers with the opportunity for job mobility, especially outside of a few big cities. Additionally, egregious hiring discrimination in Russia has limited the ability of many workers to find any alternative employment at all.

Housing   Even though enterprises no longer control who lives in the apartments that they built, the lack of available housing has kept families tied to old enterprises.

In Soviet times, enterprises used housing to attract and hold employees under conditions of systemic labor shortage. They distributed individual apartments as rewards to their best employees and could evict individuals that they wanted to punish.[87] Lack of decent housing was cited as a major reason for labor turnover in Soviet enterprises,[88] and turnover could mean difficulty in fulfilling the plan. The defense complex in Soviet times thus had good reasons for maintaining control over as much housing as possible. By 1993, though, enterprises had both economic and legal incentives for turning over their housing and other social facilities to municipal governments.[89]

Through 1995, however, most Russians lacked the ability to move to a new location. Housing remained scarce. State-supported housing construction declined as the Soviet economy worsened, and those wishing to build new private housing in urban areas often lacked access to both bank loans and a sufficient supply of appropriate construction materials.[90] Private investors also continued to face complicated bureaucratic and legal battles if they wished to receive permission for new construction, even on their own land.[91] As a result, housing was prohibitively expensive for those who had not been grandfathered in at subsidized rates. In the words of one defense enterprise trade union leader, "We have no millionaires who can purchase housing on the side. It is possible to receive it only from the enterprise, and on subsidized conditions."[92] The extravagant private *kottedzhi* ("cottages") springing up outside major Russian cities are far beyond the means of the average worker.

Much of the housing stock that did exist in Russia throughout this period was undesirable. As of 1990 40 percent of residents in one of Moscow's urban districts were forced to live in communal housing, and 25 percent of the population of both St. Petersburg and Yaroslavl' were living in communal apartments, where several family members share a single all-purpose room, and several families share a bathroom and kitchen.[93] Furthermore, much of Russia's individual apartment housing is considered by Russians to be poorly appointed, and according to the State Statistical Committee, 30 percent of apartment blocks and 80 percent of single-family houses (the latter mostly in rural areas) "lack the basic amenities of running water and sewer lines."[94] This means that if a family had obtained a good apartment from a defense factory, it had every incentive to stay there. Those who dared to seek new work in different cities have often been men who left their wives and children behind in the apartments they already occupied. These men have been living in the only places they can afford, uncomfortable communal apartments,[95] and have probably thus seen their new jobs as temporary expedients at best.

Even if one could secure an acceptable apartment, it was difficult to relocate in Russia in the early 1990s because of the lack of developed infrastructure. A basic impediment was that throughout this period, a residence permit was still required to live in several of the more desirable cities in Russia, including Moscow, even though such permits were declared unconstitutional by the Constitutional Court. These permits could be bought, but often only for the equivalent of thousands of dollars. Some enterprises provided them for recent graduates they wanted to attract, but many private businesses lacked this capability. Furthermore, relocation in Russia carried enormous transaction costs because the consumer services market was undeveloped and transportation difficulties were immense.[96]

For all these reasons, employees who wanted to leave the factory still had strong incentives to remain in the immediate vicinity of their old employment, so that they could retain their factory-supplied, state-subsidized housing. In large cities with developed markets or with natural resource industrial bases related to Russia's current export emphases (such as the energy or precious mineral sectors),[97] this may not have required remaining at the enterprise. Plenty of alternative positions may have been open nearby. But as of 1995 many regions of Russia, even those whose leaders enthusiastically support market reforms, simply didn't have developed, booming consumer economies like Moscow's, with its large variety of retail shops and kiosks on every major street corner and high levels of foreign investment. In outlying areas, the only alternative jobs available may have been such things as baby-sitting, auto repair, vegetable tending, and the semi-illegal carrying of imported goods across state boundaries. (The relatively large and defense-heavy region of Novosibirsk has been cited as an example of an area where other sectors cannot absorb those laid off from defense enterprises.)[98]

This situation may improve in the future. The World Bank has promised, for example, to provide a $400 million loan to municipal governments to leverage private investment in housing in six Russian cities—Moscow, St. Petersburg, Nizhnii Novgorod, Barnaul, Tver, and Novgorod—in the hopes of constructing 22,000 apartments, 8,200 townhouses, and 1,000 private dwellings for those with "moderate incomes."[99] This may ease the housing pressure in those cities in the long run. Meanwhile, it has made sense even for employees who are terribly underemployed to retain their factory jobs for the sake of the housing they already occupy, since relocation to a healthier economic area is not a reasonable alternative.

Health care   Good-quality publicly available health care (for example, in municipal clinics) has also been scarce in Russia. The fact that factories continued to supply relatively good health care to employees and their families, at low cost, gave families the incentive to keep at least one member employed in the enterprise. Large enterprises in Soviet times usually built health-care facilities for their employees and paid the salaries of the specialists who worked there. It seems that in most cases defense enterprises continued to try to provide their employees with free health care and subsidized medicine even in difficult economic times.[100]

While many enterprises plan simultaneously to make these services available on a profit-making basis to outsiders,[101] such plans seem not to have borne fruit during the initial transition period. Presumably, if and when they do, then as long as one's salary is high enough, buying adequate health care may no longer be a hardship. Large enterprises have a reputation for providing good-quality treatment.

As of 1995, however, high-quality affordable health care was not widely available in Russia. The quality of state-provided health care available to the general public, even in large cities, has generally been considered poor. Equipment is outdated, basic medicines such as insulin are scarce, and sanitation standards often shock visiting Western specialists.[102] While enterprise-based facilities may not all meet Western standards either, the average enterprise facility is known to be superior to the average public facility.

This situation, like the housing situation, has served to bind families to the old Soviet enterprises. Even when salaries are paid late or employees are on forced leave, the fact of continuing employment at the enterprise has allowed workers to use whatever health benefits still remain in operation, and it appears that many enterprises faced with an economic crunch continue to provide social benefits for their employees even when wages cannot be paid.

Hiring discrimination   Beyond these incentives to stay in factory jobs, many workers had to face the fact that they could not obtain new jobs because of sex or age discrimination. No enforced laws prevented hiring discrimination in Russia during this period, and such discrimination was both rampant and public. Newspaper want ads from late 1994 often clearly stated the age and sex of the person wanted for a given job. Here are some examples from a random issue of the want ads for sale in the Moscow subway:[103] "Enterprises invite to work in a security service: officers of the reserve, under 35 years old, having a Moscow residence permit." "Bookkeeper with knowledge of computers, young woman under 25." "Courier, secretary, salary negotiable, not more than 22 years old, with a pleasant appearance and good manners." "Office manager, with experience, under age 22, pleasant appearance, good manners, pay negotiable." "Guard, man under 45, for a private security enterprise in the Elektrozavodskaia region of Lobnia, working one day out of three, pay from 300,000 rubles." "Lawyer's assistant (young man or woman from 18 to 25 years old) with knowledge of computers." "Secretary-editor, productive, computers, English and Spanish, young woman under 27." "Layout artist, experience in layout of texts and newspaper ads on computer, man under 40, higher education, high pay, center [of Moscow]." "Worker—man under 45 without bad habits, Khimki." Similarly, January 1995 want ads in one of the major St. Petersburg newspapers offered the following positions: chief bookkeeper, to a woman aged twenty-five to forty; commercial director, to a man aged twenty-eight to forty-five; interpreter for a Finnish trading company, to a woman aged twenty-two to thirty-two; and trade representative for a telecommunications service, to a man aged twenty-four to thirty-two.[104]

Almost no ads express the desire to hire anyone over forty-five, and few want to hire anyone over thirty-two. The exception is that enterprises were required to set aside a certain number of positions for workers nearing pension age;[105] usually, though, they had enough older workers remaining from Soviet times that they did not need to hire anyone new to fill this quota. According to the monitoring group Human Rights Watch—Helsinki, employers often expressly refused to hire women of child-bearing age to avoid paying state-mandated maternity benefits.[106] Other reports indicate that women over age forty were almost never able to find work in the private sector.[107]

Meanwhile, the normal age at which one received a state retirement pension was fifty-five for women and sixty for men; exceptions could be made by the authorities in some cases, but only down to the age of fifty-three for women and fifty-eight for men.[108] Employees in their forties thus had little alternative except to keep their old jobs for the foreseeable future. Simultaneously, at least some Russian defense enterprises continued to offer "veterans' benefits" to workers who remained at the enterprise for more than twenty years. At the Mashinostroenie plant in Reutov, these benefits included free telephone service, payment of half of one's rent, and a one-time payment of three-months' salary on retirement.[109] Older workers had every reason to maintain their employment at the old Soviet enterprise rather than trying their luck on the market. It is thus completely understandable that younger (especially male) workers should want to leave the plant, while older (and female) workers remained behind.

Both managers and many workers therefore had clear economic incentives to keep inefficient enterprises functioning. If the enterprises died, they would be left without the means for survival. The major impediment to mobility, in all the instances examined here, was the absence of a general social safety net and enforceable fair-trade and fair-hiring laws. State-funded low-income housing; job retraining and relocation programs; adequate public-clinic healthcare or minimal health insurance; state work on improving the communications, transport, and business infrastructure; and state creation and enforcement of antidiscrimination laws would have allowed individuals to take employment risks.

In the absence of state guarantees, the enterprise fulfilled the social benefits function. This was a valuable public service, but in providing it, enterprises simultaneously acted to perpetuate themselves. The rational self-interest scholar would ideally want to ascertain who convinced the Russian state government *not* to consider instituting a general public welfare program as part of its reform program. At the moment, however, we do not know whether the absence of state programs was due primarily to abstract financial calculations

made by disinterested economists or instead to quiet lobbying efforts by directors eager to ensure that the enterprise remained the key economic unit in the
society so that they could keep their jobs. It must be noted that it is not merely
directors who had this interest. Enterprise trade unions had responsibility for
oversight of enterprise social programs, and by law they received 5.4 percent
of the enterprise wage fund to pay for the various programs they administered.
(There are reports that this money has sometimes been misappropriated for
"doubtful commercial operations.")[110] Thus trade unions too had rational
economic incentives to keep workers tied to enterprises.

Managerial Behavior that Failed to Maximize Economic Self-Interest

Despite all this evidence, however, it appears that some enterprise behavior
goes beyond what would be required for managers' rational self-interested
goals and is only explicable with reference to the power of the institutions
and norms into which people have been socialized. The continuation of
some behavior patterns in fact interfered with the economic motives to keep
the enterprise functioning.

An example of such a behavior pattern, one that was economically appropriate in Soviet times but inconsistent with rational economic considerations
in the reform era of 1992–95, was the tendency of managers to follow ingrained
habits associated with labor shortage, despite the objective circumstance of
overemployment (measured in terms of the "hidden unemployment" of workers sent on forced leave) in Russian defense industry. Economist Janos Kornai,
in his authoritative description of the socialist economy, explains that internal
labor hoarding was endemic to all enterprises in the Soviet system, particularly
those in industries such as defense that demanded highly qualified workers.[111]
Internal surpluses were necessary to ensure that mandated output plans, which
were ratcheted up every year, could be fulfilled even if qualified workers
decided to leave and even if senior members of the planning hierarchy decided
to cut labor allocations to the enterprise. The fact that other enterprises also
hoarded labor aggravated the situation, because it meant that few qualified job
candidates were available at short notice and enterprise managers faced a
seller's market.

A Russian sociologist specializing in labor economics wrote in 1991 that
managers were still behaving as if they needed excess reserves of labor.[112] In
1991 this may have been perceived as a rational economic decision for managers to make, given that, as many observers have noted, it was only in 1992
(when defense spending first plummeted in Russia) that defense industrialists

began to believe that the command economy was actually dead.[113] But if such behavior continued through 1995, it would indicate that ingrained norms, rather than rational economic calculation, had power over managers' choices.

There were of course objective economic reasons why managers would have wanted to retain a large workforce. At least some regions gave tax benefits or other privileges to enterprises with many employees. A telling example is found in the oblast (region) of Samara. The regional administration there instituted a cap on the salaries of directors of firms more than 50 percent state-owned. But the cap varies by enterprise, and its level depends on, among other factors, "the number of workers in the enterprise."[114] It makes sense that a region facing high levels of unemployment would like to provide incentives to enterprises to keep as many people employed as possible.

Several analysts have also suggested that overemployment has been the result of a pact between trade unions or STKs on one side, and directors on the other. If management refrains from mass layoffs, then the trade union and/or STK cooperates in allowing managers to take control of the enterprise stock during privatization.[115] Keeping a large workforce would thus be consistent with managers' desires to keep their jobs.

Two strands of evidence, however, are difficult to explain using this self-interested economic and political reasoning and therefore indicate the perseverance of an old cultural mindset: (1) the desire of managers to retain the same relative balance among employee profiles and qualifications within the enterprise, even as output characteristics should have changed to reflect new market demands; and (2) the unwillingness of both managers and collectives to let go of the enterprise's social assets.

Recall that the arguments of the socialization perspective are directly opposed to the rational self-interest school's stress on self-centered materialism. Instead, they predict that managers will try to maintain the health and well-being of their enterprise collectives and subdivisions because they see this as part of their fundamental obligation to society. These concerns are part and parcel of the paternalistic social role managers were allotted under the Soviet system. Managers should be willing to sacrifice personal wealth when necessary in order to help retain jobs, benefits, and other resources for those inside the *krugovaia poruka*. Furthermore, preserving the glory of these Soviet-era enterprises and the high regard in which society holds them should be seen as important, since these reflect well on managers and help them to maintain their own social reputation.

What does the evidence indicate about these arguments?

Retaining the Collective and Its Glory

Perhaps the most widespread concern articulated both by Russian defense managers and trade union leaders has been the need to "retain the collective,"[116] meaning not just a large workforce, but one resembling what the plant had always had. Managers treated as self-evident the fact that a large cadre of highly qualified scientific, engineering, and technical personnel was required at their enterprises, despite what appeared to be a permanent cost crunch. (In fact, when I asked a variety of people associated with the defense industry in Russia in fall 1994 *why* it was important to retain the collective, the most common response was bewilderment that I would raise such a question at all.) In the words of one observer, "If one asks the managers to name their two chief priorities . . . the social bloc [of answers] takes first place—stabilizing employment, retaining the core of the collective, and realizing social interests—with the expansion of markets or the development of [new] technology at an enormous distance behind."[117]

Only through maintenance of such a collective, one that had worked together on large-scale projects over the space of decades, could managers hope to retain the high-technology production profiles they had built up in Soviet times. Sometimes the intention was to use this profile in their approach to the market.[118] At other times, hope remained that the past profile would once again be required by the state for large technology projects.[119] It was not uncommon to hear managers say that because the major profile of their production had always been huge, one-of-a-kind, high-technology projects for the state customer, they needed that sort of venture now in order to survive.[120] In one case, the director of a defense electronics enterprise in Zelenograd (who was eventually unseated by his STK) is reported to have "brushed off" orders from nonstate customers throughout 1993 and 1994 because he wanted to keep his best technical workers available for future state orders that never came.[121]

There has been an overwhelming belief among Russian defense industrialists in the need to retain their enterprises as technology powerhouses, regardless of cost. Many defense enterprises have turned to bank loans to cover their employees' salaries, even though they have no clear ability to repay them.[122] This stands in stark contrast to the experience of U.S. defense enterprises undergoing restructuring since the cold war's end. In the early 1990s, many newspapers ran stories about the large number of unemployed engineers in defense-heavy regions of the United States. It was considered par for the course that downsizing meant that well-trained, highly qualified technical specialists would be laid off.[123]

Part of the difference between the Russian and U.S. views of how enterprises should approach a changed market may be economically rational, attributable to the loss of resources to support advanced education in Russia. As the state budget has contracted, universities and scientific institutes have been particularly hard hit. Most faculty members have had to take on second jobs in order to survive, and students can no longer get by on state pensions. Young Russians with skills and talent are either entering business instead of science or flocking to graduate training programs in Western countries and then entering the job market abroad. Numerous top Russian scientists, particularly physicists and mathematicians, have taken tenured positions at Western universities.[124] It is thus much harder than it used to be for enterprises to find sufficient qualified replacements for trained personnel who leave, and figuring out how to train new personnel has become a pressing concern. TsAGI, for example, used to hire 700 to 800 people per year; they are now down to hiring around 150 per year, and most of these are only minimally qualified workers. The flow from higher-training institutes has ebbed. According to TsAGI managers, it is rare for someone with great scientific potential to be looking for a job nowadays.[125]

Yet it was not always clear that these enterprises should concentrate on maintaining an extensive high-technology profile. (Note that the question of whether the Russian *state* should try to retain high-technology scientists and engineers and discourage emigration is a separate issue unrelated to the economic calculations of managers.) Little objective evidence indicates that a potential flood of orders would await these companies if they maintained sufficient personnel levels. The notion that the typical defense enterprise should continue to employ a mix of technical people similar to that used in the past indicates the pull of historically instituted norms of behavior. If it were the number of employees on the payroll alone that counted in managers' calculations, then there would have been no reason for them to hang on to the highest-paid specialists. Yet when a U.S. researcher suggested to the personnel director of one defense plant in the Moscow region in 1994 that perhaps a different mixture of employees was needed now that the plant's production profile had changed, his comment was met with polite bafflement.[126]

There are exceptions to this rule. For example, TsAGI rewards those employees who work well on outside private orders, placing them on a special list of key workers.[127] The general director, Gherman I. Zagainov, also publicly announced in internal enterprise radio broadcasts that he intended both to liquidate some sectors of the enterprise and to further decrease the number of employees in the basic subdivisions of the institute.[128] (Note that reducing the size of the workforce here had not yet entailed mass layoffs; it merely involved unequal distribution of wages and other benefits based on performance, so that less desirable workers were encouraged to go elsewhere.)

While other enterprises have also given special benefits to a particular core of valued employees, TsAGI's method for choosing who to favor appears to be exceptional. At other enterprises, the preexisting subdivisions of the enterprise were responsible for putting together for the director a list of their own core employees. This meant that the basic structural profile of the old enterprise was kept intact, even as downsizing occurred.[129]

A situation at the Impuls' enterprise in Moscow demonstrates the consequences of this line of thinking. Impuls' as a whole was basically financially sound as of late 1994 and working at a higher productivity level than in the early 1990s, although some subdivisions that managers had always considered unimportant to the enterprise's overall profile were disbanded.[130] One division, however, which used to make chemical coatings for a particular (unnamed) Impuls' product, remained in existence even though it was now running at less than a third of its former capacity. Rather than eliminating or downsizing that division, managers were instead trying to find a new customer for it.[131] In other words, the existing structure of the enterprise was driving the search for new orders. The market was not driving enterprise restructuring. Managers worked to preserve their collectives and subdivisions in the face of economic pressure to do otherwise.

To some extent, this may have reflected a belief that the state would require in the future a workforce resembling that from the Soviet era. Until mid-1994 defense enterprises were required to maintain a "mobilization base" of equipment and raw materials that would allow quick reconversion to military production in time of war.[132] Some enterprises might have felt obligated also to retain the people capable of running that equipment. Presumably, however, if this had been the only concern of managers, the necessary personnel could have been made into the equivalent of a reserve officer training corps. It wouldn't matter if employees took other jobs as long as they could be called back to defense enterprises in the event of war mobilization. But I have found no evidence indicating this to have been the case. Instead, the average manager seemed to conceive of the defense industrial enterprise as a technological powerhouse, providing products or services that remained vital to making the Russian state great. In the words of a Nizhnii Novgorod shipbuilding factory manager, "What can I say to the worker concerning his profession as shipbuilder, which always 'rang proudly'? [There are] traditions, dynasties, through which it was repeated to him over many years [that he] remained necessary for the future, the 'radiant future.' I explain [to him]—it's mistakes by the politicians."[133] Wrote another manager of a military shipbuilding firm in St. Petersburg, "Are we a great power or a banana republic? We have vast border expanses, and we must defend them."[134]

The idea of completely refiguring the plant and reorganizing the workforce to respond to changed conditions was not considered, even though ensuring the continued existence of the enterprise was the manager's highest self-interested economic goal. For example, according to press reports, some managers at the Mashinostroenie enterprise in Reutov took offense when conversion assistance promised by the U.S. government turned out to be a soft-drink bottling joint venture rather than a project related to the enterprise's primary work in aerospace technology. The head of the satellite imaging division of the enterprise said, "It was absolutely our last choice. . . . Everyone is laughing at us."[135] (The director nonetheless accepted the offer, and the enterprise welcomed the new source of funds.) The notion that a great military and space enterprise would focus on consumer goods production was hard to swallow, because high technology and highly trained employees defined what the enterprise was. Related attempts by the Soviet state in the Gorbachev era to assign low-tech conversion production plans to high-tech defense enterprises were met with disdain by enterprise managers.[136]

Not all managers were insistent that they must continue to produce *defense* orders per se. In fact, the League for Assistance to Defense Enterprises, a lobbying group made up of general directors from many large firms in the Russian defense complex, proposed to the state that 60 percent of all defense enterprises (those whose current state orders were 25 percent or less of their production levels) should be released from the official designation of the "military industrial complex," given that the state clearly lacked the resources to fund their defense production anyway.[137] Some enterprise representatives express relief in finding orders for civilian production from abroad, because foreign firms are more likely than the Russian state to pay for orders on time.[138]

The issue then was not so much the production of exactly what was made before but rather the maintenance of the enterprise's basic structure and high-technology profile. The reasoning behind such retention seems to be conditioned by a combination of three factors, none of them based on objective material calculations. First are pride in past achievements and identification with the glory heaped on the defense industrial enterprise in Soviet times. The high-technology collective made the enterprise great, and therefore it is assumed that the enterprise's further success depends on that same type of collective. Second is continued hope for large high-technology orders.

Realistically, the number of such orders does not seem likely to grow much with time, given that the Russian state has lost its raw economic ability to sustain many such projects and foreign investors continue to show ambivalence toward the Russian market. Obviously, some enterprises have found such orders and will continue to do so, but it is probably not realistic to believe that most will have such opportunities. (In any case, many of the large-scale orders placed now are one-time deals, with no guarantee of continued orders in the future.)[139] Third is the tendency to focus on sunk costs. The fact that the enterprise purchased or created high-technology equipment in Soviet times and trained people to use it seems to translate into a belief that such equipment and training must be maintained,[140] because it defines where the "advantage" of the firm lies.

Sunk costs should not be part of an objective economic calculation about what to do to keep an enterprise functioning in current conditions. In the words of a standard microeconomics textbook, "A sunk cost is an expenditure that has already been made and cannot be recovered. Because it cannot be recovered, it should have no influence whatsoever on the firm's decisions."[141] In other words, the fact that an enterprise owns particular equipment and has always employed such equipment should lead managers to turn to that equipment for future production only if its use matches the economic opportunities available from state or market. If the market for such activities exists, then a unique research group that has become more than the sum of its parts through years of cooperation should be retained to use that equipment. If a market for that activity is not on the horizon, however, the only reason to keep such a group together is grounded in a sociological, cultural attachment to a historical institution that no longer matches the enterprise's economic interests.

Pressures emanating from the trade union or STK may force a director to maintain such collectives. It is difficult for outsiders to decipher what the political balance of decision making looks like inside enterprises. We thus cannot determine for sure whether it is the director's preferences alone that matter or instead the preferences of the collective as a whole. Keeping the collective happy may have been necessary for the manager to stay employed. Regardless of who is responsible, however, the fact remains that the strategies chosen indicate the power of cultural understandings about the nature of the collective. Without such acculturation, managers could have closed old divisions without laying off workers by shifting personnel around within the enterprise. They also could have lowered costs, as TsAGI did, by selectively rewarding those who brought in the most business rather than those who helped each division the most.

Retaining Social Assets for the Collective

As was noted above, both federal laws and economic necessity have encouraged enterprises to transfer most of their housing and some of their other social assets to municipal budgets, and many have done so. A number of enterprises have nevertheless expressed their desire to hold on to some social facilities and even to continue to build new ones. Managers and workers seemed to prefer the continuation of a paternalistic system based on the transfer of real goods and services within a hierarchy rather than on cash. But if enterprises had fewer social expenditures to make, they would have more resources, which workers could then bargain into higher wages.

Some managers have indicated that they do have self-interested motives for holding on to at least some of their social facilities. For example, managers at TsAGI intend to use their easy access to land and building permits to construct housing and other facilities for profitable rent or sale to outsiders.[142] Such projects are even more attractive when local tax breaks are given in return for continued construction of facilities. This is the case in the Siberian city of Barnaul and in St. Petersburg.[143] (Reports from other regions indicate, however, that sometimes the transfer of facilities to the municipal budget gives enterprises tax savings.)[144] Enterprises' seeming desire to maintain social assets can sometimes turn out to be a desire only to maintain ownership of the building where the social assets are located, in order to use it for other purposes. This was apparently the case in the closed nuclear city of Arzamas-16, where argument centered on whether the nuclear weapons scientific institute or the city should retain control of the enterprise's preschool facilities.[145]

Despite these indications that social facilities are sometimes retained for self-interested reasons, a number of enterprises appeared to be holding on to them not for tax or outside profit reasons but because doing so aided the cause of employee retention. Once again, maintaining the collective and its benefits structure was paramount. Arguments along this line have been commonly reported in the Russian press.[146]

In 1994 the deputy general director for social services of the Mashinostroenie plant in Reutov shared such thinking, saying that his enterprise was continuing to build housing explicitly "to stabilize the collective." Every new recruit to the company was given at least a dormitory room at a subsidized rent. While a large fraction of Mashinostroenie's housing and other social facilities had been given to the city of Reutov, the plant at that time was holding on to two buildings with 110 apartments, two dormitories, a hotel, a polyclinic, a stadium, two palaces of culture, a children's summer camp, and a vacation spa.[147] Nonemployees could now use these facilities on a rental basis, but insiders still got subsidized, preferential access. The children of employees were given free lessons in six sports at the stadium, "so the kids are not out on the streets doing drugs"; workers could still buy subsidized food in Mashinostroenie's dining halls and retail shops; and the enterprise maintained contracts with local state farms for delivery of autumn potatoes to employees' homes.

Even TsAGI, an enterprise known for cost-conscious and profit-seeking disposal of its social assets, still offered its employees' children a subsidized summer camp in 1994. According to a press report, children were pleased to get luxuries at camp that were unavailable at home, such as chocolate, oranges, bananas, and meat every day. While parents had to pay part of the fee for this camp, the full cost was heavily subsidized by TsAGI.[148] Other examples abound: for instance, the military electronics firm ELMA in Zelenograd maintained two vacation areas that were paid for out of the enterprise's social insurance fund,[149] and a military spare-parts plant in the town of Nerekhta kept open its summer camps and vacation spas even when worker salaries were delayed by several months.[150]

Factory provision of housing may very well have been necessary to hire new scientific and engineering employees; as I mentioned earlier, housing was scarce and expensive, and newcomers would be unlikely to move to an area without the guarantee of a reasonable place to live. Factory provision of health care also helped to attract new employees and keep valued members of the existing core. It is unlikely, however, that other subsidized social facilities, such as stadiums and summer camps, were necessary to attract new employees fresh out of training. It would be cheaper to retain core employees by paying them more so that they could afford to buy social services themselves rather than to maintain large facilities that benefited the entire collective. Social services funds accumulated by the enterprise that were not transferrable to cash could instead have been used for projects such as vocational education or improvement of the information resources available to employees, to help them find new jobs elsewhere.

Nonhousing-, nonhealth-related social services were not provided to the collective for rational self-interested motives. Instead, there seem to have been at least two additional cultural reasons for maintaining this infrastructure. First, yet again, there was an attachment to the sunk costs that the collective had put into building the facilities in the past. Analyst Gregory Andrusz notes that in Soviet times, enterprises tried hard to hang on to their housing facilities, rather than transferring them to municipal governments when there was pressure to do so, at least in part because "the housing may seem to be 'theirs.' "[151]

This seems to be equally true of enterprises' attitudes toward their social facilities in the transition era. An example is provided by Valerii A. Radchenko, general director of the Zvezda ship engine–building factory in St. Petersburg. Zvezda was supposed to give its social facilities (including a preschool, a stadium with a swimming pool, a children's summer camp, and a vacation area) to the local government, but Radchenko was afraid that outside commercial owners would ruin them. "All this we built with factory money and have maintained in good condition up until now," he wrote.[152] A similar situation was reported in Arzamas-16, where an employee collective voted to retain ownership of an enterprise sports facility despite the financial drain it imposes. They feared that outside owners would not maintain the existing profile of the sports complex or might charge customers so much to use it that employees would not be able to afford it.[153] (This in fact happened with the preschool that the scientific institute wanted to maintain in Arzamas-16: after the institute was forced for financial reasons to give it up to the city, it was privatized, and the new owners now charge parents 10 percent of the average monthly wage for each child's care.)[154]

Again, it may be pressure from the collective as a whole that forces managers to maintain existing enterprise structures, rather than the preferences of the managers per se. Yet these situations indicate that the collectives were suffused by a paternalistic cultural attitude. Employees would rather have guaranteed access to social facilities (including nonessential ones, such as swimming pools, sports complexes, and vacation spas) than to more liquid resources that they could then bargain into wage increases. While the desire to hang on to a day-care facility can easily be explained by rational self-interested motives, the desire to keep everything the way it was cannot.

The second cultural reason for hanging on to these facilities was the managers' belief that maintaining benefits for the collective was part of their duty. In Soviet times, the pooled bonuses of the enterprise collective were funneled by the manager into facilities that served the common good. As a 1959 history of a Soviet shipyard put it, the trade union and manager decide together "how the profits of the establishment are to be spent on improving the workers' living and cultural conditions."[155] In the fall of 1994 the deputy director of the Mashinostroenie plant in Reutov made a similar statement, arguing that it remained important for employees to feel cared for by the enterprise.[156] These cultural norms of paternalism were probably reinforced by enterprise directors' desire to attract the same level of respect from their employees that they elicited in Soviet times.[157] Joseph Berliner, in his classic work on Soviet managers, argued that "the director . . . who is able to build a larger worker's club or an additional nursery for children of working mothers or make some improvements in the plant cafeteria, is likely to obtain the support of workers and the rest of management."[158] Historically, the director was responsible for implementing the common will, and the construction of social facilities constituted physical proof of the director's concern for employees. By tapping in to that institutionalized expectation, directors today may find the provision of social services a means for preserving not only the collective but also their reputations for effectiveness inside the *krugovaia poruka*.

Theoretical Conclusion: Culture Matters

The chairman of the trade union committee at the Mikron factory in Zelenograd said in 1992, "The economic basis of our life is the enterprise. No one will ever be permitted to destroy it."[159] As I have shown in the preceding pages, preservation of the Soviet defense enterprise is an economic necessity for both managers and many workers in Russia today. The rational self-interest perspective is in large part supported by the evidence, because individuals have clearly acted to protect their own economic well-being during this time of societal upheaval, and managers have acted to expand their existing property rights in order to gain more wealth.

At the same time, however, managers do not appear to value their own individual wealth above all else. While self-interest keeps enterprises open and keeps managers and workers in them, enduring cultural notions of what it means to preserve the enterprise—including preservation of its basic preexisting structural divisions and its social assets—are at odds with the notion of self-serving individualism. Managers want to fulfill their traditional social roles and to maintain their reputations as powerful providers for the common good. As enterprise budgets continue to retract, both managers and employees may find themselves harmed by these institutionalized expectations of what the enterprise should provide.

In addition, the continuing importance of Soviet-era structures—namely, the mother enterprises—limited the choices that managers were able to consider. The need to remain at the enterprise has prevented managers from taking advantage of the relative wealth they accumulated in the Soviet system (especially their ownership stakes in spin-off companies) to become independent entrepreneurs. History is path dependent; the structure of the old system continues to channel materialistic behavior in the new system. Self-interested motives are important, but they alone do not provide a complete picture of how managers have related to their enterprise collectives. Instead, attention must also focus on how cultural norms limit the choices managers can consider.

The major structural factors ensuring the continued social importance of the enterprise could all, in theory, have been changed by human action. The absence of a general social safety net and adequate public information resources served to limit employment mobility. There does not seem to be any evidence that defense managers lobbied for laws that would have aided this mobility. Instead, their lobbying seems to have revolved around the needs of their enterprises, especially in the area of credits and other subsidies. And even though the Russian state may not have been interested in pursuing general social welfare policies in any case, enterprise subsidies have certainly acted as a major drain on budgetary resources that the state might have put to other uses.

Policy Conclusions: Political Fragmentation and Enterprise Desperation

The fact that both managers and employees are structurally anchored in individual enterprises means that we should not expect the Russian defense industry to be a particularly effective force in Russian national politics. Both labor and capital are relatively immobile, because social benefits, information resources, and spin-off investments are all bound to particular enterprises and are not easily transferable. But if enterprises shared a set of common interests, this might not present a problem: shared economic interests between labor and capital within particular sectors can lead to powerful industrial lobbies.[160]

Given the coherence that many observers found in the directors' lobby during the 1992 privatization debates, one might have expected that strong sectoral pressure would continue in Russia through 1995. With time, however, so many differences have appeared in the objective interests held by various enterprises that such a lobby would be difficult to maintain. Some enterprises are privatized or in the process of privatization, while others remain on the state's not-for-privatization list. Enterprises with differing ownership structures are likely to have competing preferences about tax laws and state subsidies, because strong competitors will not want to bail out the weak.

The customers of these enterprises vary significantly as well. Some enterprises, such as the MAPO-MiG consortium that manufactures fighter jets, are primarily engaged in arms production for export to third world countries. Others, such as TsAGI, are significantly supported by lucrative high-technology civilian projects with Western companies and governments. Logically,

MAPO-MiG might favor the expansion of the Russian weapons market. If such weapons were sold to pariah countries such as Iraq or Libya, Western ire would likely be raised, and Western economic sanctions would probably be levied against Russia. Yet MAPO-MiG would emerge unscathed, because its customer base would be expanded. TsAGI, in contrast, currently has an extensive range of contracts with the Boeing Corporation, which is the primary user of one of TsAGI's giant component-testing wind tunnels, as well as with General Dynamics and McDonnell Douglas; TsAGI is also the recipient of a U.S. Air Force grant and has been negotiating with NASA.[161] Given these ties, it would not be logical for TsAGI to engage publicly in lobbying activity that favored the Russian competitors of U.S. aerospace companies, nor would it make sense for TsAGI to support Russian arms sales that might provoke U.S. retaliation against the Russian economy.[162]

Thus the fact of labor and capital immobility, combined with differing economic interests across firms, leads to fragmented, not unified, political action within the sector.[163] Given that capital and labor are enterprise specific and that economic interests vary dramatically across enterprises, it is not surprising that the mighty Russian defense industry has turned out to be somewhat of a paper tiger in national politics. Many Russian observers have noted that the defense industry has lost out to the oil and gas and agricultural lobbies in obtaining subsidies and other government assistance.[164]

Since 1992 a single, formal defense industrial pressure group has not really existed in Russia. In 1992 the RUIE lobby clearly played the decisive role in influencing state privatization policy. But by 1993 the general perception was that the old RUIE constituency had split in two. Insider privatization was well under way, and that meant that the unified interests of managers in buying up state property were no longer sufficient to hold the lobby together. The directors who owned successful factories had aligned themselves with the liberal reformist parties, while the "producers of goods that no one wants to buy at the prices set by those producers" joined the protectionist and socialist Federation of Goods Producers.[165] This latter group may regain legislative power through its coalition with Russian nationalists in the electoral party known as the Congress of Russian Communities. Given the vicissitudes of Russian politics (and the short-run orientation toward cooperation outlined in chapter 1), however, it is unlikely that such a bloc will hold together indefinitely; it was already falling apart at the time of the Duma elections in December 1995.

In 1992 a lobbying organization for defense industrialists was established. Called the League for Assistance to Defense Enterprises, it was formed "so that the voice of the 'defense complex' would be strengthened" and to "exert influence on governmental structures."[166] While its representatives have met regularly with top Russian leaders,[167] enterprise managers proved not to be very committed to this group. At its 1993 annual meeting, the league criticized the directors of two huge Moscow-area enterprises, NII Avtomatiki and TsAGI, for being "insufficiently active" in the organization despite being members of its presidium. Two additional directors who served on the presidium were chastised for having "practically withdrawn" from league activities.[168] As the rational self-interest school would have expected, the collective action problem was at work. Directors have not taken time away from managing their individual enterprises to work for abstract political gains for the sector as a whole.

The general director of one large defense enterprise told me in September 1994 that he joined the league only "so as not to be the white bird," which in Russian folklore is an outsider pecked to death by the other birds.[169] Around the same time, a senior manager of a different large defense enterprise informed me that his team sees the league as primarily a joint marketing endeavor and that its members all have their own ideas and find it hard to cooperate on any but the most basic questions.[170] One success the league prides itself on is its ability to "propagate ideas" in major Russian news publications.[171] It was also the major force behind the establishment of a slick new advertising magazine for Russian weapons, *Military Parade*.[172] These activities indicate that the league may indeed function primarily to assist enterprises with marketing, rather than as a successful lobbying group.

While defense industry does not seem to be a predominant player in the crunch of national lobbies descending on the Russian capital at the moment, this does not mean that enterprises lack political influence. As the next chapter will demonstrate, enterprises have instead made a strategic decision: rather than looking to the federal level for support, they are focusing on the local and regional levels and allowing lower-level governments to do their lobbying for them. Defense industry is actually having a major impact on the de facto, as opposed to the official, Russian state budget, and individual enterprises are quite able to win favors for arms exports and other forms of governmental support. They are just not doing it in a way that benefits the sector as a whole.[173] The next chapter will explore in more detail how both subsectoral and local lobbying groups have dealt with the collective action problem facing Russian defense industrial firms.

Employment immobility within defense enterprises, along with the varied economic interests of individual managers, has two major implications for Russia's political future. First, it means that the so-called red directors and any associated military-industrial alliance[174] are unlikely to be a unified political force. It is doubtful that they will be able to field or elect a common slate of candidates for office or to push for any particular foreign policy goal, such as the reestablishment of the Russian empire. The West should not fear that such an alliance may lead the Russian state to become a military threat in the future, because cooperation among enterprises will be hard to maintain. Yet foreign influence, either Western or anti-Western, can grow in the sector as individual enterprises become dependent on particular export markets or investors and vulnerable to the breaking of those ties.

The second, more alarming implication is that employee collectives are likely to fight tooth and nail to keep their enterprises open and their jobs intact. If the enterprises close, both managers and workers are left with nothing. This means that as state resources for subsidies decline, the number of factory-based protests should increase. The level of violence may also increase, as desperation grows.

This seems in fact to be occurring. According to one newspaper report, there were 859 enterprise strikes throughout Russian industry during the first five months of 1995, a 120 percent increase over the same period in the previous year.[175] While there is no data on what percentage of these occurred in defense industrial enterprises, strikes are common in the sector, and some have indeed involved the threat of violence. In July 1994, for example, the labor collective at the Mashinostroenie defense plant in Nizhnii Novgorod imprisoned the plant director in his office one morning and marched out on to the street, threatening local and regional authorities with beatings if back wages were not paid (their demand was met).[176] A year later, at the Uralvagonzavod plant in Nizhnii Tagil, a disgruntled worker who hadn't been paid in four months stole a tank from his own shop at the factory following a family quarrel and drove it up and down the streets of the city with the police in hot pursuit.[177] He said that his actions were "a protest against the hopeless poverty of the defense complex." It would be easy to dismiss this as the act of a single misfit, except that "the following day spontaneous mass meetings occurred around the cashier officers of the factory: the workers demanded their pay." The county prosecutor decided to drop charges against the man with the tank, "considering the social tensions in the region and the support for the transgressor inside the factory."[178] Even more recently, in mid-1996, Interior Ministry troops were sent to break up a protest by workers at the Gorokhovets Shipyard, a former production site for naval weaponry, who had blocked the major highway linking Moscow and Nizhnii Novgorod.[179]

Managers trying to protect their jobs may also employ threats of violence against those who want to replace them. For example, at the Rybinskie Motors aircraft engine plant in Yaroslavl', the old general director, Valerii Anikin, angered Goskomoboronprom (which held 37 percent of the enterprise's stock) when he failed to invite its representative to a shareholder meeting that reconfirmed him in his post. As a result, the state authorities refused to renew Anikin's contract and appointed a temporary replacement director to take charge until the next stockholder meeting. This replacement director was then told by the enterprise's chief engineer that "if he signed the contract in the name of the general director, a blood terror would be organized" against him and his team.[180] Goskomoboronprom did win in this case, at least temporarily (more will be said about this in the next chapter), and a new meeting of the stockholders was held during which a new director was elected. The night before the meeting, however, the Moscow office of Rybinskie Motors was hit by two hand grenades. While no one was injured, many of the enterprise's legal documents were destroyed in the resulting explosions and fire.[181]

Thus while labor and capital immobility, supported by an underlying network of paternalism toward the individual collective, saps the national lobbying strength of Russia's military-industrial complex, it also increases the potential for social instability and mob violence in Russia's defense-heavy regions. Each of the cases noted above, at defense enterprises in four different regions and from four different subsectors, involved either the use or the threat of violence in response to fears of lost jobs or wages. Certainly, it is not only in the defense complex that strikes and the threat of labor violence have been reported in Russia. Coal miners and energy workers, among others, have also been involved in such activities. This should not make us any less worried about the impact that defense sector unrest will have on Russia's future, however. Social unrest and strikes at enterprises where weapons and military materials are made are dangerous, because they make threats of armed violence credible. In the next chapter, I further explore the consequences of defense sector regionalism in Russia.

3 Conglomerates, Lobbies, and Soviet Connections

The previous chapter described how the old Soviet defense enterprises survived with much of their existing structures intact in the new Russia, at least through 1995. In this chapter, I will show that many of the business partnerships cemented among these enterprises (and between enterprises and government authorities) in Soviet times also endured, although the pattern of endurance here is less strong. Some of these preexisting partnerships have been formalized into conglomerates called financial-industrial groups. Other partners formed new lobbying groups along old lines in order to obtain credits and other funding from the central government.

Once again, I will match the rational self-interest and socialization approaches against each other to see which provides the most convincing explanation for why these old ties seem so strong today. Have defense enterprise directors turned to these networks primarily to uphold long-standing norms of mutual obligation? There was a long-established tradition of working together to bail each other out when hard times hit. The socialization approach argues that enterprise managers should have seen this method of business as being both appropriate and comfortable. The "circular guarantee" (*krugovaia poruka*) would have continued to provide the basis for business trust and for new information in the uncertain environment of transitional Russia. From the socialization perspective, trust is the glue of relationships, and relationships are the basis for economic interaction.

The rational self-interest approach argues, in contrast, that strong short-term material incentives must have stood behind any connections that were maintained in the new era. Self-interested defense enterprise directors should have chosen to collaborate with their former colleagues if and only if it suited their immediate interests. If former partners were maintained in the new climate, they must either have exercised some kind of power over the director's enterprise (as a monopoly supplier, for example, or as the controller of a key economic lever, such as advertising) or have had something of immediate value to offer the enterprise. Since trusting anyone was foolish and voluntary collective action was unlikely, the old network ties should otherwise have quickly faded away under new market pressures.

Before turning to the evidence that can test these arguments, I will begin by showing that cooperation based on long-standing linkages at both the ministry and local levels has indeed been a common strategy used by Russian defense enterprises in the transition era.

Conglomerates and Lobbies in Russian Defense Industry

Many of the business relationships maintained among defense enterprises in the Yeltsin era reflect connections that were established either within Soviet-era nationwide ministries or within a particular Soviet-era administrative region. One of the common forms that these relationships have taken is the so-called financial-industrial group (FIG). An enormous amount of space in the Russian press has been dedicated to discussion of FIGs, even though there seems to be general agreement that the term is so ill-defined as to be almost meaningless.[1] The term refers to conglomerates of large enterprises and banks that have either purchased portions of each other's shares or formed a new, joint, independent legal entity (such as a holding company or association) with some sort of corporate oversight or investment responsibilities. Sometimes both kinds of conglomeration have been done simultaneously. While many FIGs are purely domestic, some stretch across the Russian border, drawing state-owned enterprises in Ukraine and other former Soviet republics into their fold. Such cross-state FIGs are usually designed to reestablish supply chains that were broken when the USSR collapsed.[2]

A set of Russian state rules officially defines financial-industrial groups using very narrow and exclusive criteria and promises special state benefits (including tax breaks and credits) to conglomerates designed according to these strict guidelines.[3] Policy makers have provided a variety of justifications for state support of the formation of such FIGs. Some hope that they will convince enterprises to strive for international competitiveness and thereby attract bank investment.[4] Others instead portray them as a means for establishing a protectionist, import-substitution industrial policy that rewards domestic investment and production.[5] But most organizations that call themselves FIGs or fit the FIG description are springing up independently. Depending on how one counts them, there were by the end of 1995 somewhere between tens and hundreds of such conglomerates, many of them centered on enterprises from the defense industrial sector.[6] Most of them are making no effort to follow the federal rules to obtain the promised special federal benefits. Instead, defense managers are choosing to enter them for reasons of their own.

Not all of these FIGs are based on preexisting networks.[7] Yet most defense enterprise FIGs do seem to be based on some kind of Soviet-era connection. Two patterns in particular stand out: those formed along the lines of the Soviet-era ministries and those formed among neighboring enterprises with investment by local and regional governments.

Ministry-Based FIGs

Several of the former Soviet defense industrial ministries have supported the formation of their own FIGs, which unite privatized or privatizing enterprises into common holding companies.[8] People who held positions of authority within those ministries are often involved in running these FIGs today, even though the ministries themselves no longer exist. Perhaps the most famous example is the Aviaprom FIG, founded by Apollon S. Systov. Systov headed the Ministry of Aviation Industry (MinAviaProm, hence the name of the FIG) in Soviet times.[9]

This pattern would appear to indicate that many independent defense enterprises have turned to those who held planning authority over them in the past for help in approaching the market. Some of these ministry-based FIGs were formed by enterprises situated along common production chains dating from Soviet times.[10] In other cases, FIG-like organizations that were formed along ministry lines (such as those for manufacturers of gas weapons and light aviation planes) appear to be constituted not for production reasons but as joint-stock companies designed to lobby the federal government for credits and other benefits.[11]

These ministry-based FIGs have retained significant ties with governmental authority figures in the Russian state, even though the ministries per se no longer exist. After the Soviet defense industrial ministries were disbanded in late 1991, a new state body was created in late 1992 to oversee Russian defense enterprises. There was a direct personnel pipeline between the old ministries and this new State Committee for Defense Industry (Goskomoboronprom),[12] whose departmental structure replicated the former ministerial division of industrial oversight responsibility. Western analysts usually view Goskomoboronprom as the organization replacing the Soviet-era Military-Industrial Commission (VPK, in its Russian acronym),[13] the planning board that used to supervise the separate defense production ministries, whose membership included representatives from each of them.[14]

Privatization has meant the end of official state control over many defense enterprises, so the FIGs that formed along former defense production ministry lines are not simply branches of the former Soviet ministries. Yet Goskomoboronprom kept close watch over these FIGs nonetheless. The committee (or in some cases, its transitional predecessor organization, the Committee on Defense Branches of the short-lived Russian Ministry of Industry)[15] actually created many of the FIGs itself. This process is worth describing in more detail.

During 1992, before privatization had occurred, many ministerial FIGs were formed from above with participation by former ministry administrators who were then serving in the Ministry of Industry.[16] Systov, for example, began planning the Aviaprom FIG even before the Aviation Ministry was officially abolished.[17] As the reform era progressed, leaders of many of these new FIGs seemed to be motivated by the desire to keep administrative control over enterprise activity. Certainly, the Ministry of Industry's Committee on the Defense Branches and its Goskomoboronprom successor shared similar attitudes toward enterprise independence: both tried to maintain state ownership over a number of defense enterprises whose collectives proposed privatization.[18] Many Russian analysts believe that governmental authorities set up ministerial FIGs explicitly so that Goskomoboronprom departments (and hence the former defense industrial ministers or their associates) could regain control over privatized defense enterprises.[19]

The functional and attitudinal similarities between the production ministries and Goskomoboronprom may be largely explained by the continuity in important personnel employed by these state agencies over time. For example, the deputy chairman of Goskomoboronprom in 1994 and the man in charge of Russian participation at international aviation exhibits, Anatolii G. Bratukhin, was deputy minister of aviation industry under Systov in the mid- to late 1980s.[20] Reportedly, as of 1994 many of the same staff members from the ministries continued to occupy the same block of posh offices that they did in Soviet times.[21] And while there do not seem to be any published expositions of how personnel for Goskomoboronprom were chosen, we do know that a similar agency, Rosvooruzhenie (responsible for oversight of Russian arms exports), was intentionally constituted from "experienced and professionally trained personnel" whose pedigrees extended back through agencies responsible for Soviet arms exports during the 1950s and 1960s.[22] It thus seems likely that Goskomoboronprom personnel also had such long-standing pedigrees.

When the Aviaprom FIG began to be formed in late 1991, official government statements indicated that it would "liaise with the Russian Ministry of Industry, specifically its new department of aviation industry."[23] Close links between state subsector authorities and the FIG were envisioned. Given that the head of the Aviaprom FIG used to supervise a Goskomoboronprom administrator who in turn oversaw the FIG and provided it with exhibition space and assistance at international shows, we can surmise that those close links endured. As late as 1994 Goskomoboronprom continued to be involved in creating new FIGs based on ministerial groupings.[24] Long-standing Soviet-era business relationships were thereby maintained under a new guise.

Local and Regional Cooperation

Some FIG-like defense enterprise organizations formed at a regional rather than ministerial level. These FIGs acted as bridges across subsectors of the defense industry. A clear example of such a FIG is the Nizhnii Novgorod Banking House, created in July 1992. This bank was founded by fifty-nine of the largest enterprises in the Nizhnii Novgorod province,[25] all of them having some kind of connection to defense industry.[26] The gubernatorial administration of the province (oblast) came up with the idea for founding this bank. Its purpose was to give large, long-term, preferential loans to its founding enterprises, to allow them to pursue projects involving conversion to civilian production.[27] The Russian government provided a special tax dispensation to the oblast administration for this purpose, allowing it to set aside half of the enterprises' taxes from 1992 into an extrabudgetary "Fund for Assistance to Conversion." This fund became the founding capital for the bank,[28] and the Russian state continued to extend a similar tax privilege to the region in succeeding years.[29] According to several knowledgeable officials, other provinces were envious of the deal Nizhnii Novgorod received, and there is speculation that Nizhnii Novgorod garnered special dispensations because President Yeltsin had obtained favors from its then-governor, Boris Nemtsov.[30] Nemtsov was a strong ally of Yeltsin's during the attempted coup against Soviet president Gorbachev in August 1991; indeed, he reportedly negotiated the famous deal with the Taman Division of troops, who refused the coup leaders' order to march on Yeltsin at the Russian White House, where he stood on a tank defending Soviet constitutional order.[31]

An investment council set up by the Nizhnii Novgorod oblast government makes the decisions about how the credits resulting from the tax dispensation are to be used. In September 1994 the chairman of the oblast's Directorate on Conversion and Military-Industrial Questions, Vladimir Bessarabov, described how the council works: The council includes representatives from the group of enterprise directors who founded the bank, from the labor unions attached to their factories, and from the oblast administration. Decisions are made jointly by this council, the provincial legislature, and the oblast administration.[32] In other words, managers, unions, and local officials sit down together to decide how state credits will be disbursed among the various enterprises benefiting from them.

Regional FIGs are not the only evidence of the importance of local ties for conducting defense business in Russia today. Local and provincial governments in Russia have also obtained direct partial control over the financial decisions made by defense enterprises located on their territories. Sometimes this results from bargaining that follows regional intervention in an enterprise's federal financial relationships. For example, regional governments have often paid off back wages that the Russian Defense Ministry owed to enterprise workers for already completed weapons orders. Usually, such payments followed strikes or other labor actions at the enterprise level and involved some kind of compromise worked out between the provincial leaders and the federal government. Such payments have been documented in Sverdlovsk oblast,[33] in Vladivostok,[34] in Nizhnii Novgorod,[35] and in the republic of Tatarstan.[36]

The city of Moscow, in cooperation with Goskomoboronprom, has perhaps gone the furthest to support its defense industries with direct financing. It reportedly invested over 61 billion rubles (approximately $12 million at the late-1994 exchange rate) of its own money in conversion projects proposed by over 300 local enterprises in a 1994 competition.[37] In 1992 Moscow also offered a special credit to enterprises in its satellite electronics industry city of Zelenograd.[38] One of the largest defense industrial FIGs, MAPO-MiG (now famous as the conglomerate chosen to supply eighteen MiG-29 fighter jets to Malaysia in 1994), turned to the Moscow city government for help in getting a bank to finance new housing construction for its workers.[39] The city government has offered twelve special tax breaks to encourage the formation of FIGs on its territory, using a looser definition of what a FIG is than is officially condoned by the federal government.[40]

The Pattern: Paternalism

These regional programs were designed to keep as many old enterprises afloat as possible. But the fact that competition for the credits was involved, as in Nizhnii Novgorod and Moscow, probably indicates that local authorities were granted a substantial say in the design of the ownership structure and investment strategies followed by the subsidized enterprises. In other words, this aid limited the independence of enterprise managers. In Nizhnii Novgorod, for example, the power wielded by regional authorities over enterprises is unambiguous. Governor Boris Nemtsov repeatedly claimed that only those conversion proposals that were supported by good business plans would be funded by the region's Banking House.[41] A knowledgeable official within the regional government said that in 1992 the demand for credits from the fund totaled 17 billion rubles but that only 5 billion were available to disburse; he claimed that only those projects that seemed likely to bring a return within eighteen months were financed.[42]

At the same time, it seems likely that none of the enterprises that founded the Nizhnii Novgorod Banking House would be cut off from assistance. If founding members were excluded from the process, the bank would be weakened; its capital would shrink each year as members withdrew from the associated tax credit scheme, and battles would rage at council meetings. Credits are therefore probably offered to everyone in a bargained atmosphere, as in Soviet times, with conditions attached. Enterprises have the incentive to be responsive to regional authorities, and regional authorities have the incentive to help everyone out to one extent or another. Given what we know about the continuities in structure and personnel from the Soviet ministries to Goskomoboronprom, it is likely that some kind of similar pattern exists for the ministerial FIGs. Certainly, the heads of departments within Goskomoboronprom continued to pressure the federal government for aid to those enterprises that they oversaw when the ministries existed,[43] even as they encouraged and supervised FIG formation.

What needs to be explained, then, more than the fact of cooperation itself, is the continuation of this Soviet pattern of paternalism, where enterprises are aided by the authorities (either those in Goskomoboronprom or those from the local government) in return for their loyalty and at least partial subservience to them. For each of the two cases considered here—ministerial ties and local ties—I will first explore in more depth the Soviet cultural institutions that set the pattern for later interactions. Then for each case I will turn to the arguments from the two perspectives about why the patterns continued into the new Russia.

Ministries as Institutions

From the late 1950s onward, Soviet leaders continuously tinkered with the state planning mechanism, instituting new structures and procedures in the hope of achieving cost savings and technological innovation.[44] Yet despite the variety of reform programs put forth over the decades, control over defense enterprise planning remained, for the most part, in the hands of various centralized branch ministries. These branch ministries supervised dozens and sometimes hundreds of geographically dispersed design bureaus and production plants, all working on similar or related technologies.

Several different defense production ministries, each with responsibility for a different subsector, existed side by side throughout the Soviet era, their number and titles varying over time.[45] At one time, from the mid-1970s through the late 1980s, there were nine such ministries. By the end of the Soviet period, seven remained: the Ministry of Machine-building (responsible for design and construction of ammunition and explosives); the Ministry of General Machine-building (responsible for design and construction of missiles and space rockets); the Ministry of Aviation Industry (responsible for the design and construction of both military and civilian aircraft, including helicopters); the Ministry of the Shipbuilding Industry (responsible for the design and construction of both military and civilian vessels); the Ministry of Electronics Industry (responsible for the design and construction of a variety of advanced electronic systems); the Ministry of Radio Industry (responsible for the design and construction of radio and radar equipment); and the Ministry of Defense Industry (which despite its name was limited to responsibility for the design and construction of ground forces weapons and battle equipment). An eighth ministry, Medium Machine-building, had earlier had responsibility for the mining and processing of nuclear materials and the design and construction of nuclear warheads; in 1989 it was merged with another ministry (which earlier controlled civilian nuclear power production) and was renamed the Ministry of Atomic Energy.[46] A ninth, the Communications Equipment Industry Ministry, was carved out of the Ministry of the Radio Industry in 1974; in 1989 it was merged with the Ministry of Communications (which was earlier responsible only for civilian communication matters, including the post office).[47]

From the early 1970s through the end of the Soviet era, the structural divisions among these ministries remained fairly constant (with some minor exceptions). Even the two ministries that were eliminated in 1989 retained their structural foundations in a new and expanded setting. Departmentalism was very strong, because there was little movement of personnel from one defense industrial subsector to another.[48] Each of the ministries thus formed a fairly closed social system.

Each ministry and its associated enterprises also formed a *krugovaia poruka*, a circle of mutual aid and obligation. In Soviet times, the ministries directed both the supply chains and the type and volume of production of the enterprises they oversaw. Ministry administrators oversaw both the design and manufacturing of weapons performed within their purview, and in many cases these production functions were not integrated within a single enterprise.[49] The ministry thus had to coordinate activities between the design bureaus and the factories that used their designs. (When the Soviet Union collapsed, a number of design bureaus and component parts manufacturers found themselves separated from the weapons production factories with which they had always cooperated, on opposite sides of sometimes unfriendly international borders.)[50]

Enterprises would engage in information exchange with their ministries as the state plan was being set, hoping to influence the shape the state directives took. Complex negotiations over planning details would then ensue between enterprise managers and ministerial representatives.[51] Both sides in the negotiations wanted to ensure a balance: goals had to be high enough to ensure the receipt of the bonuses that the state bestowed for continually increasing production but low enough so that enterprises could actually fulfill the plan.[52] The ministries probably knew that the use of illegal methods (including under-the-table barter between enterprises) was necessary for each enterprise to meet the plan and unofficially sanctioned such activities.[53] Only if the plans were met and overfulfilled would both the involved enterprises and the associated ministry personnel obtain the bonuses the state handed out for good performance.

Social networks were thus built between the enterprise and its ministry and among enterprises working under a common ministry. A unified Soviet military-industrial complex did not really exist (except, perhaps, at the apex of power),[54] because enterprises pursued all their economic activity under the auspices of the separate defense industrial ministries. Managers of various enterprises within the ministry would get to know each other by attending administrative functions arranged by the ministry, by engaging in backdoor barter to get supplies for production and consumer goods for workers, and when they themselves were appointed to positions within the ministerial hierarchy.[55] The tight personnel replacement hierarchies within enterprises, described in the previous chapter, would have meant that those appointed to positions in the ministries would have kept close contact with those who took their places in their home enterprises.

Often, relations between the branch ministries and the enterprises were themselves mediated by what were known as branch associations, which monitored particular sets of enterprises within the branch and thereby encouraged the formation of even stronger personal connections among sub-sets of enterprise managers.[56] (If an enterprise were unusually large, it might be named its own branch administration. This happened, for example, to the Svetlana defense industrial firm in St. Petersburg, whose managers expressed muted pleasure in escaping the extra layer of surveillance that the branch association had earlier placed over their activities.)[57] In addition to these branch associations, another form of intermediary existed between the min-istries and enterprises: the ministerial banks. In recent times, these have evolved to include both "channel banks," which were used by the ministries to funnel state funds to enterprises, and "agent banks," which were set up within enterprises themselves, essentially to act as corporate treasurers by per-forming and clearing day-to-day transactions.[58] Many of these banks have reportedly been involved in forming FIGs.[59]

The relationship between enterprises and ministries was complex. Enterprise managers were largely dependent on the ministries for arranging the raw material and equipment supply networks they required in order to meet the plan. They also relied on them to negotiate plans that were actually possible to meet. The ministries would themselves be judged and receive resources from higher authorities based on how well the enterprises under their purview performed, so it was in their interests to act as advocates for their enterprises, to ensure that the resources received were adequate for the job. Because of this, Western analysts have sometimes argued that the interests of enterprises and ministries were "identical" and that together they acted as a unified pressure group on the center.[60] This perception was reinforced in the case of the defense industrial ministries, because, as noted above, ministerial personnel tended to be drawn from the managerial corps of the group of enterprises under the specific ministry's supervision.[61]

Yet there was also an underlying tension between managers and ministe-rial officials, because close ministerial oversight and the resulting bureau-cratic red tape limited managers' freedom to meet the needs of their indi-vidual factories when unexpected contingencies arose. In the mid-1960s Soviet Prime Minister Aleksei Kosygin began to champion the notion that too much planning inhibited flexibility, and he encouraged managers to experiment independently to a limited degree.[62] The VPK participated in drawing up the Kosygin reforms,[63] and many defense enterprise managers responded enthusiastically to the new policies. They wrote articles and books arguing that planning should be based on real cost indicators rather than on artificially mandated production volumes and stated that enterprises should be allowed to find their own suppliers and customers rather than being subject to ministerial control over these links.[64] Too much control on the part of the ministries limited the ability of managers to achieve their primary goals, which were to keep both themselves and the enterprise collective economically and socially satisfied.

Despite a lengthy history of connections within defense industrial subsectors, then, and despite the fact that the ministries had acted as funding and planning advocates for their enterprises for many years, managers would have entered the reform era with ambivalent feelings about the desirability of maintaining those old ministerial ties. The fact of the Kosygin reforms, along with their abandonment, implies that there had been some kind of contest, lasting at least a decade, over who would control the enterprises. Managers socialized into the Soviet system would have had reason to doubt the motives of their former supervisors in the new system. The opportunity finally to get out from under ministerial control might have been seen as a blessing.

In view of all this, the socialization perspective cannot adequately explain why so many managers voluntarily sold shares of their enterprises and otherwise committed the economic future of their enterprises to the officials who used to supervise them. The Soviet-era networks may have been strong, but they were not based on a shared culture of trust. Tension marred the harmony of those connections. This leaves ample room for the rational self-interest school to propose a more cynical explanation for the appearance of ministerial FIGs.

Rational Self-Interest and the Former Ministries

As I noted above, the defense industrial ministries were disbanded in 1991 and eventually replaced with Goskomoboronprom departments. Some analysts are convinced that this series of administrative changes was a slap in the face to defense industrialists and a downgrading of their status.[65] (In an apparent attempt partially to restore the status of this sector, the State Committee for Defense Industry was eventually transformed into the Ministry of Defense Industry in 1996.)

If the old ministerial authorities had indeed lost all their power during the early transition era, then the rational self-interest school would have a hard time explaining why defense managers turned to them and their successors in the early 1990s, allowing former officials to supervise the formation of new FIGs. Especially if, as I argued in chapter 1, the economic environment discouraged people from trusting each other, then selling one's shares to a larger conglomerate would have been foolish, especially if there was already a history of conflict between the enterprise and the conglomerate supervisors. We know that at least some enterprises chafed against the fetters of the Ministry of Industry departments in 1992. For example, managers in the defense electronics city of Zelenograd complained that administrators from the former Ministry of the Electronics Industry were trying to convince the government to maintain a protectionist, self-sufficient national policy in supply and customer relations, thereby harming the ability of Russian microelectronics enterprises to become internationally competitive.[66]

Yet a deeper examination of the structural incentives involved in these relationships shows that self-serving motives did indeed support them. In spite of the federal government's decision to downgrade the status of the old defense industrial ministries by uniting them into a common committee, the remnants of those ministries received important administrative perks in the new system.

The first set of perks relates to property ownership. The ministries had been the official legal owners of the sites occupied by defense enterprises in Soviet times. In the late 1980s private cooperatives began to be carved out of these state enterprises (a process discussed in detail in the following chapter). Because of their property ownership rights, it was the ministries who legally had the right to decide which cooperatives would be allowed to rent out space;[67] they could even refuse to rent out space to entrepreneurs they disliked. As I will show in the next chapter, many of these cooperatives were used by enterprise managers as a way to obtain private income through the use (and sometimes abuse) of state property. It was therefore in the economic interests of managers to keep ministry administrators happy even as privatization began.

Similar ministerial property rights then continued into the new Russia. Each defense enterprise privatization decision made by the Russian State Property Committee has been done in consultation with the relevant department from either the Ministry of Industry or its Goskomoboronprom successor.[68] In other words, every instance of defense enterprise privatization occurred under the supervision of personnel from the former ministry. There have been numerous cases reported from 1992 through 1995 where defense enterprise privatization proposals were vetoed by Goskomoboronprom.[69] In some of these cases, the State Property Committee or other reformist federal organizations overrode the Goskomoboronprom veto, but this happened only after sustained and costly lobbying efforts by the involved enterprise managers.

Goskomoboronprom further retained the authority throughout the transition period either to dismiss or keep those managers of state-owned defense enterprises whose STKs gave them a vote of no confidence.[70] In essence, this gave former ministry officials direct control over managerial appointments, and presumably they preferred managers who upheld sectoral interests. The case of Rybinskie Motors, the enterprise, discussed in the previous chapter, whose battle over the directorship involved death threats and hand grenades, is particularly instructive in this regard. Goskomoboronprom owned 37 percent of the shares in the semiprivatized Rybinskie enterprise. Such partial continuing state ownership of privatizing defense firms was quite common during this era. The man who oversaw the state-owned shares in Rybinskie was Valerii Voskoboinikov, deputy chief of the Aviation Industry Directorate within Goskomoboronprom.[71] Not surprisingly, it was the Ministry of Aviation Industry that had supervised Rybinskie in the past. Voskoboinikov used his shares to force the appointment in April 1995 of a new enterprise director. The new director, who was the former chief engineer of the enterprise, received Goskomoboronprom support because he was willing, unlike the former director, to have Rybinskie continue manufacturing airplane engines. (These engines had been made for years in cooperation with another enterprise from the Soviet Ministry of Aviation Industry, called Permskie Motors.) Voskoboinikov wanted Rybinskie to keep building both military aircraft engines for planes designed by the Tupolev and Iliushin design bureaus and PS-90 engines for the Tu-204 passenger airliner.

The displaced director of Rybinskie, Valerii Anikin, who boasted that he had given investors a 300 percent return on their shares the year before, believed that concentrating on airplane engine construction would be economically foolish. The PS-90 engine in particular has had numerous safety and performance problems and is generally perceived to need substantial modifications in order to find use in the future.[72] Anikin had wanted Rybinskie to work instead with the U.S. firm General Electric to build turbines for natural gas extraction and had urged Goskomoboronprom to sell its state-owned shares to Gazprom, the privatized firm that used to be the Soviet Natural Gas Ministry. Gazprom was reportedly very interested in the turbines, which would replace expensive imported equipment.[73] Goskomoboronprom refused to sell its shares, arguing that Rybinskie was a strategic enterprise that should be kept on the list of concerns prohibited from full privatization.[74]

Several rounds of battles ensued throughout 1995. Prime Minister Viktor Chernomyrdin, former minister of the Oil and Gas Ministry and founder of Gazprom, stepped in officially to strike Rybinskie from the "not-for-privatization" list, which would allow Gazprom to buy Goskomoboronprom's shares.[75] But a subsequent attempt by the Russian State Bankruptcy

Administration to remove the new, Goskomoboronprom-supported Rybinskie director from his office failed, even though physical force was used.
This left Rybinskie's future privatization plans in doubt.[76] Rumor had it that
Goskomoboronprom's real motives in the case were to prevent a fully privatized Rybinskie from stealing the gas turbine market share of its old partner inside the ministry, Permskie Motors. Permskie Motors, located in
Perm', was reportedly backed by Goskomoboronprom chief and Perm'
native Viktor Glukhikh.[77]

This example makes it obvious that until all shares in privatized enterprises have been sold to private actors (keeping in mind that dozens or hundreds of defense enterprises will likely never be privatized), every general
director and each enterprise collective has a strong incentive to stay on the
good side of Goskomoboronprom officials from its former ministry. If personnel from the former ministry who are still connected to Goskomoboronprom view FIG formation or other forms of sectoral cooperation as a
means for them to recapture private gain from enterprises that wiggled out of
their control, it might very well be suicidal for managers in the midst of the
privatization process to refuse to enter such conglomerates.

Authorities from the former ministries retained other perks besides property ownership that could be used to reward or punish enterprises. For example, Goskomoboronprom retained some influence in this period over the
allocation of state defense orders.[78] In fact in early 1995 First Deputy Prime
Minister Oleg Soskovets announced that future payment to defense enterprises for fulfillment of state orders would be made through Goskomoboronprom rather than through the Defense Ministry.[79] In 1991 the Ministry
of the Electronics Industry (and its follow-on Ministry of Industry department) had used its influence in allocating orders against enterprises with
which it was annoyed. Enterprise managers in Zelenograd were especially
angry at the predatory way this ministry managed defense orders. When some
enterprises began trying to get out from under the control of the ministry, its
administrators apparently retaliated by ensuring that state orders were
directed elsewhere in the sector, depriving the independence-minded enterprises of income until they could find civilian orders on the market.[80] This
example should have been sufficient to demonstrate to managers the obsta-
cles they would face if they disregarded ministerial wishes.

Other more positive economic incentives might also have led enterprises
to stick with their former ministries throughout this era. For example, organizations from within the former ministries played a key role in negotiating
arms exports in Soviet times, giving them a knowledge base and set of inter-

national contacts that enterprises would want to utilize. In an era of murky property rights, when foreign purchasers did not know whom to trust in Russia and new Russian players lacked information about markets and prices, FIGs based on ministerial connections might have ended up playing a crucial role in obtaining arms sales deals. This has certainly been the case in the field of aviation,[81] arguably the area in which Russia has the strongest chance of making headway in the competitive developing world weapons market.

Former ministerial groupings also had the power to choose which enterprises would receive the most favorable advertising opportunities. For example, Goskomoboronprom was one of the sponsors of the Russian arms fair for international audiences, "Armaments, Military Technology, Conversion," held in Nizhnii Novgorod in September 1994.[82] Exhibit space at this fair was allocated to enterprises based on their departmental affiliations within Goskomoboronprom; in other words, by officials from their former ministries.[83] Furthermore, a Goskomoboronprom affiliate, the All-Russian Scientific-Technical Institute of Interbranch Information, owns a marketing database, a consulting business in the preparation of television and newspaper advertisements, and an exhibition hall in Moscow for continuous display of conversion products to foreign visitors.[84] Goskomoboronprom, at least as of late 1994, also had to preapprove all articles appearing in the slick new international advertising magazine for Russian weaponry *Military Parade*.[85] Any enterprise that tried to fight its Goskomoboronprom department would have been unlikely to have its products well advertised; any enterprise that allowed well-connected personnel from the former ministries to buy its shares in the form of a FIG was likely to gain access to the spotlight.

In addition to exercising direct power over enterprises, several former ministerial groupings within Goskomoboronprom (including the Electronics Industry Department)[86] and subsectoral FIGs (including Aviaprom,[87] the International Aviation Engines FIG,[88] and the Russian Association of Conversion Enterprises and Manufacturers of Gas Weapons Joint Stock Co.)[89] have all publicly lobbied the federal government for changes in state policy that would bring more credits for new civilian technology development to their members. It is interesting that in each case the basis for these lobbying efforts was some kind of joint-stock company, where members had to buy shares; indeed, there appear to have been no observable efforts by general-interest groups that were *not* joint-stock companies to engage in such sectoral lobbying. This means that personnel from the former ministries were able to provide selective incentives to those participating in the cooperative effort, because the joint-stock companies they founded received and distributed the state credits. Individual managers who chose not to join would not be on the official list of beneficiaries.

At least one of these efforts appears to have been very successful: a joint-stock company sponsored by Aviaprom. Aviaprom organized a conference on small plane construction in December 1994, which led to the formation of yet another FIG, the Russian Association of Light Aviation. This association's purpose was to "represent the interests of [small-plane aircraft designers and manufacturers] in the design and implementation of the federal program" for development of civil aviation.[90] In April 1995 the Russian federal government promised to invest $2 billion over four years in this program,[91] apparently in the form of loans from "extrabudgetary" sources.[92] A state-owned company was formed to finance this investment.[93] As with much other so-called extrabudgetary financing by Russian government authorities, the precise methods used by this company are shrouded in mystery.[94] Most likely, personnel associated with Goskomoboronprom retained financial resources that did not appear on paper.

There were thus good reasons throughout the years following the collapse of the Soviet ministries for wealth-seeking managers of Russian defense enterprises to agree to form FIGs under the aegis of their former ministerial bosses. The rational self-interest school wins over the socialization school on this point; it does a better job of explaining why managers would sell shares to those who used to supervise them, in the absence of a history of trust. Personnel from the former ministries could provide selective incentives (including credits, advertising, career support, and privatization approval) to defense managers who chose to cooperate with them, while leaving those who crossed them out in the cold.

What about a different argument that the socialization perspective might make: that networks formed between enterprise *directors* within Soviet ministries should endure in the absence of state oversight? If social norms of mutual obligation were at work, then directors should have turned independently to their old friends in related enterprises to see them through rough times. Existing supply and purchase chains should have been maintained by managers entering the market. The available evidence, however, seems to indicate that the influence of such sectoral networks is declining with time. For example, Aleksandr Grigor'ev, general director of NPO Impuls' in Moscow, stated in 1994 that the horizontal ties that had previously linked enterprises within Soviet ministries had disintegrated.[95] His production manager affirmed in an interview that considerations of cost and availability, not loyalty, now determine the enterprise's choice of business partners.[96] (Note that Impuls' is not in a ministerial FIG, and its state-owned shares are controlled by the State Property Committee, not Goskomoboronprom. Based on the above discussion, this may mean that it has more freedom than some of its counterparts to choose its own business partners.)

Analysts found much the same thing to be true in a range of enterprises in St. Petersburg in 1993: only the "essential few" contacts from previous times were maintained, while others fell away under cost pressures.[97] Both the Positron enterprise in St. Petersburg and the Urals Electro-Mechanical Enterprise in Yekaterinburg have turned not merely to more cost-competitive suppliers but also to foreign suppliers, because the quality of their components is generally recognized to be superior.[98] When former ministerial personnel are not applying pressure for enterprises to engage in FIG-related activity, managers are not choosing independently to retain old ties for their own sake.

Analyst Kathryn Hendley notes that the supply manager of the Saratov Aviation Factory reported that 90 percent of the enterprise's fourteen hundred suppliers had not changed between 1991 and 1993. It turned out, however, that managers at the enterprise considered three-fourths of these partners to be monopoly suppliers.[99] To their knowledge, then, they had no alternative except to maintain previous relationships. Hendley notes that it is possible that alternative suppliers did exist and managers at the Saratov factory simply didn't know about them. If this is the case, it might in fact support the arguments of the socialization school, because it would mean that these managers were following well-worn paths in their search for new contacts and new information rather than seizing the opportunity for an independent search for new possibilities.

Yet given the absence of a developed business information infrastructure in Russia during this transition period, including the lack of public databases and the paucity of reliable assessments of the financial health of particular enterprises, turning to old networks for information may have been the only course available to those who wanted to lower their chances of being victimized by predatory behavior. While the networks themselves were no guarantee of reliability, they were better than nothing. It would have been foolish for directors whose enterprises might otherwise have gone broke to ignore the availability of this assistance, however flawed it might have been. The probability that this was the case is increased by evidence from other enterprises. In St. Petersburg, for example, researchers report that while old contacts between enterprises began to fall away in 1993, it was through preexisting networks that managers found new business partners and obtained information about their reliability.[100]

The fact that existing contacts were used as entrées to new partnerships and old networks were discarded with time indicates that the predictions of the rational self-interest perspective remain superior to those of the socialization school. Old ties were used when they benefited managers and discarded when they ceased to be optimal.

What of the relationships between enterprises and ministerial banks? Perhaps here the socialization school could make a good argument that maintaining social networks still served to establish trust in the chaotic Russian business climate. Again, though, it seems likely that something other than pure trust was at work. According to a 1993 World Bank report, the "new ownership structure" of privatized banks in Russia is one where "banks are owned largely by enterprises," making "the practice of connected and insider lending common in the Russian banking system."[101] Enterprises may thus have turned to banks they knew not merely because they trusted them but because they owned them (or at least had significant ownership stakes in them). This would make the banks a source of constant low-cost loans, with no potentially embarrassing inquiries about credit worthiness or profitability.

A claim has been made more recently that banks are now reversing the direction of control in these relationships, taking the reins away from the enterprises. According to the deputy director of Aviabank (the bank associated with the Aviaprom group, founded by thirty-seven aviation industry enterprises in 1990), "while the 'child' [bank] has grown and matured, the 'parents' [enterprises] have begun to age," allowing banks to buy up their capital.[102] Presumably, such capital purchases occur when the enterprise cannot repay its loans other than by granting shares to the bank. An additional form of increased bank control over enterprises has occurred when banks have acted as white knight investors when workers and managers have not been able to afford a sufficient number of shares during privatization to guarantee insider control.[103] In fact, it is claimed that one of the reasons so many conglomerates are avoiding the federal FIG rules is that those rules limit banks to a mere 10 percent ownership stake in firms to which they are lending. For their part, banks oppose the rule because it deprives them of control over their operations.[104]

Currently, there is insufficient evidence to prove whether banks have truly managed to turn the tables on their founders. We do know, however, that bank managers and defense enterprise directors are not always different people, and thus the question may be a red herring. Banks that call in loans through share purchases may merely be a means for some enterprise directors to gain control over additional enterprises. An example of this occurred at Promstroibank-St. Petersburg, a bank that owned shares in several defense industrial enterprises. This bank chose as its chairman of the board Valerii V. Filippov, the general director of the Ferrit company, a defense industrial enterprise,[105] and a member of the Association of Industrial Enterprises,[106] a St. Petersburg defense industrial lobbying group. Promstroibank–St. Petersburg was the largest investor in the Baltiiskii Zavod military shipbuilding enterprise; Baltiiskii Zavod was in turn a minor shareholder in the bank. In 1994 Baltiiskii received a huge loan from the bank that it could not repay. As a result, the bank took over a dormitory on Baltiiskii's property, which it planned to refurbish as a hotel.[107] One defense enterprise director in effect called in a debt from another.

Further casting doubt on the image of defense enterprises as sacrificial lambs to their own banks is the fact that some defense industrial FIGs foundered when their associated banks were shut down by the authorities for insolvency.[108] Since the manufacturing enterprises in these FIGs do not appear to have been shut down, this would indicate that enterprise managers may instead have used the banks as short-term cash cows. Thus while some banks may in fact have taken control away from opportunistic enterprise managers, clearly all have not done so.

For the most part, then, networks linking managers in Soviet times seem to have been maintained after the collapse of the old system only if they were directly economically convenient for the enterprises involved and not out of loyalty. Some enterprise managers have been more clever than others and gained at others' expense. But there is little evidence that old ministerial networks are being maintained in the absence of material rewards. The rational self-interest approach has done the best job of the two perspectives in explaining the continuation of ministerial ties. The socialization approach makes a significant contribution, however, by pointing out that established social networks at the beginning of the reform process influenced the self-interested directions that were taken later. Still, managers seem to have adapted quickly to the rules of the new game, selecting which members of their old business networks to maintain based on a recognition of the direct economic costs and benefits involved and not on established norms of propriety.

How has the second set of Soviet-era networks, those among local enterprises and authorities, withstood the transition era?

Soviet Culture: Local and Regional Connections

Like ministries, municipal and regional administrative councils (*soviets*, in the conventional English spelling) were also held responsible in Soviet times for the performance of enterprises. Those responsibilities were based on enterprises' locations, regardless of ministerial affiliations. Local governments, like ministries, would often act as advocates for "their" enterprises, lobbying higher authorities for more resources for them.[109] They had good reason for doing so. In return for such advocacy, enterprises were expected to fulfill special tasks for their cities and regions when state budget allocations left local needs unmet. These tasks included sending out "volunteers" from the enterprise to help with the local harvest, often in deep mud and cold rain with primitive tools; diverting enterprise employees, equipment, and supplies from their normal uses in order to build roads and other local infrastructure; arranging for heavy industrial enterprises to produce consumer goods for the local market when insufficient items were received from the center; and helping out nearby enterprises that were experiencing production difficulties, so that the state plan could be met on time.[110]

Defense enterprises, often representing a variety of subsectoral ministries, tended to be concentrated in specific local areas.[111] A number of large cities were dominated by defense industry or defense research facilities.[112] Some smaller towns were established solely as defense industrial or research bases; these were so closed to outsiders that residents had to lie to relatives about their domiciles and employment.[113] In each of these areas, defense enterprises would have dominated the concerns of local government.

Ties between enterprises and regional (oblast) authorities were strengthened by the *sovnarkhoz* reforms of 1957–1965. As part of continuing Soviet efforts to rationalize the economy, the central ministries in Moscow were temporarily denied some of their previous rights of control over enterprises, and planning responsibilities were given to oblast planning agencies instead. Although some Western analysts have traditionally believed that the *sovnarkhoz* reforms did not have much of an impact on defense industrial enterprises,[114] we now know that there were some real administrative effects on the defense sector. Evidence made public by the partial opening of the Moscow archives of the Central Committee of the Communist Party proves that the regional planning agencies did oversee at least some defense industrial operations.[115] There was a "handing over of [defense branches of industry] to the *sovnarkhozy* [regional administrations]."[116] Regional party administrations were reorganized at this time to oversee defense industry production in at least Leningrad and Novosibirsk (two defense-heavy regions),[117] and efforts were made to find new jobs for those let go from the ministries that oversaw aviation industry, radio-technology industry, shipbuilding, and electronics (presumably an indication that administrative employment in those ministries fell as their responsibilities were given to the regions).[118] In 1965, the year these reforms officially ended, enterprises in at least the ship-building and electronics sectors were transferred back to the ministries from the *sovnarkhozy*,[119] again indicating that administrative changes had been put into effect by the reforms.

We also know that the local *sovnarkhoz* was involved in drafting plans for the 1959–65 period at the Krasnoe Sormovo military shipbuilding plant in what was then called Gor'kii (now renamed Nizhnii Novgorod),[120] indicat-ing that it had some sort of supervisory role. Simultaneously, the Communist Youth League (Komsomol) organization at Krasnoe Sormovo worked on planning issues with its counterpart at the Dvigatel' Revoliutsii diesel ship plant in the same city,[121] again indicating strong local party ties among defense enterprises. In at least several defense-heavy regions and in at least several defense ministries, the *sovnarkhozy* did have some administrative impact on planning and did appear to cement new ties between local enter-prise personnel.

In a number of major defense-heavy regions, including Moscow, Lenin-grad, Sverdlovsk, Gor'kii, and Novosibirsk, subsectoral administrations were set up inside the *sovnarkhozy*.[122] Little ministries were thus created at the regional level. This arrangement would probably not have fostered regional crossbranch contacts between defense and nondefense enterprises, given the departmentalism inherent in the Soviet ministerial structure. Aviation facto-ries, for example, would not have been put under the same planning author-ity as pasta factories or even fuel processing plants.[123] But the fact that regional branch administrations, not just national branch associations, were now involved in enterprise oversight meant that regionally based social and economic connections would have been built among managers within the defense sector. It was reported that at least in some defense-heavy regions, for example, local suppliers were found for machine-building enterprises that had earlier received long-distance supplies.[124]

While the *sovnarkhoz* measures were temporary and are widely regarded as having failed to improve economic productivity in the Soviet Union, defense industrial enterprises would nonetheless have experienced an alternative model of economic association for almost ten years, strengthening their ties with their regional counterparts. (And regional branches of the VPK continued to operate throughout the Soviet period.) These regional ties would likely have expanded the information base available to managers and lowered their trans-action costs for under-the-table barter deals and would hence have improved their abilities to negotiate workable plans with their ministries. It would have made sense, then, for managers to maintain such contacts even after the *sov-narkhoz* reforms ended.

Another mechanism also served throughout the Soviet era to develop net-works among managers of different enterprises in the same locality. Directors of large or important enterprises tended to be given seats on the local and regional soviets by the vote of their collectives.[125] In 1959, for example, the chairman of the Sormovo district soviet of Gor'kii and the "mayor" of the city of Gor'kii itself were both from the Krasnoe Sormovo shipyard.[126] As noted above, these soviets were in turn partly responsible for oversight of the enter-prises located on their territories. The directors of neighboring enterprises would thus have formed another example of a *krugovaia poruka*, a circle of mutual aid and obligation. When a soviet asked an enterprise for help with road construction, or the harvest, or consumer goods production for the city, as described above, it would not only have cemented feelings of mutual obligation between the city and the enterprise; it would also have simulta-neously involved mutual obligations between one large enterprise director and another.

This helps to explain why municipal and regional associations of defense industry managers appeared in many locations during the late 1980s and early 1990s, as the power of the central ministries declined and the market began to open. The managers forming these associations would already have known each other well. For example, the Association of Industrial Enterprises in St. Petersburg, formed in 1989 by nine local defense enterprise directors (and later growing to include thirty-one enterprises and two banks), was based on social contacts developed during the Soviet era.[127] The ELANG Associa-tion was similarly independently created in Zelenograd in 1991 "for business purposes" by the leaders of five enterprises and production associations.[128] A comparable association of enterprises was formed in Nizhnii Novgorod in 1990.[129]

Local authorities may have needed to take action early in the reform era to bridge the gaps between enterprises that had been under the supervision of dif-ferent ministries. Yurii Solodovnikov, deputy director of the Military Industrial Complex and Conversion Commission in what was then the Leningrad City Soviet, wrote that his committee was instrumental in gathering information about local defense enterprises that had been in separate ministries, so that common conversion plans could be worked out. According to Solodovnikov, "in the first half of [1990], there was an attempt to assign the members of the commission as 'curators' of the enterprises, on the basis of what was already known to the deputies because of their previous work or domiciles."[130] In other words, defense industrial representatives sat on the city council together and used it as a means for strengthening their cooperative relationship. (The fact that managers from different enterprises had previously worked together on city business would not have led them to share what would earlier have been considered classified details about each other's production profiles.)

Other defense-heavy regions also began the reform era with a high concentration of local politicians and policy makers coming from common defense-related backgrounds. For example in Nizhnii Novgorod, the governor, the chairman of the oblast soviet, the chairmen of both the oblast Committee on Economics and the Administration for Economic Prognosis, and the chairman of the board of the Nizhnii Novgorod Banking House (the local defense industry FIG described earlier) were all graduates (from one era or another) of the Nizhnii Novgorod Radio-Physics Institute.[131] This institute acted as a feeder of scientific personnel to a number of Nizhnii Novgorod defense plants, including Nitel, Krasnoe Sormovo, and the Popov Communications Equipment Enterprise.[132] While Governor Nemtsov himself did not join the defense complex, through his work as a physicist in the 1980s he met and befriended the father of the Soviet nuclear bomb, Andrei Sakharov, the well-known dissident and peace activist.[133] Given his accomplishments, Sakharov would have been both acquainted with and respected by many defense scientists in the region where his former Arzamas-16 home was located, despite his dissident status. (And midway through the Gorbachev era, Sakharov was working actively with the support of the Soviet state once again, this time as an advocate of reform.) These networks would have served as an ideal platform for the Nizhnii Novgorod authorities to use to communicate with defense managers about conversion issues. Regardless of what we might assume were the differences in their political views, they all would have spoken a common technical language and shared a common base of work experience. As was mentioned above, Nemtsov has consistently acted as a strong advocate for local defense enterprises at the federal level.[134]

Obviously, as in the case of ministerial ties, the relationship between enterprises and regional governments would have cut two ways. The same kinds of pros and cons of paternalism would have been elements of the relationship. On the one hand, cities and regions lobbied the central government for resources for local enterprises; on the other hand, they demanded services from the enterprises in return. Local and regional authorities acted as one more set of enterprise interlopers, eager to interfere in management decisions. Sectoral ministries and local authorities existed in a state of constant tension with each other.[135] Enterprises would have found themselves caught in the middle.

Rational Self-Interest and Local Ties

The dual-faceted nature of this relationship is continuing today. Cities and regions have a direct interest in ensuring the health of the enterprises in their areas. This means that enterprises have a direct interest in maintaining good relations with the local authorities who come to their assistance.

To some extent, the concern of regional authorities is financial. This has been especially true since 1992, when responsibility for social welfare payments began to fall increasingly on the shoulders of local governments.[136] Cities and regions have good reason to help keep their factories open, through federal subsidization if need be, in order to avoid local unemployment. Simultaneously, the Russian federal government has shed its budgetary responsibilities, largely in response to demands by organizations such as the International Monetary Fund to cut federal spending, and has forced local governments to pick up its former budget items. For this reason, subnational governments now find themselves paying for the lion's share of enterprise subsidies.[137] Local authorities thus have a strong stake in their enterprises doing well on their own.

Local authorities may also have a direct personal stake in the well-being of local defense workers. As noted in the previous chapter, a wildcat strike of defense industrial workers at the Mashinostroenie plant in Nizhnii Novgorod in July 1994 included an apparently drunken threat that workers would march to the regional kremlin to beat up municipal and regional conversion authorities. In another instance, in Izhevsk, the capital of defense-heavy Udmurtiia (and itself a newly reclosed city because of fears of weapons leakage to foreigners or the mafia),[138] the mayor actually was beaten up in June 1995, when he went out to talk to irate demonstrators who were angry that the city had raised the rent on their apartments at a time of delayed wage payments, in order to fund the construction of new luxury homes.[139]

Not surprisingly, then, for both economic and social stability reasons, local and regional authorities have acted as federal lobbyists for the defense enterprises located on their territories. One particular sore point raised in these lobbying efforts has been delays in federal wage payments to those working on Defense Ministry contracts. The amount of back wages owed to defense workers has become staggering. This is reportedly in part because the

Defense Ministry placed orders for weapons without paying much attention to its actual budget.[140] According to Defense Ministry representatives, it may also be because the Finance Ministry, the banks, and Goskomoboronprom refused to release funds that had been allocated for wage payments.[141] No unified set of figures defines the limits of the defense budget—the precise share of military expenditures in Russia has reportedly remained unknown even to the legislature that approves the federal budget every year—and there have been numerous complaints about this lack of transparency from both parliamentarians and concerned outside advisers.[142]

Several local governments in defense-heavy regions have done an excellent job of convincing the state to cough up back wages (as well as subsidies) for local enterprises by using a uniquely powerful political tool: tax withholding. This is possible because the taxation system in Russia is based on what is called "upward transfer sharing." Federal taxes are collected at the local level by inspectors whose salaries come from Moscow but whose nonsalary benefits (including housing) come from local governments. (According to the World Bank, some estimates indicate that salaries account for only 30 to 40 percent of the overall compensation package received by state tax service employees.)[143] In theory, the federal government receives these transfers from local inspectors and then returns a set portion of the revenues to local governments for their own use. However, the portion returned to the local governments varies significantly across regions and is set arbitrarily through ongoing negotiations.[144] Unhappy regional leaders can use tax withholding as a tool in these negotiations. Because tax service employees are dependent on local governments for benefits, they can be convinced to collude in the decision not to send on the full measure of taxes owed to Moscow. There is little Moscow can do to collect these arrears. In one analyst's words, the system is "ad hoc, bargained, [and] nontransparent."[145]

Since 1992 at least thirty regions in Russia have used the tax-withholding tool to try to influence federal policy.[146] Efforts in the regions of Tatarstan and Omsk have led directly to new federal funding for defense conversion.[147] Several county-level cases of tax withholding have also been reported in defense-heavy Nizhnii Novgorod.[148]

The Republic of Tatarstan represents a particularly significant case in this regard.[149] This republic, with a large Muslim population, is famous for having been the first Russian region to get special federal concessions, in February 1994, over its constitutional status, at least in part because of its use of the tax-withholding weapon.[150] Throughout 1994 and into 1995 Tatarstan continued to bargain successfully with federal authorities, primarily Prime

Minister Viktor Chernomyrdin and First Deputy Prime Minister Oleg Soskovets, in order to obtain special conversion credits, tax preferences, long-term state orders, and an independent affiliate of the state arms export agency, Rosvooruzhenie, for its defense industrial enterprises.[151] (Nizhnii Novgorod oblast had been the first region to negotiate successfully an independent Rosvooruzhenie affiliate, in 1994.)[152] Tatarstan remained unsatisfied with the conduct of federal defense industrial policy despite these successes. In July 1995, after Prime Minister Chernomyrdin failed to respond to the republican leadership's requests for Defense Ministry debts to be paid off, Tatarstan once more began withholding its tax payments. This time authorities announced that they would save all the funds they owed to the federal government and send them directly to the republic's defense industry workers instead.[153]

Like the former ministries, local governments also have the power to threaten their enterprises with negative incentives. A December 1993 presidential decree gave regions the right to impose their own taxes on local enterprises as they see fit, without central government oversight.[154] Because enterprises lack capital mobility, managers find themselves caught in whatever tax structure their region hands down to them. (There is no evidence that anything has emerged in Russia that resembles the U.S. system of competition between states to attract businesses to relocate.) Furthermore (as was noted in the previous chapter), in the new system enterprises depend on subnational governments to assume their Soviet-era housing and social infrastructure burdens. Relief from expenditures on housing can mean the difference between enterprise survival and bankruptcy.

Since it is in the interests of regions to maintain as much employment as possible to avoid social welfare payments and social instability, it is unlikely that threats of induced bankruptcy will be used at the local level. Managers share with local and regional officials an interest in the endurance of enterprises, and thus there is every rational economic incentive to continue to work together. Even so, as in Soviet times, local and regional authorities continue to extract favors from the enterprises they assist. In particular, enterprises have faced pressures to give "donations" of resources to local governments.[155] Sometimes, these donations include cash loans,[156] something managers probably provide with gritted teeth during this era of scarce funds. Enterprises and local authorities depend on each other's success; the *krugovaia poruka* reasserts itself.

A Special Case of Self-Interested Behavior: St. Petersburg

There are some cases where local authorities and enterprises have not seen eye to eye, however. In St. Petersburg, for example, the mayor during the immediate post-Soviet era, Anatolii Sobchak, had a more ambivalent attitude toward his city's defense enterprise directors than that held by leaders in Moscow, Nizhnii Novgorod, or Tatarstan. Sobchak had the reputation in some circles of preferring to develop the city's potential as a tourist spot rather than trying to salvage its ailing high-tech defense enterprises.[157] A number of defense enterprise directors reportedly said in 1993 that Sobchak "regarded the survival of defense industry as irrelevant."[158] City officials early in the reform period in fact encouraged the formation of new small businesses as a means for countering pressures from the old state enterprises for bailouts to keep the city economy functioning.[159] In June 1994 Sobchak accused enterprise directors of prospering at the expense of their workers, which not surprisingly caused directors to respond with outrage and claims of unfairness.[160] In the 1995 words of one analyst, "The military-industrial complex doesn't love him."[161]

Although an article in one of the city's newspapers in January 1995 praised Sobchak for deciding to give city support to military-industrial enterprises,[162] it seems that this support came only in response to harsh pressure from an alliance uniting local defense industrialists, trade union leaders, and, in a surprise move early on in the reform process, federal authorities. The problem began in January 1993. The St. Petersburg city government announced that 70 percent of a credit package it was to receive from the Russian federal government for economic restructuring had already been allocated. The money would go to light industrial and food production firms that had solid plans for the future. A newspaper report said, "Enterprises of the MIC [military-industrial complex] and heavy industry still have not presented such programs. Therefore, for them to receive a part of the credit is problematic."[163] Apparently, defense industry was scheduled to receive only 400 million rubles from a 9.5 billion ruble program,[164] even though it was claimed that 35 percent of the local working population was employed in defense industrial enterprises.[165]

By early February, it had been discovered that the proposed federal credit to St. Petersburg had been frozen, apparently by the Russian Central Bank and Ministry of Finance. An article in a local newspaper explicitly linked this credit freeze to the disappointment of defense enterprises, saying that they "used (in this case with frozen credits) their lobby in the government. Now it is hoped that there will be a revision of the existing order for disbursing credits."[166] The first deputy mayor for industry of St. Petersburg, Dmitrii Sergeev, went to Moscow to argue with Prime Minister Chernomyrdin, and it was subsequently announced that the Central Bank had decided to unfreeze the credits. Once again, city leaders emphasized that the credit was to be used to support concrete production, not for debt relief for ailing enterprises.[167] Within a week, however, the promise to unfreeze the credits still had not been fulfilled. Chernomyrdin at this point publicly stated, perhaps coincidentally, that four areas were to be given credit preference throughout Russia: oil and gas production, the social sphere, science, and the defense industry.[168] The prime minister refused several invitations to visit the city to negotiate with local authorities; when his deputy for economics, Boris Federov, did visit St. Petersburg, he announced, "We don't have the resources to finance even the most important directions. . . . There will be no more credits."[169]

After several more invitations to visit the city, Chernomyrdin finally arrived in April 1993, apparently at least in part on the invitation of the Association of Industrial Enterprises in St. Petersburg (a defense managers' lobbying group). While he was touring the shopfloor at one defense enterprise, according to a newspaper report, the Association directors got together to "agree on a position." They prepared a request to the government, asking for more budgetary support and describing as "very complicated" the social situation in the city, where "every new day a social explosion threatens [to occur]."[170] Chernomyrdin was reportedly "disappointed" after his meeting with the defense directors, telling them they had to do more to adapt to the market, but he repeated during this visit his earlier statement about the four sectors—among them, the defense industry—that were to receive credit priority. He is reported to have said that he would provide means for the support of the St. Petersburg economy if city leaders could present a "complex program" for using such funds.[171] In mid-April, the government finally gave the credits to the city, which announced that they would be used for two purposes: defense industry conversion programs and housing construction.[172]

It is clear that the Association of Industrial Enterprises must have used a federal connection to pressure the local government. Only such a connection could explain the freezing and unfreezing of the credits, the visit of Chernomyrdin, and the redirection of credits toward enterprises that the mayor did not wish to support. One key individual probably played an important role.

Georgii Khizha had been the general director of the Svetlana Association military production facilities and was the man responsible for founding the Association of Industrial Enterprises in 1989.[173] In May 1992 Yeltsin appointed him deputy prime minister of Russia, with responsibility for both industry and arms sales. Up to that point, Khizha had been deputy mayor of St. Petersburg under Sobchak, and he had the reputation for being a skillful go-between who was able to bridge the often yawning gap between the mayor and local defense enterprise directors.[174] After Khizha went to Moscow, the organization he founded expanded from nine to thirty-one enterprises. While no direct evidence is available on this point, it makes sense that selective incentives favoring lobbying activity would have played a role in this expansion. Khizha viewed it as his "duty" to support defense industrial interests[175] and was thus likely to do all he could to help out members of "his" Association.

The story of relations between the mayor and defense enterprises didn't end in April 1993. Within a month, Khizha had been fired by Yeltsin. Although an apparently unsubstantiated rumor circulated that he was implicated in an arms-smuggling scheme,[176] the standard explanation for his removal was that he was not reform-minded enough for the Russian leadership.[177] While there is no direct evidence on this point, it is always possible that Khizha's intervention in St. Petersburg finances played a role in his departure, given that Yeltsin and Sobchak were reported to be close friends.

The conversion credits that Moscow had promised to enterprises in St. Petersburg, like those promised everywhere else, were delayed by the ongoing Russian defense budget crisis and only began arriving in late spring 1994.[178] In February 1994 the Association of Industrial Enterprises sent appeals to Yeltsin, Chernomyrdin, both houses of parliament, and the Federal Security Council on the matter. The Association approached Sobchak and asked him to join their appeal, but he responded that he was too busy and sent his deputy Dmitrii Sergeev in his place.[179] Shortly thereafter, the local affiliates of the Federation of Independent Trade Unions of Russia (FNPR, in its Russian abbreviation), the follow-on organization to the official Communist Party–controlled "trade unions" of Soviet times, formed a strike committee that united the labor forces of thirty of the largest enterprises in the city. They held their meetings at the Kirovskii tank factory. Complaints about the back wages owed to defense workers—and the unresponsiveness of city authorities to this situation—were central to their concerns.[180] At the end of April 1994 the FNPR began sending representatives to picket the Smol'nyi, the building that served as the head offices of the city administration.[181] These pickets continued throughout the summer.

In October 1994, the local FNPR chairman, Yevgenii I. Makarov, said that unless the city fulfilled its obligations to local workers, "a series of sharp conflicts may follow in a host of enterprises in the city."[182] He explicitly cited "tense situations" at a number of defense factories.[183] One week later, a national FNPR strike and demonstration was held in cities throughout Russia, to protest the direction of economic reforms. This action had been planned far in advance, and despite FNPR claims about the effect it might have, most

Russian authorities did not appear to be anxious on the eve of the event. It was assumed that participation rates would be low.

Yet Makarov managed to get somewhere between forty and seventy thousand demonstrators out on the streets of St. Petersburg,[184] dwarfing the protests held elsewhere (for comparative purposes, only four to five thousand demonstrators turned out in Moscow, even though the FNPR had expected seventy thousand there, too).[185] A few days later, Makarov reminded city authorities of the FNPR's earlier demands for a city program of industrial support, complete with tax relief, credits, and loans.[186] By the start of the new year, Sobchak announced the formation of a new St. Petersburg Fund for Support of Industry,[187] which gave defense enterprises a 15 billion ruble tax break and sent a matching amount of money to local electricity and water supply companies to pay off defense enterprises' utility debts.[188] A couple of months later, Sobchak invested city funds in a new defense conversion joint venture for the manufacture of city buses. The home of this joint venture was the Kirovskii factory,[189] the point of origin for the FNPR strike activity. In the words of one press report, "Credit for the fact that the situation has not become even worse, in the opinion of [industrialists], belongs to the city's mayor."[190] He just needed a little push.

In this second half of the St. Petersburg saga, it is not clear why the city authorities gave in. Khizha was long gone from the corridors of power, and there was no evidence of federal involvement in Sobchak's decision to create the support fund or aid the Kirovskii venture. Furthermore, St. Petersburg has had a sufficient influx of market activity, including foreign investment, that it is unlikely that its overall economy is truly dependent on the health of defense enterprises. In addition, Sobchak demonstrated that at least in early 1995 he had nothing to fear from local elections. In October 1993 Yeltsin disbanded local soviets throughout Russia for reelection following the national parliamentary crisis of that same month. At that time, Sobchak effectively transferred all real power over policy to the mayor's office. Robert Orttung claims that a fax Yeltsin sent announcing the closure of the soviet's meeting hall was actually written by Sobchak for Yeltsin to sign.[191] Later, St. Petersburg repeatedly made the national news because throughout 1994 it was only with difficulty that voting in the new local parliamentary elections achieved the 25 percent participation rate necessary to have the results declared valid.[192]

Because neither federal intervention nor immediate electoral pressure appears adequate to explain Sobchak's move and because he withstood pressure from the local defense industrial lobby for so long before agreeing to help them, it is probable that it took the show of strength made by the FNPR at the October 1994 rally to persuade Sobchak to give in to defense industrialists' demands. Perhaps he, like the Nizhnii Novgorod authorities, feared the possibility of social unrest and violence. St. Petersburg newspapers throughout 1994 stated that at various defense enterprises "the situation in the collective is such that there are sufficient sparks to set off a fire" (referring to the Baltiiskii Shipbuilding Factory) and "the production areas literally boil with passion in spontaneous meetings" (regarding Svetlana).[193] Perhaps it merely took Sobchak several years and uncounted battles to understand the political lay of his own land. By the end of 1995 he was facing a summer 1996 electoral battle against Viacheslav Shcherbakov, the former head of the regional division of the state arms export agency Rosvooruzhenie and a man closely connected to St. Petersburg's trade unions.[194] And in fact in June 1996 Sobchak lost his reelection bid for the newly titled position of governor of St. Petersburg. Shcherbakov had withdrawn from the race in favor of the winner, Vladimir Yakovlev, but Yakovlev then appointed Shcherbakov as his chief deputy.[195]

As the experience of St. Petersburg makes clear, local lobbying and conglomeration in Russian defense industry are not merely a result of pressure emanating from local authorities. Sometimes, local enterprise networking is pursued as a means for influencing those authorities rather than being a tool influenced by them.

Rational Self-Interest or Socialization?

Both sectoral and regional cooperation among defense enterprises and government authorities seem to be strongly supported by self-interested motives. Through cooperation, enterprises gain subsidies, lobbying support, and access to marketing and advertising services. In turn, former ministry officials get ownership shares in privatized enterprises and continuing control over the decisions of those that remain state-owned. Local and regional officials in defense-heavy areas gain both popularity among the citizenry and relief from social support service payments that they would otherwise face.

It would seem that local governments and enterprise directors had more genuine interest in each other's well-being than did Goskomoboronprom and the ministerial FIGs. If the ministerial authorities were to disappear, only the least innovative managers would likely mourn their passing, given that these authorities have had a tendency to interfere in privatization and reprofiling plans. But the healthier the regional economy is, the more credits and subsidies may be available to local enterprises now that the federal government has shed its responsibilities in that arena. The healthier local enterprises are, the fewer resources the local government will have to spend on unemployment compensation and poverty relief. This means that local and regional defense enterprise connections are likely to remain politically important into the future. This mutual dependence clearly results from Russia's reform-era economic and legal structures. The rational self-interest perspective is correct in pointing to objective environmental institutions as the source for behavioral incentives. Everyone participating in these reconstituted networks gains great benefit from them.

Yet it must be recognized that actors at the local and regional levels have used existing, long-standing relationships to take advantage of this structure rather than merely being constrained by it. Soviet patterns of network interaction and mutual help, especially the pattern ensuring that enterprise directors would form a local elite network in defense-heavy areas, helped to determine which economic incentives would be important in the new system. In the words of one socialization theorist, "Economic institutions do not emerge automatically in response to economic needs. Rather, they are constructed by individuals whose action is both facilitated and constrained by the structure and resources available in the social networks in which they are embedded."[196] Continuity in old norms and networks caused the emergence of the particular structural pattern that appears to be dominating defense industrial lobbying and conglomeration activities today.

The socialization perspective did not do a good job of explaining the pattern of ministerial links in the reform era. Managers should have distrusted the ministries but trusted each other, if history was their guide. Networks with suppliers and buyers should have been maintained even as networks with former planning supervisors were severed. Instead, the opposite occurred: as new market opportunities presented themselves, managers turned away from enterprises with which they had traditional production links but joined FIGs headed by former ministry authorities. Rational self-interested motives explain their actions better than do cultural norms or habits.

Yet the reform-era pattern of enhanced local and regional ties is best explained when both material interests and cultural norms are considered. Self-interest and socialization reinforce each other here, making locally based social and economic institutions even more powerful. As a result, Russia finds itself in a unique situation. Arguably, the most important political-economic decisions made in Russia today are not the national laws officially passed by the federal government. Nor are they the declarations of sovereignty and other acts passed by regional governments acting in isolation, given that few Russian regions today can survive without a strong economic connection to

Moscow. (And considering the reaction of Moscow to events in Chechnia, future violent attempts to obtain regional sovereignty seem unlikely.) Instead, it is the bargained nexus between federal and local government policies that matters most, on issues ranging from the budget to foreign policy design.

With time, the remnants of the former ministries are likely to matter less and less in the decisions that defense industrial managers make. Privatized enterprises, especially those that have developed independent international business contacts as reforms have progressed, are less likely to retreat into ministerial relationships in the future. Their independence will be sealed as competent independent advertising agencies and other business services spring up for them to use. Defense enterprise issues should come more and more to be seen as local affairs rather than national sectoral ones. (The two major exceptions here may be aviation industry, where ministerial FIGs seem to have solidified and to be exerting effective lobbying pressure on the state, and the defense nuclear science and production complex, which is still under the control of the Ministry of Atomic Energy.) What will localization of most defense industrial interests mean for Russian stability and international security?

Think Locally, Act Globally

Local governments have already been able to obtain payment of federal back wages, special subsidies, and arms export administrative preferences for defense enterprises located on their territories. In addition to the examples cited earlier, the region of Sverdlovsk signed an agreement with the federal government in January 1996 to allow federal taxes collected there to be diverted directly into conversion projects at local plants.[197] In mid-1995, Tatarstan appeared to be pushing the envelope even further. The vice premier, Ravil' Muratov, visited Baghdad and announced that Tatarstan planned to begin limited trade with Iraq by the end of the year. According to one report, he declared that this would happen whether or not Russia continued officially to abide by the United Nations economic embargo against Iraq.[198] According to another report, Muratov interpreted the UN sanctions to mean that a variety of products could legally be shipped to Iraq even with the sanctions in place.[199] Both reports agree that Muratov said that this trade shipment would include sales of two hundred KamAZ trucks.

While there has been no public mention that any military goods might be involved in this trade, it should be kept in mind that KamAZ trucks have been used as troop carriers. In 1980 the U.S. Commerce Department forced the cancellation of 250 détente-era private business contracts with KamAZ after photographs indicated that KamAZ trucks were used in the Soviet invasion of Afghanistan.[200] Even if no military-use items were traded in this case, however, Muratov's statement provides evidence that local authorities have started to challenge Moscow's control over Russian diplomacy in order to help defense-related enterprises. Tatarstan's boldness may reflect a sentiment prevalent in Russia's arms export community: Russia should try to convince the United Nations to lift all embargoes against both Iraq and Libya and should break Yeltsin's September 1994 promise to the United States not to sell more arms to Iran.[201]

So far, Rosvooruzhenie, the state arms export agency, appears to have maintained control over *legal* arms exports in Russia (illegal arms exports have been frequently reported). The regional affiliates of Rosvooruzhenie, including those established in Nizhnii Novgorod and Tatarstan, are administratively subordinate to the agency, although they are separate corporations. Directorates within both the Foreign Ministry and Defense Ministry in Russia have veto power over extending any weapons export permission.[202] Since May 1994 it has been legal for individual enterprises to seek the right to bargain with foreign arms purchasers on their own;[203] MAPO-MiG, the FIG receiving support from Moscow city authorities, was the first private actor to be granted this right, in October 1994.[204] The enterprise, however, must get a license through normal channels for any deals ensuing from such negotiations. The right to independent bargaining (or to use a regional affiliate) merely saves the enterprise Rosvooruzhenie's standard 5 to 10 percent middleman fee and payments delay[205] and overcomes weaknesses that enterprises have perceived in Rosvooruzhenie's choice of markets for deal making.[206] Given the indictment of various Rosvooruzhenie functionaries on currency and tax fraud charges in the spring of 1995, the ability to avoid using that agency as a middleman is an asset indeed.[207]

Yet if the Tatarstan trend of independent province-level diplomacy continues, then the current loosening of Rosvooruzhenie procedures means that an administrative framework (complete with independent advertising and direct international contacts) has been created for authorities in several defense-heavy regions—Tatarstan, Nizhnii Novgorod, and the city of Moscow (through MAPO-MiG), at a minimum—to assume control over the arms export process. It is impossible to predict with any certainty what such regional control might mean; there is no evidence that regional leaders would want to foster uncontrolled proliferation any more than the central authorities do. (Tatarstan, in particular, is potentially both geographically and ethnically vulnerable if its arms fuel conflicts in the Caucasus or Central Asia.) It would definitely mean, however, that any future international arms embargoes or arms transfer control agreements would have to be negotiated with several semi-independent Russian players rather than with one state alone. This would be bound to make such agreements harder to reach, which in and of itself could make proliferation more likely.

Whether or not defense industrial regionalism has an effect on arms exports, it certainly has a negative effect on the ability of the Russian state to control the federal budget. This is especially true because tax rates and credits are on the bargaining table, not just back wages. And even the issue of back wages may threaten the promises Russian officials have made, to organizations such as the International Monetary Fund, of tighter federal budgets to control inflation, because such wages may not be adequately budgeted. Then–defense minister Pavel Grachev revealed this when he said, in an interview at the Nizhnii Novgorod arms fair in September 1994, "There is no money, and we will not pay. . . . I await extrabudgetary resources, in order to transfer them to the places where strikes because of wage debt have begun in MIC (military-industrial complex) enterprises."[208] The president of the Russian Weapons Corporation stated at almost the same time, in August 1994, that extrabudgetary funds for the defense complex included such things as (unspecified) credits and private capital generated by FIGs, which were coordinated by government authorities.[209] Some federal wage payments do not originate in the official budget, in other words; they, like conversion credits and tax relief, come from the shadowy extrabudgetary sources that are not under parliamentary oversight.

When elections loom, tight federal budgets are likely to come under particular threat. In part, this is because regional interests dominate the Federation Council (Russia's upper house of parliament) by design. In part, it is precisely because the legislature does not have complete control over the budget. In 1994 and 1995 regional bargaining with central authorities was always done through the office of Prime Minister Viktor Chernomyrdin, who had meanwhile founded his own political bloc ("Russia Is Our Home"). Speculation was rife that Chernomyrdin's favors to regional administrations were granted only with the expectation of political payback in return.[210]

This means that the power of uncompetitive defense enterprises in certain Russian regions indirectly threatens the ability of the Russian state to use fiscal measures to control inflation. Because tax rates, credits, and wage payment levels are bargained on the fly, the official budget adopted by the legislature and signed by the president may bear little resemblance to actual income and expenditures. This feeds the cycle of low domestic investment levels and doubts about the future, because it threatens economic stability. The fact of regional opportunism encourages more short-term thinking and predation, further undermining the establishment of the rule of law and contract in Russian business.

At the beginning of the reform process in Russia, many observers saw cooperation between dynamic regional authorities and established high-technology enterprises as a means for accelerating the establishment of stable markets and long-term investments. Certainly, regional influence is obvious in many of the success stories emerging from Russian defense industry. The NITEL corporation in Nizhnii Novgorod is building VCRs with the Sharp Electronics corporation of Japan, using credits from the local Banking House, and selling them at a profit on the world market.[211] The KamAZ enterprise in Tatarstan has attracted significant investment from the Cummins corporation of the United States and is widely regarded to be capable of becoming a competitive international truck manufacturer.[212] MAPO-MiG in Moscow is capturing a wide export market for its jet fighters.

Yet the success of these firms and others like them may have come at a price. The institutionalization of provincial influence over Russian taxation, credit, and trade policy may actually undermine Russia's long-term political and economic stability. As regions compete against each other for more budgetary and extrabudgetary favors, as well as for more diplomatic independence, the fragility of the Russian constitution is highlighted. If the Russian state is decapitated, and dozens of regions find themselves fighting for a place in a system that is never institutionalized, then the result will not be prosperity for Russia or integration into the developed world economy. Instead, it will be the reestablishment of a kind of feudalism.

Regional authorities by definition have fewer resources than a unified state does, and disagreement between regions and the federal government is likely to continue over who has responsibility for what. This means that organized crime and a general absence of rule of law are more likely to endure in a quasi-feudal system than in a strong and unified state. Consider, for example, how much more difficult local and state tax collection would be in the United States in the absence of the Internal Revenue Service database or how hard it would be to interdict drug dealers or terrorists without the Federal Bureau of Investigation or the Bureau of Alcohol, Tobacco, and Firearms. National coordination makes it easier both to control crime and to implement a successful fiscal policy. An efficient set of unified economic and legal institutions is unlikely to be established otherwise. Continuing competition among regions for dominance over resources may also lead to festering civil conflict in a time of widespread poverty. In short, regionalism is in and of itself dangerous.

But feudalism in Russia may be more dangerous and more costly this time around than it was in the Middle Ages. Defense enterprise collectives will continue to agitate for more resources, and the local "lords" will discover that they have the ability to manufacture and sell advanced weaponry and mass-destruction materials. If control by the Russian state continues to evaporate, outside monitoring of national stocks of weapons and materials will become increasingly difficult. In fact, as I will show in the next chapter, the Russian state may already have lost the ability to control proliferation from Russian defense enterprises.

4 Spin-offs and Start-ups

Most U.S. analysts view the appearance of spin-off and start-up companies from the old Soviet defense enterprises as a positive trend.[1] Small, private, high-technology firms are an integral element of U.S. capitalism, and U.S. observers thus see them as a sign of Russian entrepreneurs' increasing efforts at market competitiveness. Russian spin-offs usually have much lower overhead costs than do their mother enterprises (because they receive preferential tax treatment and because their revenues do not go to support unprofitable subdivisions), and their managers have more freedom to set differential salary levels within job grades. Small firms are thus judged more likely to operate at a profit than are their mother enterprises. Western investors are also attracted by the fact that these firms are legally separate from their mother companies, which eases the ability of outsiders to monitor the uses to which their investments are put.[2] Hence defense enterprise spin-offs and start-ups are usually cited as evidence of the success of market reforms and of the rational responsiveness of former Soviet managers to capitalist opportunities.

As the analysis below will demonstrate, however, this new competitiveness and market responsiveness has been achieved only at significant social cost. In many cases, the formation of independent spin-off companies from old Soviet defense enterprises has been met with suspicion and hostility by those workers who remain behind at the old enterprises and has thus led to conflict between STKs (the Labor Collective Councils) and the owner-managers of the newly formed companies. These owner-managers are often also mid- or upper-level managers at the mother enterprise, and many spin-off employees work simultaneously in mother enterprise shops. As a result, such conflicts often erupt as management/labor disputes on the shopfloors of the mother enterprises. In at least one case, that of the nuclear weapons research institute in the closed city of Arzamas-16, conflict has led to accusations that the spin-offs are insufficiently regulated and may therefore leak classified information or materials to the outside world. Simultaneously, the owner-managers of spin-offs and start-ups often feel threatened or smothered by the mother enterprises, on whom they depend for floorspace, supply contracts, and other resources.

I begin this chapter by showing that labor-management conflicts regarding spin-off activities have been common in Russian defense enterprises during the initial transition era. I then turn to the rational self-interest explanation for such behavior. These conflicts are clearly propelled by individuals fighting over wealth and property rights under conditions of resource scarcity and uneven power distribution, a classic self-interest scenario. Yet including the arguments of the socialization perspective in the analysis allows us to add important information to our understanding of these conflicts. These arguments make it clear that the specific characteristics of these spin-off conflicts have a basis in cultural patterns dating from Soviet times. Thus, while the rational self-interest explanation may be sufficient to explain the existence of these conflicts, their intensity is probably magnified by the fact that core social groups dating from Soviet times are involved in fighting them. Finally, I close with a discussion of how these management/labor conflicts within Russian defense enterprises may affect both Russian domestic stability and the likelihood of weapons and nuclear materials proliferation across Russian borders.

Evidence of the Problem

Virtually every Russian defense enterprise during the initial transition period created a number of small, often relatively independent new firms, usually on the basis of existing enterprise subdivisions and shops.[3] (Managers at the TsAGI enterprise in Zhukovskii say that the new firms located on their floorspace do not all have connections to the old TsAGI workforce, but this situation appears to be unusual.)[4] As noted above, the owner-managers of these new firms have tended to be current or former mid- to upper-level managers from the old enterprises, often scientists or engineers who supervised research and development or end-product subdivisions in Soviet times. Many of the spin-offs operate under a dual-employment system, where managers and workers retain their positions in mother enterprises while simultaneously working for the new independent companies.

The new firms have been engaged in a variety of activities. Some have continued to fill the social asset functions formerly performed by the mother enterprise, for example, food service to the factory, car and truck repair, or local housing construction. These firms tend to be highly valued by their mother enterprises, because they can operate more efficiently and with better quality than the mother enterprises could manage with their declining budgets. Others have explicitly used patents and production knowledge garnered by their mother enterprises over their decades of experience. Some in this second group began producing variations of the consumer goods that Soviet defense industrial factories had been ordered to make along with their military output.[5] Others have made high-technology civilian or dual-use equipment or components related to their mother enterprises' former major production profile.[6] Some have become sales offices for merchandise resulting from the parent enterprises' past production; reportedly, profits from these sales are not always shared (for example, through a licensing arrangement) with those whose intellectual property was used to create the merchandise.[7] In other words, those who by happenstance had possession of finished goods as the old economy disintegrated could resell or remanufacture them without worrying about patent rights. At least a few of these spin-offs are themselves engaged in defense production, either for Russia or for export abroad.[8]

The economic incentives for creating these small firms were overwhelmingly strong, beginning with the cost-accounting planning reforms of the Gorbachev era. While the actual effect of the Gorbachev reforms was muddy,[9] many enterprises chose in the late 1980s to adopt a planning model that made employee bonuses dependent on the profitability of the enterprise as a whole and of their individual shops and subdivisions within the enterprise.[10] That is, the old focus on meeting plan targets regardless of cost was replaced by a new focus on cost effectiveness. In 1988 new small businesses called "cooperatives" were allowed to form for the first time, and many arose inside existing state enterprises. These were not really privately owned, but their employee collectives could keep the profits they made on the open market. As Simon Johnson and Heidi Kroll make clear in their investigative report on what they call "spontaneous privatization," these cooperatives received both tax privileges and exemption from state wage ceilings, making profitability easier. They tended to be constructed on the basis of existing enterprise shops and subdivisions.[11] This meant that as cost accounting became more prevalent, it was to the advantage of managers to parcel out their existing orders to the new bodies springing up under their roofs within existing shops.

The wages paid by these cooperatives depended on productivity, and higher productivity levels provided both better bonuses for state employees and new opportunities for independent sales of output to customers other than the state. The cooperatives, made up mostly of people who worked simultaneously in the shops at the large state enterprises whose areas they occupied, were allowed to use the floorspace and equipment of "low-profit or loss-making enterprises, production divisions, shops, or sectors,"[12] renting it from the supervising ministries at minimal cost to perform essentially the same work as the mother enterprise did and gaining access to the state supply system.[13] Cooperatives did attract new market orders on their own, but they also worked on state orders that previously would have gone directly to the mother enterprise.[14] The mother enterprise's ministry got better plan results by subsidizing the spin-offs, granting them low-cost access to space, tools, and supplies and encouraging the cooperatives to share in the enterprise's business.

In this era, intellectual property rights did not matter. Defense enterprise directors could not have expected in the late 1980s that within a few years their firms would be privatized and forced to face the market. The cooperatives provided a way for managers to lower the overall production costs of the large factory while using state property and resources to make a profit for themselves on the side. Legislation in 1990 and 1991 gave further tax privileges to cooperatives that reregistered as "small enterprises" that were legally subordinate to the mother enterprise but financially independent.[15]

When the first stage of the privatization program went into effect in Russia in 1992, workers and managers in these small enterprises were some of the earliest beneficiaries.[16] In many cases, spin-off and start-up companies have been allowed to privatize even within those defense enterprises that remain on the state's not-for-privatization list because of the strategic nature of their production.[17] Not all spin-offs are privatized; some remain wholly state-owned "daughter companies" of state enterprises. Of those that have privatized, sometimes the mother enterprise retains a controlling packet of the spin-off or start-up shares; at other times, the founders of the start-up have taken control of all the shares on their own. Regardless of the ownership structure chosen, the symbiosis between mother enterprises and these small spin-offs seemed to be continuing universally through 1995. The vast majority of spin-offs and start-ups remained dependent on their mother enterprises' largesse for profitable operation; many were still heavily subsidized by their mother enterprises. It is from this set of circumstances that worker/manager conflict arose.

In each case, the conflict was over the question of who had the right to share in the profits of these spin-offs—for example, through licensing fees, increased wages, or other benefits—and who bore the obligation for their production costs, including such things as water and power usage, floorspace rental, and raw materials and components. Because current or former mid- or upper-level managers of the mother enterprises have usually been the managers of the spin-offs and because the spin-offs continued to operate on floorspace owned by the mother enterprises, often employing workers from the mother enterprise in their "spare time," the question naturally translated into one of equitable wage distribution in the mother enterprises during times of economic hardship. (I use examples to detail the exact nature of the conflicts below.)

It is hard to find reliable evidence concerning the frequency of labor/management conflicts over the structure and activities of spin-offs from Russian defense industry. The central Russian press covers such conflicts only occasionally and never in much depth. When questioned directly, the managers of mother enterprises tend merely to speak vaguely of such things as internal misunderstandings on the tactics of restructuring and do not wish to go into details about labor council disputes.

One sign that such conflict may be endemic to defense industry was a stunning April 1994 article written by Arkadii Vol'skii, head of the Russian Union of Industrialists and Entrepreneurs and a man known to be a passionate advocate for the interests of defense industrial managers. Vol'skii said that he had visited enterprises in eleven regions of Russia and was dismayed at the level of conflict between STKs and directors everywhere. Most striking, he confirmed that directors were using state property to run small enterprises for enormous personal profit at a time when many of their workers were not receiving their wages,[18] an unusual statement from one who proudly bills himself as a political advocate of the military-industrial complex. Another sign that managers may be engaged in opportunistic activities is the response of many enterprise directors to threats by the state to declare them bankrupt. By mid-1994 Russian federal bankruptcy laws began to be enforced against enterprises with significant state ownership, including defense enterprises. It was reported then that many directors faced with the threat of enterprise liquidation were able to find new cash resources that they had "mislaid,"[19] at least some of which had reportedly been laundered through daughter companies for the personal benefit of managers. According to one Russian observer, "No one who is in the know doubts that two-thirds of nonpayments are caused by these machinations. . . . Any firm has from one to two to tens of daughter firms, in which sit either close relatives or schoolfellows of the leaders."[20]

Clear evidence of the duration and severity of management/labor conflicts over property rights and wage equity in the spin-offs emerges from local newspaper reports in defense-heavy cities, as well as from Western researchers' interviews of the managers of spin-off companies. Particularly useful are the newspapers of such small defense-dominated cities as Zelenograd (a formerly closed defense electronics city just northwest of Moscow) and Arzamas-16 (the still-closed flagship city of Soviet nuclear warhead construction in the Nizhnii Novgorod region).[21] These newspapers tend to allocate a lot of column space to the internal politics of defense enterprises and seem less concerned than Russian big-city newspapers are to paint a happy picture of their cities for outside investors. Such reports, as well as occasional references in more major newspapers and evidence uncovered by Western interviewers reveal that there have been disputes regarding spin-offs at a variety of enterprises, including Zelenograd's ELAS Scientific-Production Company, which made electronic equipment for satellite communication and data transmission;[22] the Angstrem enterprise (which works on large integrated systems)[23] and the Kvant enterprise (which produced personal computers under one of the defense industrial ministries),[24] both also in Zelenograd; the All-Russian Scientific Institute for Experimental Physics (VNIIEF), the defense nuclear institute in Arzamas-16;[25] Moscow's Institute of Precision Mechanics and Computer Technology;[26] St. Petersburg's Svetlana defense radio electronics enterprise;[27] and St. Petersburg's Izhorskie Zavody enterprise, where nuclear submarine reactors are produced.[28] An internal institute newspaper also indicates that G. I. Zagainov, the general director of TsAGI (Russia's major aerodynamics testing and design institute), was so concerned about the unregulated activities of spin-offs and start-ups within his enterprise that in February 1994 he instituted a temporary ban on the conclusion of contracts by spin-offs using TsAGI technology.[29] (His primary concern was the uncontrolled loss of TsAGI's intellectual property.) At another huge Moscow-area aerospace enterprise, I was told by the deputy director for financing in September 1994 that I could not see issues of the factory's internal newspaper because it revealed "family quarrels" and the enterprise did not wish to air its dirty laundry in public.

Given the geographical and profile diversity of these enterprises, it is a good bet that such conflicts are widespread. Across the board, the conflict can be viewed from two perspectives: that of the owner-managers of the spin-offs and start-ups, who wanted the freedom to avoid enterprise-imposed conditions on their profits, and that of the mother enterprise STKs, whose workers wanted the collective to be reimbursed for the subsidies the spin-offs received. The director's corps of the mother enterprise could fall into either camp, depending on the degree that the managers' interests coincided with spin-off interests. Sometimes the mother enterprise director and his cohort received shares or other economic benefits from the spin-offs, while at other times they struggled desperately to reassert control over spin-offs that had successfully escaped their purview in the preprivatization era, when property rights and factory profitability did not matter.

Rational Self-Interest: The Perspective of Spin-off Managers

From the viewpoint of frustrated spin-off and start-up owner-managers, eager to make a go of it in the market, the cause of these conflicts was greedy labor councils and the mother enterprise managers who supported them. The labor council leaders were perceived as socialist holdovers who wanted to keep control over independently generated profits in order to spread the wealth among the less able workers left behind.

The major structural problem that the freedom-seeking spin-off owners faced was their inability to obtain independent floorspace. Rental space is scarce in Russia, and the laws allowing new construction are very complicated and heavily favor existing large enterprises.[30] It is thus usually inconceivable for a private spin-off carved out of a mother enterprise subdivision to obtain floorspace for operation without the mother enterprise's help.

Sometimes, this meant that potential new businesses were quashed at inception. For example, as of early 1993 there were reportedly two thousand small enterprises in Zelenograd that wanted to begin business operations but lacked the space to do it.[31] The chairman of the Society of Scientists of Zelenograd, B. Sedunov (an obviously passionate defender of the rights of spin-off managers), reported to the society in 1992 how different the situation was in California's Silicon Valley. Having visited the defense-heavy U.S. electronics region, he "was struck by the enormous reserve they have of production space. There, someone wishing to found a business doesn't have to solicit space or build it from scratch. In Zelenograd, out of 800,000 square meters [of unused industrial space], small businesses rent out no more than 10,000 [square meters of it]."[32] The large enterprises have the power to decide who may engage in business and who will be left out in the cold.

Large enterprises thus have a disproportionate control over the shape of local economies in defense-heavy regions. When mother enterprise managers have a stake in the spin-off firm, the spin-off finds itself rewarded; if the mother enterprise managers are excluded from the firm's profits, the spin-off suffers. For example, one Zelenograd spin-off that was still state-owned, SIC ELVIS, wanted to privatize and as of late 1994 was continuing to pursue privatization options. The SIC ELVIS manager reported, however, that after learning that their facilities (owned by the old Soviet enterprise called ELAS) could not be "privatized" or purchased, the new company's interest in privatization waned.[33] Presumably, denied the option of buying their space, privatization would have left the new firm vulnerable to whatever rental costs ELAS wanted to impose; retention of their status as an independent state-owned enterprise under the ELAS umbrella, on the other hand, gave them preferential operating conditions. David Bernstein reports that another Moscow defense enterprise spin-off, which did privatize in a parallel situation, has complained of the "excessive" rent charged by its mother company for the property it uses.[34]

It is not merely rental costs that are at issue. The dependency relationship set up by the floorspace problem goes much deeper. Aleksandr Galitskii, the general director of an ELAS spin-off that did privatize, ELVIS+, points out that more than simple square meters are involved. Conducting world-class, high-technology business demands that a firm invest in items of physical infrastructure, including such things as specialized cables and precision-quality telephone systems.[35] Such items, always expensive to rip out and re-create, were especially so in the Russia of the early 1990s, where such equipment was not yet standard and the quality of trunk systems was variable and often poor. Thus as time went on the fact that spin-offs had become established in space owned by the mother company made the prospect of relocation more and more costly. Because spin-offs began to form in the late 1980s, when a space crunch did exist and land ownership laws didn't, the mother enterprises won long-term advantages in their ability to control the activities of spin-off managers.

Control of facilities also meant control over the flow of resources, such as heat, electricity, and water, that spin-off firms use. Mother enterprises also controlled the building's security services,[36] a vital resource in a time of heavy organized crime activity. When mother enterprises didn't pay their utility bills on time, spin-offs also suffered from the ensuing cut-offs.

The director of one Russian defense industry spin-off was proud that he managed to get independent control over the provision of part of his firm's electricity. When the lights went out in the building as a whole because of the mother enterprise's failure to pay the power bill, his company was still able to operate, because it paid part of its electricity bill directly to the power company.[37] One of this man's coworkers later revealed that this arrangement was possible only because some sort of special deal had been made directly with the mother enterprise employee who controlled the building's power usage.[38] Apparently, attempts by the mother enterprise as a whole to maintain control over spin-off resource provision can be circumvented by the judicious inclusion of certain employees in the spin-off's profit-sharing calculations.

Beyond control over space and production resource flows, the mother enterprise often also has the power to control access to suppliers and customers that the spin-offs need. This becomes an issue when the managers of the mother enterprises are not supportive of spin-off activities (obviously, when mother enterprise managers are engaged in spin-off activities, these old contacts work to the spin-off's advantage). Because the spin-offs are often engaged in a business that somehow relates to the mother enterprise's past business, unsupportive enterprise managers can use their networks of contacts to try to shut a wayward spin-off out of the market. As I noted in the previous chapter, these old Soviet business circles are probably becoming less important levers with time. They may have been significant in shutting out fledgling businesses early in the reform era, however, when managers turned to their established connections for advice on whom to trust in the new market.

Sometimes, the mother enterprise itself has refused to accept the spin-off's output. For example, the Institute of Precision Technology and Design, formerly Shop No. 2 of the Angstrem enterprise in Zelenograd, wanted to sell its designs to Angstrem, keeping the proceeds of these sales for itself so that the mother enterprise could not gobble up all the value it generated. Angstrem leaders, however, believed that the Institute was unfairly using the mother enterprise's intellectual property in its work. As a result, the Institute had difficulty getting its designs accepted at Angstrem for serial production, even though many of the patterns it had developed were specifically designed for Angstrem activities and had no market elsewhere.[39] In another case reported by Petra Opitz, one plant of the Almaz Shipyard in St. Petersburg tried to privatize on its own but was forced to return to the fold of the mother enterprise because the second major plant of the enterprise refused to share contracts with it.[40] In other words, spin-offs have sometimes had to learn the hard way about monopsony power (that is, the power wielded by a single buyer when there are no other buyers in the market).

In many cases, perhaps the majority, the mother enterprise's control over spin-off activities is even stronger than these examples indicate, because the mother enterprise often owns a significant share of the spin-off's stock.[41] As in the case of enterprise privatization involving outside share purchases (discussed in chapter 2), directors who have lost control over spin-offs have often tried to regain ownership of them. An example is provided by the ELAS enterprise in Zelenograd, whose general director, Gennady Guskov, saw a dozen spin-offs privatize independently in the early 1990s. It is not clear how these spin-offs managed to gain their freedom; ELAS managers must either have been slow to understand the consequences of such privatization or insufficiently powerful to stop it. At least one of the start-ups, ELVIS+, privatized in order to begin a business relationship with the U.S. company Sun Microsystems.[42] Guskov tried both to woo these firms back into a closed joint-stock company, using a press campaign,[43] and to annul the previous building usage contracts reached through an aggressive appeal to the Russian State Property Committee.[44] As of mid-1995 he had not yet succeeded.

Rational Self-Interest:
The Perspective of the Former Collectives

On the other side of the conflict over spin-offs, the labor collectives of many mother enterprises have understandable reasons to resent the good fortune of the new small firms. As I noted earlier, there is evidence that a large number of spin-offs have been using the intellectual property of their mother enterprises without compensating them adequately. There is also evidence that when mother enterprise managers have owned spin-off stock, the spin-offs have obtained access to floorspace and other physical resources at below-market cost, thereby increasing the expenses of the mother enterprise without contributing to its revenues. Obviously, such costs limit the amount of money that can be spent on wages.

It has only been in the past few years that Soviet-era defense industrial enterprises have begun to recognize the costs involved in losing control over the use of intellectual property. In the past, ownership of patents was not an issue of particular concern, and exactly who owned a particular patent was not always clear. According to one report from the closed defense nuclear city of Arzamas-16, "in past years, many designs and even inventions were not patented."[45] It is thus not surprising that when cooperatives began to form in the late 1980s, control over intellectual property was not a major concern for the mother enterprises, especially since privatization and tight budgets were not yet on the agenda. By the time the mother enterprises realized that their control over the spin-offs was evaporating, an important source of potential income was gone.

Small spin-off enterprises have freely admitted (and even boasted) to local newspaper reporters that one of their major advantages in dealing with the market was the specific technical and design knowledge (i.e., intellectual property) that they gained through their work with defense enterprises.[46] This phenomenon would be unheard of in countries with developed intellectual property laws. In the United States, for example, it is not uncommon for designers and engineers to be asked to sign an employment contract prohibiting them from working for a competitor in similar product areas using related methods for a certain number of years after termination. In Russia, by contrast, defense directors encouraged their employees to go out and found what would later become competing firms, employing not only the identical technology but the identical equipment, floorspace, and workers used by the mother enterprise.

It may be useful here to compare the property rights situation in one sub-field of U.S. defense technology that remains state-owned: the national nuclear weapons laboratories. Back when a generous U.S. government budget for the work of such labs was assured, patents, as in Soviet defense enterprises, were not a major concern of the labs. New technologies were either "kept hidden for security reasons or released to the public for anyone to use," and the fact of public release meant that private companies were reluctant to invest in developing the technologies, because they could not keep their processes commercial secrets under the Freedom of Information Act.[47] Thus no one reaped exclusive private benefit from public research expenditure. Under federal legislation passed in the late 1980s, however, the government labs have recently been able to issue proprietary rights and licenses to private firms using Cooperative Research and Development Agreements (CRADAs), under which the costs and risks of new technology development are shared.[48] This arrangement is attractive to the labs, which are able to profit from the royalties that these patents bring in and to keep valuable employees whose limited salaries might otherwise tempt them to leave. In the case of the Lawrence Livermore lab, for example, the California Board of Regents (which operates the lab as a U.S. Department of Energy contractor) often receives at least a portion of the royalties,[49] and the federal employees responsible for the invention get a share as well.[50] In some cases, federal lab employees are granted leave to pursue private joint projects; for example, the Sandia lab helped the McDonald's hamburger chain to develop a better glue for its recyclable paper bags.[51] There have been numerous complaints about the inefficiencies of utilizing CRADA property rights in practice.[52] Yet it is clear that in the U.S. case (to use terms from the Russian example) the mother enterprise managers that encourage spin-offs' use of lab intellectual property have both legal support and economic incentives for seeing that the proceeds benefit those in the collective responsible for developing them. In the U.S. case, independent spin-off efforts are cooperating with the labs, not feeding off them. Furthermore, conversations with several Lawrence Livermore employees make clear the fact that private enterprise is strictly separated from lab business and that any employee found using lab facilities for private business will be fired.

Recently, directors of at least some Russian defense industrial mother enterprises seem to have become wiser about the money-making potential of intellectual property and have implemented rule changes to try to curb its loss. For example, VNIIEF, the defense nuclear institute in Arzamas-16, faced complaints from employees about the "random selling-off [*razbazarivaniia*] of intellectual property created over many years by an enormous collective."[53] Later, a U.S. delegation was told that VNIIEF now charges a licensing fee of 12 percent on all profits made by any spin-offs using VNIIEF intellectual property.[54] Using another set of tactics, by September 1994 TsAGI, which, as reported above, was so concerned about the loss of intellectual property that it temporarily banned spin-offs from making contracts early in 1994, had begun to solve the problem by ending the right of individuals to hold shares in spin-offs that relied on TsAGI core technology.[55] TsAGI's managers believed that if ownership was required to be corporate, this would allow them more control over intellectual property use, although the exact mechanism allowing such control was not made specific. In a similar vein, the Mashinostroenie enterprise in Reutov assured a U.S. delegation in September 1994 that the plant had "learned from [its] past mistakes" and now had a special subdivision whose duty was to oversee intellectual property rights and defend patents.[56] And Guskov, the unfortunate general director of ELAS in Zelenograd, was trying to entice privatized spin-offs back into his closed joint-stock company explicitly in order to forestall "the practice of 'free' transfer of scientific and technological results obtained by NIIMP [the subsidiary scientific institute] to other subdivisions and even completely different organizations," which he believed was "in wide practice."[57] As time goes by, then, the "borrowing" by spin-offs of mother enterprise intellectual property may decline, and licensing control may be reestablished.

Another form of "borrowing" has continued to cause shop-floor conflicts, however. As I mentioned earlier, managers of mother enterprises who own significant stock in spin-offs have had a tendency to charge those spin-offs exceedingly low rent and resource usage rates. This is the flip side of the dependency of spin-offs on mother enterprise floorspace: while those attempting to break free from the mother enterprise are punished, those that have provided side income to mother enterprise managers have received special privileges.

Accusations that defense enterprise managers are engaged in such behavior appear frequently in small defense-city newspapers. For example, a deputy of the Zelenograd city council wrote in 1991 that "in many contracts it is stipulated that NIIME and Mikron [a defense electronics factory and its associated research institute] are obligated to provide the small enterprises with free equipment, space, raw materials, and energy. The result is that the small enterprises are acting as parasites."[58] He blamed this arrangement on the association's former director, Aleksandr Nesterov, claiming in particular that Shop no. 5 of the association, which housed a cooperative called Star, "experienced a deficit in its finished goods, leading to a dearth of full-time work for the workers of the shop," while Star simultaneously achieved smashing success on the market. The head and deputy head of the shop were, coincidentally, the head and deputy head of the cooperative.[59] The managers, then, benefited personally from expenditures borne by mother enterprise employees. They did not identify the interests of the collective with their own interests but instead put their individual material interests first.

More recently, in Zelenograd, in a shop at the ELION defense electronics enterprise, the STK complained that a spin-off was using the enterprise kiln during normal working hours, presumably with the enterprise paying the power bill.[60] Yet again, an enterprise was bearing costs that detracted from its ability to pay wages, while simultaneously the spin-off was gaining what economists would call a monopolistic market advantage (that is, the ability to set an artificially low price for a product and drive competitors out of the market) because of its free access to the kiln. A city council deputy explained that most STKs "considered and continue to consider the newly born cooperatives and small joint-stock companies their most evil enemy. The conviction exists [among the STKs] that they [the spin-offs] are all stealing everything and that unscrupulous administrators are giving material and monetary resources to them. To deny this is useless; sufficient facts exist."[61] He argued, however, that such arrangements constitute a "crime" and an exception and that rather than attributing such activities to all small enterprises, the affected STKs should bring legal suit against those responsible for such theft.[62] (This suggestion was rather naive, given the undeveloped state of the Russian corporate legal system.) There are other reports that in Zelenograd spin-off arrangements constituting "theft of state property" continued through 1994.[63] Similar accusations have appeared in the press concerning enterprises in St. Petersburg.[64]

There do seem to be some examples where spin-offs have reached contractual accommodation regarding these costs with the workers of the mother enterprises. For instance, managers of the ELAS state enterprise, home to ELVIS+ and SIC ELVIS, apparently chose to include the rental and energy bill arrangements for the small enterprises in its yearly labor contract with the STK. They also chose to charge the small enterprises a contribution fee to the enterprise social defense fund.[65] The ELAS labor force has thus avoided turmoil over the issue. Yet this is probably because ELAS managers, who lacked personal access to the income of many of these spin-offs, were using the STK to limit spin-off independence.

VNIIEF

A clear example of shopfloor conflict over spin-off activity occurred in Arzamas-16 (now called Sarov), where in March 1994 a dispute was reported between the administration and the STK at the VNIIEF defense nuclear institute. The labor contract for the year was under negotiation. In its contract meeting, the STK complained that it was being wrongly excluded from decisions about the pay that institute managers received.

These managers, constituting about 5 percent of the institute workforce (or 1,000 individuals), were said to be profiting as individuals from spin-offs that were essentially funded by the institute. There was anger that as a result these managers' take-home pay was much higher than their official salaries and they were thus compensated at a stupendous level compared to the wages of those still working only on VNIIEF business. Around 4,000 VNI-IEF employees, or 20 percent of the institute's total workforce, were said to hold spin-off jobs as of June 1993.[66] While this meant that a large proportion of workers were engaged in private market activities, it also left 80 percent of the workforce excluded from the benefits that spin-off employees received.

The STK demanded "an extraordinary confidential report concerning the leaders of the institute (beginning at the level of chiefs of independent laboratories), whose pay in the small enterprises is higher than their pay at VNI-IEF."[67] The STK chairman said, "We have an evident situation where in the divisions a significant fraction of the workers are not kept fully occupied or are idle, but this is not reflected in the pay of division leaders."[68] A report of the STK meeting continued, "The administration of VNIIEF continues to accept the commercial structures, granting them a roof and other unmeasured internal resources: after all, most of the leaders are numbered among the appointments in such firms. [To put it] simply, who will hack off the bough on which he likes to sit?"[69] Earlier reports had indicated that spin-offs were operating with institute resources on institute time, even though this was against regulations,[70] and that the rents charged for spin-off floorspace were far below market prices.[71]

The STK proposed that the yearly contract be amended to include a provision that managers "not occupy themselves during the [institute] workday with entrepreneurial activities that are not connected with the programs, themes, orders, or contracts of VNIIEF."[72] In the end, however, the STK and the director apparently agreed to disagree about the role the STK should play in pay-grade negotiations, and the contract was approved without resolution of some key points.[73] Still, STK pressure did lead the institute's director, Vladimir Belugin, to order an internal audit of spin-off activity. This audit recommended (without much reported commentary) that the institute cease its support for nine of its forty-four spin-offs but found that the rest of them "work for the benefit of the institute."[74]

In 1996 a member of the VNIIEF financial management team confirmed in a private interview that "many" of the STK accusations, which were reported in the local Arzamas-16 newspaper, were accurate: state intellectual property was sometimes used by private entrepreneurs without proper compensation to the institute, and private businesses did use VNIIEF equipment and floorspace (such as computers and labs) on VNIIEF time. But this manager explained that VNIIEF leaders lacked the time, resources, and skills to ensure that restructuring was being done by the book and expressed a belief that the necessity of restructuring, and of providing profitable opportunities for people whose skills would otherwise be wasted, justified the actions taken. Said the manager, "The STK must understand our situation."[75]

The interpretation one puts on this series of events obviously depends on one's perspective. The STK had earlier accused Belugin of a "confrontational, rude style of relations" and in mid-1993 had asked the Ministry of Atomic Energy to replace him.[76] (The financial manager I interviewed in 1996 said that Belugin was a fine person with whom to work and that while the STK as a whole was also polite and cordial, some of the STK leaders were rude.) From the STK's perspective, then, the collective was working to root out managerial corruption, and neither the word of the director nor an internal audit done under his supervision would indicate a good-faith effort by managers to uphold the collective's interests. Instead, because the workforce was located in a closed city with no alternative opportunities nearby and because the ministry appeared to support the director, the STK was bereft of any real control.

On the other hand, from the perspective of the institute and spin-off managers, the majority of the spin-offs have been run well and fairly, providing licensing fees to the institute, and were one of the only avenues available to residents in the closed city to make a profit through hard work. The director repeatedly stressed that the primary reason for establishing the small enterprises was to "retain the collective,"[77] a function that may very well be necessary for proper maintenance of the sensitive materials housed at the installation. In this view, the STK leaders are old thinkers mired in expectations of socialist leveling and are unable to adapt to market-based salary differentials. The STK has too much power, not too little, and that is why Belugin decided in 1993 to ban its unsanctioned meetings during working hours.[78]

From the outside, it is impossible to know which side's arguments have the most truth behind them. Given that similar perceptions on both sides are frequently found throughout Russian defense industry, it is likely that both are at least partially correct in their perceptions.

The Sociological Explanation: Added Value

As I have shown, there are clear underlying structural reasons for the disputes that seem endemic in Russian defense industrial enterprises at the moment. Managers exercise a great deal of power within their enterprises, and they can use this power both to restrict the activities of uncooperative competitor spin-offs and to subsidize the activities of spin-offs that bring them personal income. The fact that the old Soviet enterprises continue to endure and that spin-off assets are specific and tied to those enterprises means that managers have a great deal of control over the spin-off economy.

The activities of spin-offs themselves also have clear structural explanations. Some spin-offs—those not controlled by mother enterprises—are acting in accordance with the expectations of transaction-costs market economists. Having detached themselves from their mother enterprises, they protect their resources from "raids" by centralized authorities within parent organizations.[79] Such spin-offs provide genuine market income opportunities for their members, opportunities that would otherwise be swallowed up by the cumbersome overhead and tax structure of the mother enterprises. Simultaneously, many spin-offs (particularly those favored by current mother enterprise managers) have for all practical purposes stolen the intellectual property of their mother enterprises and have gained enormous exclusive competitive advantages (in economic terms, quasi-rents) by using the facilities and contacts of those mother enterprises at below-market cost.

I could stop here and say that the rational self-interest explanation is sufficient for understanding this case: spin-off managers have clearly not sacrificed individual gain for the sake of the collective. However, this would leave us with an incomplete understanding of the important variables that affect the choices managers make in these situations. Despite the strength of structural explanations for spin-off activity and conflict, historically ingrained cultural patterns have insinuated themselves here and there within the story.

For example, directors see the benefits of spin-offs as part and parcel of retaining the collective, since spin-offs provide market opportunities for workers while keeping them within the factory fold. This clearly harks back to the discussion in chapter 2 about the endurance of behavior patterns appropriate to a scarce labor market, under conditions of overemployment. It is particularly poignant in the case of the closed nuclear cities, because the very viability of these enclaves in a market economy is questionable, even though most of the residents of these cities do not want to leave and do not want to open them to outsiders.[80]

Furthermore, as previously noted, the root of the conflict over spin-offs is often attributed by spin-off managers to a cultural factor: the "psychology of leveling" that is thought still to permeate the labor collectives of defense industrial enterprises. In Soviet days, both floor and ceiling salaries for each job grade were set by the state, and individual innovation and entrepreneurship were not rewarded. Many spin-off owner-managers believe that it is primarily their own willingness to work hard in order to achieve higher salaries that has alienated them from their former coworkers today. They object to what they see as the perseverance of an old collectivist mindset that no longer fits the new market realities. A certain amount of the tension between the spin-offs and mother enterprises may be attributable, then, to the paternalistic expectations of both directors and workers: the notion that the factory will take care of everyone, even those who are not productive.

Further indication that socialization may be at work in this relationship is the simple fact, noted above in the case of Zelenograd, that at least some directors would rather leave floorspace unused rather than renting it out to any private firm that can pay for it. These defense directors apparently prefer to exercise power at the expense of making money. A sociological study of managers in defense-heavy Cheliabinsk found that Russian managers valued having power over the lives of others much more than U.S. managers did,[81] and perhaps this is part of the ingrained paternalism they practice. While there is no evidence on this point (except for journalistic claims about spin-off firms employing friends and family), it is reasonable to speculate that managers are probably renting out floorspace to their friends sooner than to strangers, thus maintaining the links of the old *krugovaia poruka*.

One would think that if rents and utility rates were set at high enough levels, leasing space to outsiders would meet one of two self-interested managerial goals: either lining the personal pockets of those who make the rental arrangements or providing income to keep the mother enterprise afloat for as long as possible so that the managers keep their jobs. Of course, the accusation that floorspace is arbitrarily controlled is made by those involved in spin-off activities; it is possible that in fact managers have acted in their own economic self-interest to stop those rogue or criminal firms who have been eager to take unfair advantage of enterprise resources (or who at least have appeared unwilling to give managers their cut). It is also possible in theory that directors are holding on to unused space now to keep it available for their own projects later, although that would indicate a faith in the future of both their enterprises and their own jobs that is probably unwarranted.

Despite these cultural overtones, when we look at the situation of the spin-offs overall, what has been most striking is the apparent willingness by many managers, especially midlevel managers, to sacrifice the good of the collective for the private individual gain of themselves and their closest associates from within the old factories. While this would at first glance appear to undercut the arguments of the sociological school, it can in fact be used to support them, once the specifics of the Soviet case are understood.

Loyalty within Subdivisions of the Soviet Enterprise

Joseph Berliner, in his classic book on Soviet managerial behavior, noted that central planning dictates focused on the productivity of shops within the enterprise rather than on the productivity of the enterprise as a whole. Shops were encouraged to be in competition against each other, instead of being given incentives to cooperate together for the good of the enterprise. This often meant that overall enterprise goals were sacrificed so that shop goals could be pursued. Shop stewards focused their attention on the ability of the shop to overfulfill its plan, not on the ability of the enterprise to do so. This could be done, for example, by overproducing large components that received big bonuses because of their size but were not needed by the enterprise, while failing to produce smaller but more necessary components. If the shop overfulfilled its part of the plan, the shop manager could receive a premium on top of his or her regular salary, regardless of what happened to the enterprise.[82]

To get this premium, the shop manager would have to motivate shop employees to work for the common good of the shop. Because any worker in a Soviet factory had the right to take any concern to the top of the factory hierarchy—remember from chapter 2 that the director set aside a certain number of office hours to listen to employee complaints—this probably meant that the shop steward could not get away with demanding output that was above the standard set in the factory as a whole. To get their premiums, then, shop managers had to treat their employees well, and the social bargain made within the shop would thus mimic, writ small, the bargain struck between enterprise director and workforce. (Although, as Berliner notes, shop stewards did not have distribution rights over the housing and other social benefits that enterprise directors controlled.)

In a 1990 study, a joint task force of researchers from the Harvard Business School and Soviet management institutes in fact revealed that Soviet workers' identification with the shop *superseded* their identification with the enterprise and that their identification with the smaller work brigade within the shop was even higher. According to the Soviet participants in the study, the core unit in every enterprise was the "structural task unit" or subdivision (*podrazdelenie*), the small group charged with completing a specific, limited task for the enterprise. At various levels in the enterprise, as subdivisions were joined together to form larger units further up the hierarchical structure (from brigade to shop to plant to enterprise), group identification became progressively weaker.[83]

This study's assessment of how the subgroup affected enterprise sociology is striking and worth reproducing here:

> Members of STUs [structural task units] refer to themselves as "we," and show an astounding cohesion, solidarity, camaraderie, and loyalty to one another and to their leader. These characteristics of the STU often lead to excessive compartmentalization of the affairs of organizations. In cases of weak leadership at the top, they can diminish the unity of the enterprise and enhance the tendency of an STU to give priority to its own interests over those of the enterprise. STU members are bound to one another by total confidentiality as to the inner workings of the group. In fact, divulging information to outsiders, even on trivial matters, needs the leaders' clear approval. STUs function as a collective entity that is practically impossible for outsiders to penetrate.[84]

In other words, the *krugovaia poruka* of Soviet economic life exerted the strongest magnetic pull among immediate coworkers, and social networks became more and more secondary to people's core identities as the distance from the immediate work group increased.

This institutionalized identification with the subgroup is reflected in the fact that most of the start-ups and spin-offs operating within Russian defense industrial enterprises seem to be delineated by the personnel makeup of the old shop boundaries. This gives Russian spin-offs unique structural characteristics in the market. For example, while many spin-offs in the United States are also former subdivisions of larger corporations, such breakaways do not necessarily maintain old employment links.

In the United States, divestiture of a subdivision—the sale of one part of the business to a different set of owners (much like the newly privatized small enterprises formed from divisions of Soviet enterprises)—most often occurs when the parent corporation considers the subdivision unprofitable and wants to free up cash for other uses. Divestiture is seen primarily as a response to overdiversification; it is a means for a firm facing pressure (from stockholders, for example, or from the threat of an outside takeover) to return to its core competencies, which makes it better able to stake out a market niche.[85] In the words of one observer, "divestiture is essentially an admission that an inappropriate project choice was made initially."[86] (This may parallel the spinning-off of privatized consumer service shops from Soviet defense enterprises, where the activities pursued are only indirectly related to the enterprise's high-tech core competency. It is not what one would expected to happen to high-technology subdivisions with high profit potential.) In the U.S. case, divestiture to new owners means that there is no expectation that the management staff or other personnel of the division will retain their jobs. In fact, *divestiture* is often interpreted by workers as a code word for downsizing and layoffs, as new owners come in and clean house.

True spin-offs in the United States, where the parent corporation retains ownership of a newly independent subdivision (much like the daughter companies in which Russian defense enterprises retain significant stock holdings), tend to occur when the parent firm wants to explore a potentially risky new market niche or when government regulation affecting the output of only one subdivision imposes significant costs on a parent firm that would otherwise not be subject to them; spin-offs are also useful when centralized management has become an inefficient mechanism to oversee the variety of activities undertaken.[87]

In a regulation-avoiding spin-off, one would expect the same basic personnel policies to be followed in the new company that were followed when it was a subdivision, much as occurs in Russia. But when new market niches or new managerial independence are being explored, there is no reason to expect that a unified set of employees will necessarily move from the old to the new business. Instead, a subset of employees from the parent firm may be encouraged to create a new small business from scratch,[88] or a new set of corporate overseers with different expectations may be appointed.[89] In U.S. high-tech start-ups, not only new employees but often new cofounders are sought to contribute new expertise to the business and to participate in the financial risk involved. According to a U.S. consultant who specializes in providing assistance to start-ups, "Most start-ups search for their founders and key personnel in the following areas: (a) parallel companies which manufacture similar products, (b) competitive companies . . . , (c) college and night-school campuses, (d) consultants . . . , (e) associations and societies, (f) referrals from bankers, lawyers, accountants, venture capitalists, management associations, friends, and contacts, (g) recruitment agencies . . . , and (h) advertisements."[90] In Russia, in stark contrast, the desire to explore new market niches and increase managerial independence at a lower level seems to be associated not with the search for new employees but instead with new job opportunities for old work groups.

If these innovative companies were truly trying to maximize their market performance, one would assume that they would not replicate the old subdivision employee structure but instead try to hire the best individuals available, as many foreign joint ventures in Russia have done. The fact that résumés and letters of recommendation tend not to be reliable indicators of ability in the uncertainty of reform-era Russia means that alternative personnel selection mechanisms must be used, such as standardized psychological and aptitude tests. But open job searches do tend to be held by foreign joint-venture firms (for example, Moscow-McDonald's gives out tray liners that are advertisements for new employees).

Even in the innovative Russian defense industry spin-offs, however, open job searches do not seem to be common. Instead, work groups from the old enterprise continue to form the core of the new endeavor. It is true that the individuals who formed enterprise work groups do not correspond perfectly to the employees of spin-off companies; many spin-offs now employ a significant number of "outsiders,"[91] especially in the areas of finance and marketing. Yet the management core of the old shop remains, and most new employees seem to be the personal friends of those who make up this core. In the words of Aleksandr Sokolov, executive vice president of the ELVIS+ spin-off, "everyone knows everyone else," and new employees are hired because of their personal connections to existing employees. Sokolov argues that placing an employment ad tends only to "jam up the phone lines," without turning up "good specialists."[92] In less entrepreneurial spin-offs and daughter companies, the workforce appears to bear an even closer resemblance to the makeup of previous personnel.

As in the case of business-to-business relationships, discussed in chapter 3, an argument can be made that prior acquaintance provides a means for establishing the trust necessary for business dealings in an uncertain environment (and even the typical U.S. hiring search described above cites "referrals from . . . friends" as a potential resource). Furthermore, in the case of those who worked side by side for years within a subdivision, the information provided by the history of the relationship is indeed relevant to the formation of self-interested capitalist business relationships. Once cost accounting became a real concern for the subdivisions in the late 1980s, those who worked together in research and engineering groups would have been able to judge who among them was a hard worker or a slacker, who was skillful and ingenious or slow and clumsy, and to what extent each member worked for the good of the group or took advantage of it. An argument could thus be made from the rational self-interest perspective that keeping old work groups together made good business sense.

Yet the experience of at least one spin-off company (whose representative did not wish to go on the record) supports the argument made in chapter 1 that in an environment where the temptation to cheat is everywhere, even a long history of personal acquaintance provides an insufficient basis for making rational business judgments. A representative of this company ruefully told a U.S. audience in September 1994 that one of the original founders of his company (someone from his work group within the Soviet enterprise), "a Ph.D. engineer with a Mercedes and a bodyguard," was "forced into criminal activity." The subdivision circle, then, does not actually provide the self-interested actor with adequate information for making wise business choices. Friends may be more trustworthy than outsiders, but old friendships often crack under the pressure of new temptations and new threats.

It is also possible that old work groups are kept together because they provide a synergy that leads to higher productivity. Those who are familiar with each other's habits and thought patterns save resources because they need to gather less information about each other's preferences and intentions in order to work together, and so the sum can become more than the parts in terms of creativity. There is no means to distinguish whether synergistic efficiency or the intrinsic emotional value of maintaining old networks is responsible for keeping existing work groups together. However, synergy would not explain the tendency of spin-offs to hire old, but outside, acquaintances of their personnel to new positions when they need to expand. It makes sense to put somewhat more trust in existing network contacts than in outsiders during a period of systemic upheaval, but the habit of hiring acquaintances probably also reflects the intrinsic value placed by the society on helping out fellow members of the circle when hard times hit.

In the end, the apparent dominance of subdivision personnel in spin-off and start-up companies from Russian defense industry probably reflects the importance that managers attach to retaining the social networks with which they have traditionally had the strongest links at least as much as it reflects cold economic calculation. The emotional and moral pull of the broken interenterprise supply networks, discussed in chapter 3, undoubtedly waned in comparison to that of the *krugovaia poruka* of the immediate work group.

This means that while the rational self-interest explanation may be sufficient to explain conflicts between the old collectives and the new spin-offs in Russia, the socialization perspective contributes to our understanding of the institutional lines such conflicts have followed. It is not unexpected that the good of the collective would be sacrificed for the good of the shop or that the good of the shop would be sacrificed for the good of the work group. Further supporting the notion that it is not mere individualistic materialism that is operating in spin-off activities is the fact that many spin-offs seem to be replicating the social service functions provided by Soviet mother enterprises.

Paternalism in Spin-offs

Binar, a privatized high-tech spin-off from VNIIEF that has made (among other items) computerized equipment to control natural gas extraction compressors, has provided its employees with a family doctor and subsidized medicines, loans for large household appliance purchases, credit to allow them to buy their apartments, and maternity benefits. It has also thrown, on average, one employee birthday party per week[93]—a long-standing Soviet workplace tradition. TOFIS, a privatized conglomerate of twenty-one consumer-goods suppliers and retail outlets that used to be run by the Ministry of Atomic Energy for the convenience of Arzamas-16 employees, has continued to pay its employees' health insurance and nursery school costs, provided a doctor on contract for employees to visit, given interest-free loans to employees to buy furniture and television sets, and sold its products to employees at wholesale prices.[94] SIC ELVIS in Zelenograd lacks the resources to build housing for its employees but has sometimes paid for repairs to their apartments and has also paid for their children's summer vacations, for their right to use a free polyclinic, and for medical treatments of handicapped family members.[95] Another privatized defense enterprise spin-off, the Moscow Center for SPARC Technology, has provided a corporate membership for its employees to use at the American Medical Center in Moscow (using funds provided by its U.S. partner, Sun Microsystems)[96] and in 1994 was considering investing in housing for its employees to spare them commuting on crime-ridden intercity trains.[97]

The behavior of each of these spin-offs contrasts sharply with the practice of those forming start-up companies in the United States. While well-established companies in the United States that have large and certain markets often provide noncash perks to their employees, new firms tend not to do so. According to a standard legal manual used by many such firms, "Since most start-up companies are unprofitable in the early years, equity and profit par-

ticipation replace the more generous salary and [fringe benefit] compensation arrangements of seasoned concerns."[98] In U.S. start-ups, in other words,
employee stock equity (and its associated risk) replaces both cash and social
services that employers might otherwise provide. This helps a new business
ensure the likelihood of both profit and employee loyalty, especially where
there is a temptation to walk away with a new and struggling firm's hard-
earned innovations.[99]

Not all Russian spin-offs are so paternalistic. The privatized ELVIS+, for
example, has not provided medical services for its workers, explicitly preferring to give them the higher pay that would allow them to buy their own.[100]
Clifford Gaddy has suggested that the transition economy of Russia is sepa-
rating those individuals who prefer paternalistic treatment by their employers from those who prefer cash benefits.[101]

But the fact that so many spin-offs are providing social services of one kind
or another—and note that many of those mentioned above go beyond the
standard expectations of access to housing and subsidized health care—indicates that even the young and worldly former employees of Russian defense
industrial enterprises seem to prefer a measure of paternalism over pure cash.
Whether or not spin-off managers themselves receive intrinsic emotional
value from such paternalism, this pattern indicates that the society of the
Russian defense sector as a whole continues to see at least limited paternalism
as a moral good, owed by employers to their workers. Otherwise, all spin-offs
would look more like ELVIS+. It seems clear that managers still feel responsible for the well-being of their "in-groups" and that the drive for profits and
high salaries does not always translate into a cash-centered market ethic.

Implications for Russian Stability and International Security

Why should the outside world care about the labor/management conflicts
generated by Russian defense industrial spin-offs or about the loyalty that
subdivision employees feel toward each other? What practical political
effects can spin-off activities have, above and beyond the impact made by the
old enterprises themselves?

One important economic effect that spin-off activities can have is to inten-
sify large enterprises' struggle for survival and the resulting battle over how to
carve up the shrinking Russian federal budget pie. When a spin-off siphons
away resources from the mother enterprise, for example by using power and
water supplies for free, then that enterprise loses money and becomes even
more dependent on government largesse for its continued existence (and
even more vulnerable to real bankruptcy). When enterprise managers fail to

receive licensing fees for intellectual property use or to rent out at fair cost space that is clearly in demand by private firms (witness the Zelenograd complaints about enterprises' hoarding of empty space), they also lose money that could help to balance their books. Any unused or underutilized asset counts as a loss. These lost profits translate into lower and later-paid wages, which along with the threat of bankruptcy serve to aggravate the likelihood of enterprise-based strike and protest activity (discussed in chapter 2).

Furthermore, when managers benefit in underhanded or inequitable ways from spin-off activities, as many STKs charge, they have strong incentives to hide those personal benefits from enterprise workers, who might otherwise go to the authorities or to outside shareholders with demands for their dismissal.[102] To conceal the truth about their activities, managers must operate without the benefit of public documentation, which by definition further exacerbates the current trend of tax evasion in Russia. Such behavior in spin-offs thereby not only directly fans the flames of enterprise-based protests by undercutting the solvency of the enterprise; it also deprives the government of the means for performing the bailouts these protests demand, making competition over dwindling funds more and more acute.

Spin-offs that do not plunder the mother enterprise or engender labor conflicts can have either stabilizing or destabilizing political effects, depending on how successful they are. Those that provide long-term profitable job alternatives to people who have talent and initiative will reinforce societal belief in the efficacy of the market and thus serve as agents for reform in Russia. As their numbers grow, presumably Russian integration with other market economies will grow as well. But spin-offs that fail are likely to drive former enterprise employees back into the arms of the old enterprises.

As one analyst notes, Russian defense enterprise spin-offs are unlikely to receive state protection from bankruptcy, because they employ a small number of workers and thus have minimal political and economic impact as firms.[103] Given the poor track record of small businesses in the United States (even the most optimistic reports indicate that only "about half of all small businesses survive their first five years"),[104] where most entrepreneurs have at least grown up in a market economy, we should not expect that the majority of defense enterprise spin-offs in Russia will survive. Those dependent on foreign investment may be hurt by Western skittishness. (For example, IBM decided to end its production of personal computers at a spin-off of the Kvant enterprise in Zelenograd when the Russian federal government revoked a tax exemption it had earlier allowed on component parts imports.)[105]

In defense-heavy regions, those whose spin-offs fail may lack job opportunities, unless they return to their old enterprises. Once again, lack of employment mobility is a vital factor in understanding the political economy of the defense sector. In fact, many enterprises seem to be extending their social safety nets to those who work in their associated spin-offs. Some enterprises, such as Mashinostroenie in Reutov, tell those who leave to work in daughter companies that they are guaranteed their old jobs back if they want them.[106] Other enterprises, such as TsAGI, provide a significant fraction of spin-off employees with some type of minimal backup employment at the enterprise so that those willing to pursue riskier market opportunities have "a guarantee behind the risk."[107] As enterprise budgets continue to tighten and layoffs accelerate, such guarantees are likely to become more tenuous, however. In the absence of a state-supported social safety net and opportunities for geographic relocation of workers, spin-off failures are thus likely to heighten local and regional unemployment problems and the resulting centripetal pressure of cities and oblasts on the federal budget.

Beyond their domestic political-economic impact, spin-offs from Russian defense enterprises may pose new international threats in the area of arms proliferation. One of the more frightening examples of such a possibility is the case of spin-offs in Arzamas-16. A local newspaper report from August 1993 claimed that most small enterprises from the defense nuclear institute there had not properly registered their rental agreements with the regional representatives of the State Property Committee and that "there has been no list [made] of the economic control rights on property attached to VNIIEF [and other parts of the nuclear installation]." The report went on to state that there were ten "secret [small] enterprises" founded by VNIIEF, whose contract specifics were closed to outside auditors.[108] A January 1994 follow-up report claimed that some of the contracts signed by the nuclear installation were highly unusual: they stipulated that small enterprises that rented state property for a certain number of years would then be granted outright ownership of that property (the period given was five years for movable property, and fifteen for fixed property). The colorful article stated: "To speak simply, the guys from these associations, those who are the most brazen, in five years can say, on a legal basis, 'Excuse me, friends, but these machines and equipment are mine.' And after another ten years, they can say it about the buildings of the shop or laboratory." Perhaps most disturbing, the report quoted an investigator from the state prosecutor's office as saying: "There is no legislation whatsoever on nuclear security. Correspondingly, there are no violations of it."[109]

While no publicly available evidence confirms that any spin-offs in Arzamas-16 are responsible for instances of nuclear materials proliferation (and even though the representative of VNIIEF's financial management team interviewed in January 1996 insisted that no rental contracts with private firms had been signed for lab space or other work areas actually located inside the highly secured fence of the main installation)[110], the fact that outside investigators are prevented from seeing the property rental contracts of some spin-offs means that nuclear security depends completely on the honesty and wisdom of the managers involved.

Regardless of whether the rental contracts are suspect, it is an accepted fact—admitted by managers—that spin-off personnel here, as elsewhere, are engaged in private business on enterprise time and using enterprise equipment (including computers and labs inside the secured installation). This means that the transfer of classified information and materials to private sources may be difficult to control.[111] The Los Alamos National Laboratory in the United States has worked with Arzamas-16 to develop a sophisticated computer and video monitoring system for use in areas where nuclear materials are present. Reportedly, however, by May 1995 that system had only been was installed at a demonstration site. According to a Russian source, until such systems go into effect, "the specialist working with nuclear materials carries personal responsibility for their security. And, in order to prevent loss, [the specialist] personally controls the presence of uranium and plutonium in locations with highly radioactive background levels."[112] If that specialist is working for an unregistered private company, the problem of control is magnified, especially when the predominant security system is one of human guards with guns and Geiger counters rather than computerized gates, cameras, and sensors.

Employees of the closed nuclear installations have always had the reputation of being some of the most moral and disciplined members of Soviet society. They take extremely seriously their responsibility for the safekeeping of nuclear materials.[113] However, as elsewhere in Russia's defense complex, economic hardship has spiraled upward in Arzamas-16 in recent years.[114] When such hardship means that access to food and medicine for one's family is imperiled, there is no assurance that morality and discipline will prevail in the face of criminal opportunity. Since December 1992 institute employees—one publicly identified as a janitor—have made at least three failed attempts to steal nonweapons-grade uranium-238 from Arzamas-16,[115] proving that insiders who need money are willing to engage in the illegal trafficking of radioactive state property. When managers approve of employees engaging in private business on company time, control over these illegal activities becomes that much more difficult, as managers can no longer be certain who is legitimately using lab facilities when.

The experience of Arzamas-16 is hardly unique. Members of a spin-off from the Elektropribor enterprise under the Ministry of Atomic Energy's control in the Sverdlovsk region were found in 1995 to have stolen 48 billion rubles worth of stable isotopes (not militarily related) from their mother enterprise, exporting them to unsuspecting industrial customers in the West.[116] The existence of poorly regulated, potentially parasitic spin-offs is thus cause for grave concern, especially until sophisticated monitoring systems are installed in all enterprises (including those in Russia's other nine closed nuclear cities) that work with weapons-grade plutonium.

The problem extends beyond nuclear materials, as well. There have been many reports that machine guns and other small weapons are being made illegally in factory shops and smuggled out on factory planes throughout Russia.[117] A defense plant in Izhevsk, Udmurtiia, apparently sold 7,000 machine guns to Chechen rebels in Russia, and a second plant in the Russian Far East is reported to have sold them sixteen artillery pieces.[118] The Russian Federal Counterintelligence Service claimed that spin-off companies from the Hydrofoil Central Design Bureau in Nizhnii Novgorod divulged to foreigners classified information about the design of Russian military wing-in-ground aircraft.[119] Virtually the entire defense complex in Russia may thus be fertile hunting ground for rogue states or terrorist groups looking for ways to purchase military equipment to which they would otherwise be denied access. When managers have incentives to hide spin-off financial activities from the general public, the rogues' job is made much easier.

Organized crime groups have also begun to infiltrate the Russian defense complex, which is hardly surprising, given the mafia influence in the Russian economy in general. For example, there were reportedly two mafia contract killings inside the closed gates of Arzamas-16 in 1995,[120] and inside the P'ezo defense electronics enterprise in Moscow in March 1995 a bomb exploded prematurely as it was being laid at night by an intruder.[121] In early 1996 the head of the Novator military enterprise in Yekaterinburg was gunned down in an apparent contract killing, and a Russian television commentary noted that "a number of other prominent figures in the military-industrial complex have been murdered over the past 18 months."[122] The possibility that organized crime groups interested in illegal weapons or technology purchases can find connections to private businesses being run from defense enterprises is thus not far-fetched.

Beyond worry about theft of classified information or materials, the existence of labor conflicts at sensitive enterprises is in itself alarming. As I noted in chapter 2, some labor disputes at Russian defense industrial enterprises have already involved the threat or use of violence. Occasionally one hears in an interview an ominous reminder from those associated with the Russian defense complex that unhappy defense enterprise workers have access to weapons. (Recall from chapter 2 the tank-plant worker who commandeered one of his plant's own vehicles.) Directors themselves sometimes use the specter of hazardous materials accidents at defense plants as a bargaining chip for more funds. For example, in the summer of 1993 work in Arzamas-16 involving the disassembly of a particular type of nuclear warhead was temporarily halted when wages were delayed, because authorities "fear[ed] the consequences of possible carelessness in the work of employees who haven't received their salaries for two months."[123] Similar measures were recommended by institute authorities in June 1995.[124]

It is easy to dismiss such threats as mere fear mongering, designed to pressure the state into bailing out troubled defense factories. However, when economic conflicts are not merely between enterprise and state but between long-term coworkers who now feel slighted by former comrades, the danger that passions will boil over is greater. The element of paternalistic in-group identification contained within these disputes makes their possible ultimate consequences even more unpredictable.

Conflicts within Russian defense industrial enterprises thus contain the seeds of real danger, both for domestic stability in Russia and for international security. Unregulated spin-off borrowing of intellectual property can lead to the unregistered dissemination of classified information and controlled materials. Financial conflicts between spin-offs and mother enterprises, and an associated desire on both sides to keep various expenditures off the public record, can contribute to the inability of state authorities to control illegal weapons proliferation. Desperate personal anger within enterprises manufacturing weapons and explosive materials can lead to rash threats or acts of violence. Once again, these problems are exacerbated by the lack of alternative employment and relocation opportunities and by the fact that enterprises, not the state, control the disbursal of social safety-net benefits.

Thus the continued structural and social importance in Russian defense industry of all three of the institutions examined in this book—the paternalistic enterprise, which limits labor mobility; the linkage of enterprises and elites at a regional level, which foments independence from Moscow's financial and foreign policies; and the formation of spin-offs based on in-groups, with incentives to conceal their activities from the inspections of outsiders—contributes to the potentially lethal mix of political instability and weapons proliferation in Russia's defense complex. Both structure and culture matter for policy outcomes.

5 Conclusions and Implications

In the preceding chapters, I have posed against each other arguments drawn from two competing perspectives on political and economic behavior—rational self-interest and socialization—to see how they serve to explain the actions of defense enterprise managers in the new Russia. I examined three arenas of managerial activity: the enterprise itself, the business and lobbying networks connecting enterprises and authorities at the ministry and local levels, and the spin-off firms that have emerged from mother enterprises. In each arena, the fundamental logic driving managerial behavior has important real-world implications for Russian domestic stability and international security. In this chapter, I will first summarize the findings of chapters 2, 3, and 4. Then I will spend some time discussing the implications these findings have for three endeavors: analysis of postsocialist transitions, theorizing about political economy more generally, and designing practical Western aid, trade, and investment policy toward the Russian defense sector.

Summary of Findings

In chapter 2, I noted that Soviet-era defense enterprises have endured in the new Russia with much of their old structures intact. Through 1995 they tended to retain large workforces (where older workers were particularly well represented) even in the absence of orders and markets. Managers continued to show a great deal of concern for maintaining worker housing and health care benefits.

This particular list of findings is very well explained by the rational self-interest model, but it does not contradict any of the predictions made by the socialization model. From the socialization perspective, those who had spent the longest time in the old system would be most likely to seek the comfort of continuing paternalistic care and job provision by the enterprise, whereas the youngest and most worldly members of the community would be more likely to adopt market values of independence and self-sufficiency and thus would be the most likely to leave. Managers would see it as their appropriate role to continue to fulfill the obligations of "mayor" at the enterprise and would value the continuation of paternalism as much as their collectives did.

From the rational self-interest perspective, older and female workers often would have had little economic choice except to stay at their old positions, since families depended on the health care and housing they provided, even if younger people and men went off in search of other opportunities. Hiring discrimination would furthermore have prevented many of them from obtaining good jobs on the open market. In addition, managers would have found that their specialized skills and information networks were fairly useless outside their home enterprises and would have been bound by their economic interests in linked spin-off firms to retain their footholds in the mother enterprises. People had strong economic motives to stay in Soviet-era institutions.

For this set of findings, then, the structure of the economic situation created incentives for managers and many workers to continue to make the kinds of choices that reflected long-standing cultural norms. Economic and political change in Russia was insufficient to unbind rational self-interest from Soviet-era behavior patterns. Capitalism there has unique attributes because the aftereffects of the Soviet system linger on. In particular, the enterprise as an institution has continued to take on the kind of social welfare duties that the state fulfills in other countries. Capital and labor immobility have acted as a brake on deeper market restructuring.

But two additional strands of evidence indicate that cultural norms mattered more than rational self-interest calculations in explaining the particular form that enterprise continuity took. First, many enterprise managers gave more attention to retaining (or making only minor modifications to) the enterprise's old mission and divisional structure than they did to the economic health of the enterprise as a whole. Managers at enterprises ranging from scientific institutes (including VNIIEF in Arzamas-16 and TsAGI in Zhukovskii) to design bureaus (Malakhit in St. Petersburg) to production facilities (the Sokol aircraft plant in Nizhnii Novgorod, the Mashinostroenie aerospace facility in Reutov, the Elektron Association in St. Petersburg, and the Almaz and Krasnoe Sormovo shipbuilding plants) all expressed an overwhelming desire to retain their enterprises' high-technology profiles and the associated high-priced collectives, sometimes even in the absence of sufficient orders to keep the enterprises solvent. While keeping a large workforce served the self-interested ends of managers, basing the activity of most enterprises on high-tech, one-of-a-kind orders did not. Managers focused on maintaining the profiles their enterprises had acquired over the years (even in the absence of present orders) and on fostering their enterprises' reputations for glory. The strategies that enterprise managers pursued in the transition era bear the marks of a unique Soviet defense sector heritage.

In at least several cases, including those of Reutov's Mashinostroenie and the Impuls' facility in downtown Moscow, retaining the profile also meant retaining essentially the same divisional structure that had existed before, even if some divisions lacked customers. The exception on this last point is TsAGI, which actively discouraged the maintenance of certain divisions. TsAGI's example indicates that some enterprise managers are less culture-bound than others and more willing to force their enterprises to adapt their behavior to the structural incentives provided by the new economic system. TsAGI managers have probably learned a great deal from the opportunities provided by their well-established and extensive relationships with a variety of U.S. and other Western firms and governments. It seems unlikely that such contact alone is responsible for the willingness to adapt, however, given that many Westerners have privately expressed the opinion that TsAGI's managers are unusually receptive to change and to Western-style business practices. Variation in the attitudes of individuals matters, despite the existence of generalizable patterns of continuity across enterprises.

The second strand of evidence indicating that cultural norms endure in Russian defense enterprises today is the fact that a great number of enterprises, including those that were unable to pay their workers for many months (such as plants in Zelenograd and Nerekhta, as well as Mashinostroenie in Reutov and VNIIEF in Arzamas-16), continued to put significant resources into maintaining family-oriented social facilities for their employees. Provision of housing and health care was probably necessary for the enterprises to function at all. The maintenance of other costly facilities, however, indicated that managers were responding to employees' social expectations, above and beyond what the enterprise needed to survive. Even the most seemingly market-oriented enterprises, such as the successful world arms dealer MAPO and the strong U.S. investment partner TsAGI, made budget allocations for such things as heavily subsidized children's camps, rather than distributing those resources as cash wages or reinvesting them in future ventures. Russian defense enterprises continued to operate under norms of paternalism that differ from those of their U.S. counterparts.

It is impossible to tell whether managers preferred to retain old profiles, divisions, and social facilities in the absence of outside pressures or whether instead the collectives pressured the managers into keeping them. What we can say definitively, however, is that cultural norms continue to operate within this sector and these patterns of expectations have constrained directors' pursuit of rational self-interested goals. Socialization has limited enterprise flexibility to respond to economic upheaval.

Chapter 3 revealed that the rational self-interest perspective and the socialization perspective do an equally good job of explaining the endurance of one type of Soviet-era social network: the links tying managers to each other and to authorities at the local and regional levels. The strength of these networks supports the socialization model's argument that there should be continuing feelings of obligation toward a primary circle of mutual help (the *krugovaia poruka*) and that the nurturing and expansion of those trust-based relationships should have eased the transition to the market. Defense enterprises in particular had always been connected to each other and to figures of authority through local and regional soviets (and for a significant period, through the *sovnarkhozy*) and always came to each other's aid in times of need. These norms were upheld as local authorities continued to provide benefits to enterprises in exchange for loyalty and cooperation.

At the same time, under the rational self-interest model, it is clear that both enterprises and local and regional governments objectively needed each other and benefited from their relationship with each other during this transition period. Local governments wanted to ensure the functioning and health of enterprises located nearby in order to avoid paying subsidies and unemployment benefits, to limit the potential for mob unrest (which was realized in both Nizhnii Novgorod and Nizhnii Tagil), and to prevent the kind of influence wielded by trade union unity in St. Petersburg. Enterprise directors, in regions ranging from Moscow and Nizhnii Novgorod to Yekaterinburg and Tatarstan, saw the maintenance of close ties with regional leaders as a means for expanding their lobbying influence on the federal government. Managers were rewarded for maintaining these relationships in areas ranging from tax relief and state credits to arms export independence.

But chapter 3 also showed that the socialization perspective cannot explain the pattern of ties that remained at the ministry level, a pattern the rational self-interest model can explain quite well. Enterprise managers socialized into the old system should have been wary of their old ministerial bosses, given their experiences in Soviet times when they tried to free themselves from strict planning oversight. At the same time, if the *krugovaia poruka* mattered, managers should have continued to feel obligated to help each other (as opposed to the political authorities) and to maintain ties to the enterprises that had been their buyers and suppliers in the previous era. Instead the pattern is exactly the opposite: enterprise directors from Yekaterinburg to St. Petersburg and Moscow deserted their former business partners when more profitable opportunities presented themselves but allowed former ministry personnel operating inside Goskomoboronprom to regain control over parts of their operations in the guise of financial-industrial groups (particularly in the field of aviation).

Immediate self-interest easily explains these relationships. Goskomoboronprom flexed its muscles and punished managers who sought too much independence, using its legal ability to influence state military orders (as in the case of several electronics firms in Zelenograd), to hinder the privatization process (in a legion of cases cited in the press), and to unseat directors in enterprises where it retained share ownership (as in the case of Rybinskie Motors). Goskomoboronprom also held out a variety of positive incentives that encouraged defense enterprise cooperation during the transition era, organizing international arms exhibitions, providing advertising assistance to enterprises, and setting up corporations to distribute the booty of sectoral lobbying efforts.

What chapter 3 indicates overall is that the *krugovaia poruka* of inter-enterprise ties in and of itself is not very strong, except when immediate material interests are at stake. Yet the particular incentives that structured business activity in the Soviet Union have continued to shape those interactions in Russia today. Directors used their old connections to gain information about new business opportunities, and long-standing ties to local and regional political bodies allowed directors to find a means for influence in the new era. It did not seem to be *trust* that mattered here so much as the convenience of turning to established connections that remained useful under new conditions. Economic history turned out to be path-dependent, because the structures of the old system channeled the options considered when that system fell apart. New channels of influence and economic activity did not arise from scratch but instead out of the well-worn procedures of the old system.

Chapter 4 returned once more to the notion of the manager having moral obligations to the collective. It became clear that the continuing authority of such collectivist norms was very limited indeed when the possibility for profit through spin-off activity presented itself. Many managers (especially midlevel managers) running spin-off firms used enterprise intellectual property, equipment, and resources such as heat and electricity without compensating mother enterprise budgets, thereby draining resources from collectives whose members were on reduced wages or forced leaves. Such cases were documented in a multitude of examples, ranging from electronics enterprises in Zelenograd to the nuclear scientific institute in Arzamas-16 and including many cases from Moscow, St. Petersburg, and their surrounding regions. Managers did not give up opportunities for private gain in order to support the larger group, even though the collectives who were left behind complained vociferously about the lack of paternalistic care showed to them by the new entrepreneurs.

Yet norms and old social connections still mattered to managers at the level where they had always had the greatest emotional impact: the subdivision and the work group. The new small firms tended to be based on old workplace personnel connections more than is the case in the United States, and many of the spin-offs (as I illustrated with examples from Arzamas-16, Moscow, and Zelenograd) continued to supply the same kind of paternalistic social benefits to their employees that the old mother enterprises had given them. The exception here was ELVIS+, which gave its employees cash instead of benefits. Undoubtedly other such exceptions exist, but the variety of cases where paternalistic care continued was striking.

Once again, as in the case of benefits provided by the old enterprises, this paternalism on the part of new spin-offs may be due to pressure emanating from the employees themselves, rather than from ingrained managerial preferences. If this is the case, then cultural norms are nevertheless limiting the flexibility of many new firms emerging from the Russian defense complex. Those norms seem to carry resonance even for the young, talented, and worldly workers who have left the safety of their mother enterprises to strike off in new directions.

One additional cultural factor may also be operating in the case of spin-offs: the apparent preference of managers to rent out space to insiders and friends and to keep outsiders from utilizing areas that are otherwise empty. It is difficult to know, however, whether this is a reflection of the fact that managers have been socialized into exercising power over the lives of those who depend on them or whether instead it is a rational response to the possibility of mafia infiltration.

Implications for the Study of Transition Economies

The first obvious conclusion to be drawn from these findings is that rational self-interest is operating very strongly within the Russian defense complex. Managers from the Soviet system have quickly adapted to new structural incentives. They immediately recognized the value of enterprise ownership; they used the state property available to them (including intellectual property, floorspace, and equipment and flow resources) for their own individual profit; and they worked with local authorities to align themselves into powerful blocs that can manipulate the fragility of Russia's federal constitution to their own economic and political benefit. Once it became clear that intellectual property mattered, managers did all they could to control it or to take it back, even though their initial naïveté about the market may have cost many of them dearly in this regard.

Interestingly enough, ministerial figures and Goskomoboronprom personnel have also acted in ways that Western positive political economists could have prescribed for them if the goal were resource maximization. They have formed lobbying groups as exclusive (and hence selective incentive-based) corporations, gaining partial control over members by exchanging ownership shares for credit assistance. They have also held on to the shares of privatizing enterprises for as long as possible, in order to influence directoral appointments and the strategic direction of enterprise activities.

In other words, rational actor models arising from the Western political economy tradition are not culture-bound. Some scholars have argued that it is inappropriate to apply such models to postsocialist transitions.[1] This study proves that argument false. While it may have been naive for Western economists to believe that they could transplant market reform models appropriate to the United States and Western Europe wholesale to the post-Soviet context, culture was not the major impediment to the success of reforms. Instead, political and economic considerations were at work that may have been hidden from Western observers lacking experience in the Soviet context. It makes perfect sense that managers whose skills and resources were meaningless outside the context of their particular enterprises would do everything possible (from lobbying to lying to organizing worker protests) to maintain those enterprises and their workforces rather than allowing them to go bankrupt (as a neoclassical economist might have preferred). It also makes perfect sense that workers who lacked the opportunity for job mobility would do everything possible to keep their enterprises open and to subvert the spin-offs that refused to employ them.

The two major factors impeding the smooth progress of defense enterprise reform in Russia—namely, the refusal of the old enterprises to die and the fights between mother enterprise collectives and spin-off managers—can be easily explained using objective structural variables such as property rights and asset immobility. This means that, at least in theory, reform policies that took those considerations into account could have been implemented successfully. One could imagine a Russia in 1992 where budget resources previously allocated toward enterprise subsidization and weapons purchases were newly channeled into programs designed to jump-start the market and relieve worker dependency on old enterprises. The state could have created subsidized retraining programs resembling U.S. community and technical colleges, encouraged the free flow of information about relocation and job opportunities by subsidizing reading rooms at local libraries throughout Russia, established better business bureaus and local chambers of commerce to encourage business information exchange across sectors, and enacted and enforced fair hiring and fair trade laws.

Of course, as always, politics intervenes. It is not clear that any of these measures would have received the support they needed for implementation from the variety of sectoral and regional actors whose power depended on the endurance of old operational structures. But it is rational economic motives that are at work here, not culture.

At the same time, we must recognize that enduring cultural values and patterns do matter. Russian capitalism is uniquely Russian. There are two levels in particular where culture has repeatedly insinuated itself into the story presented here. First is the manager's conception of what his or her own social role involves. The manager must protect the core definition of the enterprise, including its high-technology profile and collective and its past glory and achievements. The manager must also protect his or her immediate social group. Second is the matching societal conception of what duties the manager owes to the collective. Under new economic circumstances, it is especially the immediate work group that imposes these obligations, which center on the paternalistic provision of family-related goods and services, such as summer camps for the children, sports facilities, and assistance with major appliance purchases.

The fact that many managers are willing so blatantly to use the resources of the collective for their own private ends indicates that it is not simple moral considerations that are at work here, nor is it some general set of communitarian and other-oriented norms. Many managers do not appear to be altruistically oriented toward their employees. The fact that many Labor Collective Councils (STKs) have criticized managers stridently for predatory behavior indicates that the expectations of the two sides on that issue often do not converge. And the fact that former ties outside the enterprise are sacrificed when they do not serve managers' self-interested ends further indicates that the perceived obligations of managers are centered on a very limited definition of insiders. They do not extend out along the entire chain of social and economic relationships dating from Soviet times.

Yet it is also clear that the Russian defense-related economy continues to be characterized by both an in-group orientation and a level of paternalism with regard to insider social services that leaves it distinct from the U.S. experience of the market. Socialization into long-standing cultural norms matters. This means that where such norms are powerful, the post-Soviet transition is likely to differ from the trajectories of other democratic and free-market reform efforts.

It also means, however, that the search for areas where those norms matter must be painstaking and complex, since the rational self-interest model has done such a good job of explaining much of what has happened in the Russian defense political economy. Surface-level stereotypes about managers' inabilities to adapt to new structural constraints have proven inaccurate. Instead it is obvious that those new structural constraints differ from what the distant observer might have believed. This finding could extend to other areas of inquiry. It would not be surprising, for example, to find that some common surface-level stereotypes about the inability of post-Soviet Russia to adapt to and accept a system of institutionalized representative democracy were also faulty. Yet at the same time it would not be surprising to find at a more fine-tuned level that strong and unique political norms continue to operate in post-Soviet Russia. Russia could in the future have a strong and legitimate democratic governance structure while still maintaining its own set of social expectations about how politicians and officeholders should act, norms that might differ significantly from those found in the United States.

What we obviously cannot know yet, given that the transition is still in progress, is how long these unique norms will endure as Russia faces the global economy. Nevertheless, given that even the new defense sector spin-offs seem to exhibit a degree of managerial paternalism that separates them from most U.S. companies and given that hardly any of the old defense enterprise managers have voluntarily given up their local social roles (and were in fact continuing as of 1996 to receive state subsidies whenever possible, especially at election time, to maintain enterprise existence), it is a good bet that these norms will be around for at least a generation.

When we take into account the variety of forms of capitalism that exist among large states today, we should not be surprised that unique Russian economic norms might survive for the foreseeable future. Despite all the talk in the press, for example, of pressures for social and economic change in Japan and Germany, we know that these countries continue to operate under versions of capitalism that are recognizably their own.[2] Yet these are countries that (given the postwar occupation) encountered much stronger U.S. pressure and many more structural reasons than Russia has faced to adopt U.S. economic norms. In fact, in areas ranging from managerial paternalism to the structure of financial-industrial groups, the economies of Germany and Japan bear more than a passing resemblance to the type of capitalism emerging in Russia today.

Implications for Theories of Political Economy

What this means is that scholars from the rational self-interest perspective would be wrong to dismiss the independent effects of culture on economic behavior. Informal societal norms, never codified into explicit laws, rules, or taboos, continue to shape the behavior of powerful actors even in revolutionary circumstances and even when a long-term reputation for trustworthiness is irrelevant. Culture, in this sense, and culture's unwritten norms of social interaction are part and parcel of the structure faced by economic actors.

Some positive political economists have looked at culture as if it were a tool to be created and then used by self-interested actors to achieve their own ends.[3] They have viewed social norms as if they were constituted for functional reasons, to enhance economic and political efficiency by causing actors' expectations to converge or to ease the difficulty of monitoring the behavior of others.[4] But although there is a great deal of truth in these utilitarian descriptions of culture, what this book suggests is that cultural expectations are not merely objects utilized by self-interested actors; they also have an independent life of their own that constrains self-interest, even when the ultimate effect impedes efficiency. Politics and the drive for power over resources are not the only human tendencies that interfere with the real-world accuracy of the "economic man" model so dear to neoclassical economists. Culture and the drive to maintain long-standing social norms also intrude.

In recent years, some rational self-interest scholars have been willing to listen to psychologists who have told them that underlying tendencies in human behavior are incompatible with perfect rationality.[5] For example, some economists have accepted the psychological arguments of what is called "prospect theory." This theory says that actors facing uncertain situations fear the potential loss of what they already own more than they welcome the potential gain of something new. People tend to avoid risky choices more often when a situation is framed in terms of potential losses than they do when the same situation is framed in terms of potential gains.[6] Many rational self-interest scholars more or less accept the notion of bounded rationality:[7] that the wiring of the human brain prevents people from being as objective as a computer might be in the same situation.

The findings of this study suggest that the psychological limits inherent in human information processing are not the only boundaries that rational self-interest faces. Culture and informal social norms also limit self-interested action. The complexity of my findings indicates that general, inculcated moral consideration for one's fellow human beings is not what limits behavior. And given that conflict over issues of intellectual property and resource ownership and theft is running rampant between managers and collectives, it is also not preservation of reputation per se that matters. Yet if preexisting norms and roles did not matter at all, then enterprise managers would not be so concerned about preserving enterprise glory or retaining the collective, and spin-off managers would not be providing paternalistic care to their employees. (One could even make the argument that this same expectation of paternalistic care from the enterprise has made enterprise provision of a low-cost "roof" for manager-sponsored spin-off activities such a common occurrence in Russia.)

The boundaries limiting and shaping self-interested behavior have their origins in well-defined expectations about roles. These expectations are likely to vary across national societies as well as across occupational and other social groups within those societies. Overall, the assumption of universal individual rational self-interest is not wrong and should not be discarded, but in order to explain the real-world choices made by individuals, we need an in-depth understanding of the social roles that those individuals adhere to within the culture where they are comfortable. Even revolutionary circumstances will not destroy the expectations held by both individuals and the broader society of what those roles mean. Self-interest is seen through the lens of those role conceptions.

At the same time, culture alone does not explain the continuity between the Soviet and Russian defense economies. Many of the objective structural attributes of the Russian polity and economy are unique and lasting by-products of the Soviet system. Political institutions, such as the connections between enterprise directors and local authorities, and legal institutions, such as the fact that ministries were the owners of enterprise property, both tend to take on lives of their own. Once in place, they limit the range of choices that people can consider. They confer privileges on particular actors, such as gubernatorial or mayoral administrations or Goskomoboronprom personnel, who can then use these privileges to their long-term advantage. These powerful people can thereby gain control over the future policy agenda. This argument is not new. It has been forcefully made by positive political economist Terry Moe, who writes that political institutions in the U.S. context are "weapons of coercion and redistribution" ensuring that the winners of any one round of a game can set the rules of the next round.[8]

Although the argument is not new, its applicability to the Russian context has a consequence that most positive political economists have overlooked: any relatively closed economic system, including any state whose domestic political economy is even partially resistant to foreign influence, will have unique *political* structural attributes that significantly affect its economy. These political attributes go beyond such basic factors of structural *economic* difference as the quality and size of land, labor, and manufacturing capabilities. Natural endowments are not all that determines national differences or even what economists call comparative advantage, that is, the particular strengths and weaknesses of a country facing the global economy. Politics limits the flexibility people have when they try to respond to economic signals. It can even distort those signals. In Russia labor and capital mobility are currently artificially constrained by politics, even though it is obvious to outside observers that a potentially huge consumer market and a highly qualified labor force are waiting there to be utilized, if only the economic incentive structure were changed. The power structure of any existing system continues to shape system change in any particular country. Thus it should not be surprising to anyone that history is path-dependent and that different varieties of capitalism endure.

When social norms developed in the old system continue to act on people's choices in new circumstances, they serve to cement further and even extend existing structural power relationships. As the cases reviewed here have shown, this has meant that employees may actually have more control over the behavior of managers than it might seem, because the webs of ingroup paternalism appear to be limiting the choices that managers make. At some level, despite massive economic eruption and dislocation and incredible political upheaval, something fundamental has not changed in Russia. Yet it is not some mythical national character that endures. Instead, it is the mutually reinforcing impact of objective economic and political structures and the socialization patterns shared by those inside a common system.

Implications for Western Policy

Three basic intertwined problems have impeded (and will likely continue to impede) the prospects for the successful market transition or fadeout of Russia's defense complex: (1) the dependence of large communities of workers and locally powerful enterprise directors on the continued existence of the old enterprises and their paternalistic functions; (2) the financial and political dependence of many local and regional authorities on the well-being of those enterprises, accompanied by opportunities to pressure or subvert relevant national policy in order to serve those ends; and (3) the mutual resentment and resulting economic gamesmanship that exists between many old enterprise collectives and new spin-off firms. As I demonstrated in the empirical chapters, each of these problems carries with it the possibility of negative consequences for Russian domestic stability or international arms control and proliferation.

What the theory employed in this study makes clear is that there is nothing that any outsider can do to end these problems, which all really center on the limits of labor and capital mobility in Russia and are supported by the continuation of paternalistic cultural expectations. Recently there have been a number of international calls for Russia to implement a universal social welfare system not based on the old enterprises,[9] in the hopes that this might sever the connections to the old system. Yet no such policy seems forthcoming, and given the structural incentives and cultural norms noted here, it is unlikely that one will arise in the near future. Such calls, then, are not the basis for a realistic Western relationship with the Russian defense complex. Yet there are things that Western governments and private aid agencies can do to try to prevent the defense complex from moving in a direction inimical to Western interests in Russian political stability and international security. I will suggest three in particular.

First, Western states can use their trade promotion and investment insurance programs to help domestic firms to establish significant economic relationships with large Russian defense enterprises that might otherwise seek primary partners in rogue states or terrorist groups.[10] The United States in particular has a tendency to view such promotion as a business activity separate from (or even opposed to) national security interests. As a result, there is a reluctance (especially in the U.S. Congress) to allow governmental agencies to assume the kind of political and economic risk that goes along with investment insurance and trade support, because it is sometimes seen as giving welfare to particular private businesses or even as providing economic aid to a once and possibly future military enemy.

But what this book suggests is that such enterprise-to-enterprise relationships should not be looked at only from a business economics perspective. They also have very positive national security repercussions. The interests of Russian defense enterprises differ from each other, and there is no evidence of the kind of sectoral cohesion that would allow a national conspiracy to undermine the West by misappropriating defense-related funds. Russian defense enterprises that become dependent on ties to Western businesses or government agencies are much less likely to risk offending Western governments through their arms sales or illegal proliferation practices than are enterprises that have no connections to the West.

Obviously, governments in democratic free-market economies cannot instruct their firms about where they should consider investing their resources. What they can do, however, if political will allows, is to make business concerns about political and economic risk less salient, thereby encouraging private firms to consider such connections more readily. Business ties can have positive international security implications.

Second, Western investors in joint-venture or trading relationships with defense industrial spin-offs should be encouraged to take seriously the question of how their work will affect labor relations within the spin-offs' mother enterprises. Obviously, foreign firms are already highly attuned to the problem of intellectual property ownership and licensing, because they do not want to find themselves legally liable for patent or property theft committed by their Russian partners. This study suggests, however, that the interests of the broader international community extend beyond the simple question of legal ownership to include the perceptions of unfairness and the conflictual personnel relationships inside factories and institutes. Disputes between enterprises and spin-offs at a time when resources are tightly constrained but illegality is entrenched can both foment worker unrest and provide opportunities for smuggling and illegal proliferation. If a Western firm is involved in supporting a spin-off company, this can add fuel to the fire, even leading the West as a whole to be blamed for the inequities and impoverishment that the unfortunate mother enterprise workers perceive.

Such concerns will not often affect the profit calculations of the Western enterprises involved in these relationships, especially if the spin-offs are privatized and consider themselves separate from the mother companies. As a result these issues will not arise naturally in business dealings. An argument can be made, however, that spin-off activities' effects on labor relations with mother enterprises are an externality of the business relationship and thus morally equivalent to such societal concerns as industrial pollution or monopoly pricing. They are part and parcel of the national interest that any domestic company with international interests can either support through goodwill ambassadorship or undermine through bad reputation.

Attempting to force such concerns on Western investors would be counterproductive, in that it would serve to discourage the kind of investment in the

Russian defense complex that the previous policy recommendation suggests we should promote. However, positive incentives might be created to encourage Western investors to confront such effects as part of their relationships with Russian firms. The raising of the issue alone would encourage Russian spin-off managers to resolve key mother enterprise conflicts in advance, because otherwise those conflicts would become a potential embarrassment for them. For example, a simple requirement could be added to Western investment assistance programs, mandating that Western firms receiving aid for joint ventures or trade with Russian spin-off companies hold annual informational exchange meetings with the Labor Collective Councils of the spin-offs' mother enterprises. From the perspective of the outside investor, the holding of such meetings need not be onerous, given that they would provide an ideal venue for public and community relations activities. At a minimum, such meetings would prevent Western support of the Russian defense complex from having the unpleasant side effect of encouraging anti-Western attitudes among the Russian populace.

Third, aid agencies (ranging from the International Monetary Fund and World Bank to the Soros Foundation) might focus their concerns on the construction of better information infrastructure in Russia's outlying areas, especially because the Russian state seems to be doing little in this regard itself. In particular, aid agencies could target their efforts on programs that would encourage the creation of the kinds of private firms and voluntary public organizations that aid economic relocation and business risk taking in capitalist countries.

Potential examples are legion. Aid agencies might focus in particular on providing seed money for the formation of the kinds of simple institutions that aid job mobility in the West: (1) privately owned employment services, ranging from headhunter consulting firms to temporary help agencies; (2) independent community colleges and vocational-technical institutes offering two-year training programs in fields ranging from translating and accounting work to plumbing and electrical repair, preferably under the direction of teachers with experience in a market economy; (3) local better business bureaus supported by those who own consumer goods and services companies in the area; (4) national and regional want-ad newspapers; and (5) independent local libraries stocked with training and educational manuals, newspaper and journal subscriptions (including local newspapers from other cities), and photocopy machines. The aid programs already in place to encourage private housing construction and transportation facility upgrades would also help in achieving these goals.

Whether or not these simple suggestions bear fruit, this study indicates that Western governments should take into consideration the potential unintended consequences of their policies toward the Russian defense complex. Conversion of the Russian defense complex has consequences for international security and stability that go beyond the more obvious and long-standing Western concern of military threat reduction. The political effects of conversion assistance also extend far beyond the more obvious financial concerns of risk and profitability assessment.

The end of the cold war and the resulting decline in the Russian defense budget has had profound social effects on members of the Soviet military-industrial complex. The fact that Russian political and legal institutions and Russia's underlying economic culture differ so markedly from those of the United States means that defense complex reform in the two countries is not really comparable. It is sometimes tempting to believe that the advent of the free market will somehow provide all those who have lost their previous jobs or status in Russia with new opportunities equivalent to those available to engineers or scientists laid off from U.S. defense enterprises. It might thus seem that these opportunities would be adequate to prevent instability. But this book suggests that a different and darker future might lie ahead, in view of the structural and cultural realities of the Russian political economy as it now stands. Rather than complacently lauding the decline of the Russian defense complex as evidence of U.S. victory in the cold war, the outside world must regard with both sympathy and wariness the social, political, and international implications of the restructuring of this crucial sector of the Soviet economy.

Notes

1. Soviet Defense Managers and Economic Upheaval

1. Around 75 percent of Soviet defense enterprises were located on Russian territory. See Julian Cooper, *The Soviet Defence Industry: Conversion and Economic Reform* (New York: Council on Foreign Relations Press, 1991), p. 21.

2. For discussions of how this divide permeates social science literature, see James N. Rosenau, "Before Cooperation: Hegemons, Regimes, and Habit-Driven Actors in World Politics," *International Organization* 40, no. 4 (fall 1986): 849–94; and Stephen Krasner, "Sovereignty: An Institutional Perspective," *Comparative Political Studies* 21 (April 1988): 66–94.

3. See Edward Kolodziej, "Renaissance in Security Studies? Caveat Lector!" *International Studies Quarterly* 36 (Dec. 1992): 421–38, esp. pp. 427–8, 433; Theodore H. Moran, "An Economics Agenda for Neorealists," *International Security* 18 (fall 1993): 211–15; James A. Caporaso, "False Divisions: Security Studies and Global Political Economy," *Mershon International Studies Review* 39 (April 1995): 117–22; and Robert Latham, "Thinking about Security after the Cold War," *International Studies Notes* 20 (fall 1995): 9–16.

4. See Kevin O'Prey, *A Farewell to Arms? Russia's Struggles with Defense Conversion* (New York: Twentieth Century Fund Press, 1995); Michael McFaul and Tova Perlmutter, eds., *Privatization, Conversion and Enterprise Reform in Russia* (Stanford, Calif.: Stanford University Center for International Security and Arms Control, 1994); Petra Opitz and Wolfgang Pfaffenberger, eds., *Adjustment Processes in Russian Defence Enterprises within the Framework of Conversion and Transition* (Hamburg: Lit, 1994); and Lars B. Wallin, ed., *The Post-Soviet Military Industrial Complex: Proceedings of a Symposium* (Stockholm: Swedish National Defense Research Establishment, 1994).

5. Leonid Zagalsky, "Gold into Straw," *Bulletin of the Atomic Scientists* 51, no. 5 (Sept./Oct. 1995):10.

6. It is important to note that both the rational self-interest perspective and the socialization perspective see people making reasoned choices about how to act. The debate between the two is over how the menu of choice is defined. The first views individualistic, materialistic behavior as natural and universal and thus as the dominant choice of people everywhere. The second believes that certain societies cause individuals to link their sense of well-being to their membership in (or even sublimation to) a group and a set of group values, leaving individualistic materialism lower on the scale of actors' priorities. Both perspectives could therefore fit comfortably into the procedural rational choice approach, which simply states that individuals choose to act in ways that they believe will allow them to satisfy their goals. For a clear exposition of what procedural rational choice entails, see William H. Riker, "Political Science and Rational Choice," in *Perspectives on Positive Political Economy*, ed. James E. Alt and Kenneth A. Shepsle (New York: Cambridge University Press, 1990), pp. 173–74. My book is not designed to test or challenge the broader rational choice perspective, because rational choice per se does not make assumptions about what people's preferences are. Instead, it examines two common but competing models of what people's preference structures look like. The argument here is over what individuals' goals are and how they go about trying to achieve them.

7. See Ronald Dore, "Goodwill and the Spirit of Market Capitalism," *British Journal of Sociology* 34 (1983), as reprinted in *The Sociology of Economic Life*, ed. Mark Granovetter and Richard Swedberg (Boulder, Colo.: Westview, 1992).

8. See, for example, Robert H. Bates, "Macropolitical Economy in the Field of Development," and David M. Kreps, "Corporate Culture and Economic Theory," both in *Perspectives on Positive Political Economy*.

9. Examples of scholarship from this perspective, which focus on a variety of geographical regions, include Robert H. Bates, *Essays on the Political Economy of Rural Africa* (Berkeley: University of California Press, 1983); Douglass C. North and Barry R. Weingast, "Constitutions and Commitment: The Evolution of Institutions Governing Public Choice in Seventeenth-Century England," *Journal of Economic History* 49 (Dec. 1989): 803–32; and Mancur Olson, "Dictatorship, Democracy, and Development," *American Political Science Review* 87 (Sept. 1993): 567–76.

10. See Bates, "Macropolitical Economy in the Field of Development."

11. For support of the notion that this is exactly what Russian defense managers did, see Michael McFaul, "State Power, Institutional Change, and the Politics of Privatization in Russia," *World Politics* 47 (Jan. 1995): 210–43.

12. See *Socio-Economics: Toward a New Synthesis*, ed. Amitai Etzioni and Paul R. Lawrence (Armonk, N.Y.: Sharpe, 1991); and *Sociology of Economic Life*.

13. See Peter L. Berger and Thomas Luckmann, *The Social Construction of Reality: A Treatise in the Sociology of Knowledge* (New York: Irvington, 1966).

14. Representative examples of scholarship under this paradigm include Dore, "Goodwill and the Spirit of Market Capitalism"; Richard Swedberg and Mark Granovetter, introduction to *Sociology of Economic Life*; and Kathleen Thelen and Sven Steinmo, "Historical Institutionalism in Comparative Politics," in *Structuring Politics: Historical Institutionalism in Comparative Analysis* (New York: Cambridge University Press, 1992). Although I cited Douglass North above as an author whose work reflects the assumptions of the rational self-interest paradigm, that work is ambiguous and difficult to categorize, because North has emphasized the influence of different mixes of objective structures and subjective understandings on economic behavior at various points in his career. The portion of his work that most clearly falls into the socialization perspective is "Informal Constraints," chapter 5 of his *Institutions, Institutional Change and Economic Performance* (New York: Cambridge University Press, 1990), pp. 36–45.

15. For an example of such reasoning applied to state behavior, see Krasner, "Sovereignty."

16. Thrainn Eggertsson, *Economic Behavior and Institutions* (New York: Cambridge University Press, 1990), p. 56.

17. For examples of the argument that managers socialized into the old norms cannot perform well under market conditions, see Kenneth L. Adelman and Norman R. Augustine, "Defense Conversion: Bulldozing the Management," *Foreign Affairs* 71 (spring 1992): 26–47; and Peter Murrell, "Evolution in Economics and in the Economic Reform of the Centrally Planned Economies," in *The Emergence of Market Economies in Eastern Europe*, ed. Christopher Clague and Gordon C. Rausser (Cambridge, Mass.: Basil Blackwell, 1992).

18. The contrast between institutional constraint over behavior and institutional conditioning of preferences is made by Krasner, "Sovereignty."

19. For example, Bates appears to condemn all "cultural theorists" who do not use game theoretic or collective choice models for their failure to recognize the power of individual choice but criticizes by name only those from the 1950s and 1960s who got their data wrong in rural Africa; see his "Macropolitical Economy in the Field of Development." Similarly, Swedberg and Granovetter make a relatively radical argument that economic institutions influence behavior based on their social construction of reality, but they choose to differentiate themselves from "the new institutional economics" only on the question of whether political power constrains economic efficiency, an issue where Bates and Weingast would share their stance, even though those two authors would fundamentally disagree with Granovetter and Swedberg on the role played by socialization in economic behavior. See Swedberg and Granovetter, introduction to *Sociology of Economic Life*, pp. 13–16.

20. Newspapers that report frequently on defense industry matters include *Segodnia*, *Kommersant-Daily*, and *Inzhenernaia Gazeta*.

21. These newspaper searches were carried out at the U.S. Library of Congress, at the Centre for Russian and East European Studies at the University of Birmingham, and at the Newspaper Reading Room of the Russian State Library in Khimki. My search of some local newspapers (unavailable in the United States) was halted in mid-October 1994, when issues I requested at the Khimki reading room were suddenly and without explanation unavailable for perusal.

22. I visited these enterprises as a member of a group sponsored by the Stanford University Center for International Security and Arms Control (CISAC). Some findings are from interviews conducted jointly by the CISAC group as a whole and are noted as such in the notes.

23. Robert H. Bates, *Beyond the Miracle of the Market: The Political Economy of Agrarian Development in Kenya* (New York: Cambridge University Press, 1989).

24. See, for example, Robert D. Cooter, "Organizational Property and Privatization in Russia," in *Law and Democracy in the New Russia*, ed. Bruce L. R. Smith and Gennady M. Danilenko (Washington, D.C.: Brookings, 1993); McFaul, "State Power"; and Anders Aslund, "Russia's Sleaze Sector," *New York Times*, July 11, 1995.

25. See Terry M. Moe, "Political Institutions: The Neglected Side of the Story," *Journal of Law, Economics and Organization*, special issue, 6 (1990): 213–53.

26. For a non-Soviet example of this theoretical argument, see Bates, "Macropolitical Economy." For an empirical example of how such connections were used by members of the Soviet Communist Youth League, see Svetlana G. Klimova and Leonid V. Dunaevskii, "Novye Predprinimateli i Staraia Kult'tura" (New entrepreneurs and the old culture), *Sotsiologicheskie Issledovanie*, no. 5 (1993): 64–69.

27. Janos Kornai, *The Socialist System: The Political Economy of Socialism* (Princeton: Princeton University Press, 1992), pp. 64–66; Gertrude E. Schroeder, "Property Rights Issues in Economic Reforms in Socialist Countries," *Studies in Comparative Communism* 21 (summer 1988): 175–88; Frederic C. Pryor, *Property and Industrial Organization in Communist and Capitalist Nations* (Bloomington: Indiana University Press, 1973); and Jan Winiecki, "Large Industrial Enterprises in Soviet-type Economies: The Ruling Stratum's Major Rent-Seeking Arena," *Communist Economies* 1 (1989): 363–83.

28. See William H. Riker and David L. Weimer, "Economic and Political Liberalization of Socialism," in *Liberalism and the Economic Order*, ed. Ellen Frankel Paul, Fred D. Miller Jr., and Jeffrey Paul (New York: Cambridge University Press, 1993), pp. 86–87; and Cooter, "Organizational Property," pp. 67–68.

29. While some have argued that organized criminal protection rackets can serve as an alternate means for contract enforcement (and hence business stability) in Russia today, it is hard to imagine that organized crime as an institution, with its attendant gang rivalry and murderous techniques, would provide a basis for confidence in long-term domestic investment. See Jim Leitzel, Clifford Gaddy,

and Michael Alexeev, "Mafiosi and Matrioshki," *Brookings Review* 13 (winter 1995): 26–29.

30. "Russia to Crack Down on Importers' Capital Flight," Reuters, July 28, 1995.

31. Lynnley Browning, "Russia Has New-Look Economy but Lacks Investment," Reuters, Aug. 10, 1995.

32. Penny Morvant, "Inflation 6.7% in June," *OMRI Daily Digest*, no. 128 (July 3, 1995).

33. For example, Rockwell International's chairman and CEO, Donald R. Beale, said in 1994: "We are taking proactive steps in forming alliances with many industrial enterprises in Russia in most of our major business areas. . . . We believe Russia will become a major player in the world market and we are building a solid foundation for the future" ("Rockwell Executives Visit Russia in Separate Delegations," PR Newswire Association, Mar. 31, 1994).

34. Ol'ga Romanova, "Sumasshedshie vkladyvaiut v Rossiu ne bolee 2 dollarov" (Lunatics invest no more than two dollars in Russia), *Segodnia*, July 15, 1995. The title is an editorial pun on the statement made by the anonymous Western conference participant.

35. The report cited, among other risk factors, "uncertainty in politics, lack of [a] legal base and stable tax system, inefficient and overzealous bureaucracy" ("Russian Lawmakers Hope for Interventionist Involvement," *Kommersant*, no. 3, Feb. 6, 1996, as reported in *Foreign Broadcast Information Service Daily Report—Central Eurasia* (FBIS-SOV), Mar. 11, 1996, p. 53.

36. This proposition arises from the folk theorem of game theory, which states that in noncooperative games, it is only the expectation of long-term, repeated interactions that leads actors to cooperate in the short run so that they can develop reputations for cooperativeness that can maximize their long-term gains. See David M. Kreps, *Game Theory and Economic Modeling* (New York: Oxford University Press, 1990), esp. pp. 65–82; and Robert Axelrod, *The Evolution of Cooperation* (New York: Basic, 1984).

37. The first article to make this point was Benjamin Klein, Robert A. Crawford, and Armen A. Alchian, "Vertical Integration, Appropriable Rents, and the Competitive Contracting Process," *Journal of Law and Economics* 21 (1978): 297–336. For literature reviews on related issues, see Paul L. Joskow, "Asset Specificity and the Structure of Vertical Relationships," and Harold Demsetz, "The Theory of the Firm Revisited," both in *The Nature of the Firm: Origins, Evolution, and Development*, ed. Oliver E. Williamson and Sidney G. Winter (New York: Oxford University Press, 1991).

38. Mark Granovetter, "Economic Action and Social Structure: The Problem of Embeddedness," *American Journal of Sociology* 91 (Nov. 1985): 481–510, as reprinted in *Sociology of Economic Life*.

39. North, *Institutions*, pp. 34–35; and Robert H. Bates, "*Contra* Contractarianism: Some Reflections on the New Institutionalism," *Politics and Society* 16, nos. 2–3

(1988): 387–401. See also Robert O. Keohane and Lisa L. Martin, "The Promise of Institutionalist Theory," *International Security* 20 (summer 1995): 43–44.

40. See Bates, "Macropolitical Economy," for an argument about how opportunistic behavior lessens social efficiency.

41. Mancur Olson, *The Logic of Collective Action: Public Goods and the Theory of Groups* (Cambridge: Harvard University Press, 1965), esp. pp. 10–12.

42. The author observed such notices along the Ohio River in summer 1992. This fits Olson's discussion of labor groups in ibid., pp. 66–97.

43. Ibid., pp. 53–65, notes that small groups can accomplish a great deal cooperatively, since the input of each member leads demonstrably to benefits for that member.

44. Bates, "Macropolitical Economy," p. 44.

45. Examples include Adelman and Augustine, "Defense Conversion"; James M. Buchanan, "Asymmetrical Reciprocity in Market Exchange: Implications for Economies in Transition," in *Liberalism and the Economic Order*; and James R. Millar, "From Utopian Socialism to Utopian Capitalism," *Problems of Post-Communism* 42, no. 3 (May/June 1995): 7–14.

46. The notion that behavior is oriented toward doing what is appropriate has also been applied to the behavior of organizations; see John W. Meyer and Brian Rowan, "Institutionalized Organizations: Formal Structure as Myth and Ceremony," *American Journal of Sociology* 83 (1977): 340–60, as reprinted in *Organizational Environments: Ritual and Rationality*, ed. John W. Meyer and Richard Scott (Newbury Park, Calif.: Sage, 1992); and James G. March, "Footnotes to Organizational Change," *Administrative Science Quarterly* 26 (1981): 563–77.

47. Harry Eckstein, "A Culturalist Theory of Political Change," *American Political Science Review* 82, no. 3 (Sept. 1988): 789–804.

48. Some socialization scholars have adopted the term of paleontologists Stephen Jay Gould and Niles Eldredge, "punctuated equilibrium," to describe the results of a sudden revolutionary jolt. See Thelen and Steinmo, "Historical Institutionalism," p. 15, who refer to Stephen Krasner, who developed this model for change in state systems in "Approaches to the State: Alternative Conceptions and Historical Dynamics," *Comparative Politics* 16 (Jan. 1984): 223–46. However, Gould and Eldredge do not argue that such punctuation means that all organisms suddenly alter to adapt themselves to new circumstances. Instead, certain organisms that already existed on the margins find themselves well suited for the new niches opened by the shock, and they now thrive and multiply. Those who were well adapted to a system that no longer exists are more likely to suffer and die off. A clear explanation is found in Stephen Jay Gould, *The Panda's Thumb: More Reflections in Natural History* (New York: Norton, 1980), pp. 179–85.

49. Murrell, "Evolution in Economics."

50. Key sources include Joseph S. Berliner, *Factory and Manager in the USSR* (Cambridge: Harvard University Press, 1957); Blair A. Ruble, *Leningrad: Shaping a Soviet City* (Berkeley: University of California Press, 1990); Peter Almquist, *Red Forge: Soviet Military Industry since 1965* (New York: Columbia University Press, 1990); and Cooper, *Soviet Defense Industry*. Also see Julian Cooper's "The Civilian Production of the Soviet Defence Industry," in *Technical Progress and Soviet Economic Development*, ed. Ronald Amann and Julian Cooper (New York: Basil Blackwell, 1986). For an in-depth comparison of U.S. and Soviet business practices, see Paul R. Lawrence and Charalambo A. Vlachoutsicos, eds., *Behind the Factory Walls: Decision Making in Soviet and U.S. Enterprises* (Boston: Harvard Business School Press, 1990).

51. Vladimir Gimpel'son, "Politika rossiiskogo menedzhmenta v sfere zaniatosti" (The politics of Russian management in the employment sphere), *Mirovaia Ekonomika i Mezhdunarodnye Otnoshenie*, no. 6 (1994): 5–20; and Clifford Gaddy, "Notes for a Theory of the Paternalistic Russian Enterprise," unpublished paper prepared for the annual convention of the American Association for the Advancement of Slavic Studies, Philadelphia, Pa., Nov. 1994. Also see Linda J. Cook and Vladimir E. Gimpelson, "Exit and Voice in Russian Managers' Privatization Strategies," *Communist Economies and Economic Transformation* 7 (Dec. 1995): 475.

52. This latter, regional set of ties is in fact the subject of controversy among area specialists and therefore demonstrates the inherent subjectivity of the socialization perspective. For example, Tarja Cronberg, in "Enterprise Strategies to Cope with Reduced Defense Spending—the Experience of the Perm Region," in *Adjustment Processes in Russian Defence Enterprises*, p. 77, finds that there was little regional interaction among defense enterprises in the region of Perm' in Soviet times and calls the recent trend toward conducting regional business there an example of independent restructuring of contacts. However, the evidence that I will present in chapter 3 indicates that if the basis for these ties was not present in Perm' in Soviet times, then Perm' was an exception. Local or regional interaction appears to have been present throughout Soviet defense enterprises in general. Direct contracting between enterprises may have been a minor or nonexistent part of that relationship. (See Julian Cooper, "Regional'naia fokusirovka konversii oboronnoi promyshlennosti" [A regional focus on defense industry conversion], *Voprosy Ekonomiki i Konversii*, special issue, "Materials from an International Symposium on Investing in Conversion, May 25–26, 1993, Birmingham, U.K.": 61.) Yet local political networks and informal economic ties across enterprises were certainly crucial to enterprise success.

53. Gregory Grossman, "The 'Second Economy' of the USSR," *Problems of Communism* 26 (Sept.–Oct. 1977): 25–40, as reprinted in *The Soviet Economy: Continuity and Change*, ed. Morris Bornstein (Boulder, Colo.: Westview,

1981). Also see Mancur Olson, "The Hidden Path to a Successful Economy," in *Emergence of Market Economies in Eastern Europe.*

54. See John M. Litwack, "Legality and Market Reform in Soviet-Type Economies," *Journal of Economic Perspectives* 5 (fall 1991): 77–89; Berliner, *Factory and Manager in the USSR,* p. 192; and Steven J. Staats, "Corruption in the Soviet System," *Problems of Communism* (Jan.–Feb. 1972): 40–47.

55. Path dependency is accepted by most of the socialization school and many members of the opportunism school. See Thelen and Steinmo, "Historical Institutionalism"; Swedberg and Granovetter, "Introduction to *Sociology of Economic Life*; Bates, "Macropolitical Economy," p. 54; and North, *Institutions.*

56. In addition to the work of Ronald Dore on Japanese capitalism, such conclusions would lend support to the controversial work of Francis Fukuyama, *Trust: The Social Virtues and the Creation of Prosperity* (New York: Free Press, 1995). Interestingly, Fukuyama (p. 28) calls Russia "a truly individualistic societ[y] with little capacity for association," where "both families and voluntary associations are weak." While Russians today may not join many voluntary associations, it is my personal observation that Russian parents are much more involved in their children's daily education than are parents in the United States and that adults in Russia are much more likely to include their parents and other members of their extended families in social activities on a regular basis than U.S. adults are.

57. For one attempt to make just this argument, see Gary S. Becker and Richard A. Posner, "Cross-Cultural Differences in Family and Sexual Life," *Rationality and Society* 5, no. 4 (Oct. 1993): 421–31. The authors present data indicating that marriage, bloodwealth, polygyny, and tolerance of homosexuality across so-called primitive societies are correlated with the production modes available to those societies.

58. See the historical summary and literature review provided by Murray Weidenbaum, "The Future of the U.S. Defense Industry," unpublished paper prepared for the 1991 annual meeting of the Western Economic Association, Seattle, Wash., July 1, 1991; and Bernard Udis, "Adjustments to Reduced Domestic Defense Spending in Western Europe," in *Downsizing Defense,* ed. Ethan B. Kapstein (Washington, D.C.: Congressional Quarterly, 1993).

59. Kevin O'Prey, *The Arms Export Challenge: Cooperative Approaches to Export Management and Defense Conversion,* Brookings Institution Occasional Papers, Washington, D.C., 1995, pp. 5–15. Also see Laure Després, "Conversion of the Defence Industry in Russia and Arms Exports to the South," *Communist Economies and Economic Transformation* 6, no. 3 (1994): 367–83; and Ethan B. Kapstein, *The Political Economy of National Security* (Columbia: University of South Carolina Press, 1992), p. 155.

60. "Russian Arms Exports up 80 Pct," Associated Press, Mar. 5, 1996.

61. See Patrick E. Tyler, "Russia and China Sign a Military Agreement," *New York Times,* Nov. 10, 1993; Stanislav Fillin (deputy director of Rosvooruzhenie, the

state arms export agency), "A New Stage in Partnership," *Military Parade*, Nov./Dec. 1994, p. 15; Aleksandr Koretskii, "Vooruzhat' soseda—pribyl'no. No do razumnogo predela" (To arm one's neighbor is profitable. Up to a certain point), *Kommersant-Daily*, May 4, 1995; and Nigel Stephenson, "Russia Plans $3.5 Bln Arms Deals with India in 96," Reuters, Feb. 20, 1996.

62. For example, see the comments on Iraq and Libya made by General Sergei Oslikovskii, first deputy director of Rosvooruzhenie, as reported in Pavel Fel'gengauer, "Yel'tsin obeshchaet ne prodavat' oruzhie Iranu" (Yeltsin promises not to sell weapons to Iran), *Segodnia*, Sept. 29, 1994.

2. The Endurance of Soviet Enterprises

1. James R. Lecky, "American Experiences in Diversification: Ideas for Nizhniy Novgorod," unpublished paper prepared for the International Conference on Defense Conversion in Nizhnii Novgorod, Nizhnii Novgorod, Russia, May 1994, p. 7.

2. For examples, see U.S. Arms Control and Disarmament Agency, "Report to the Congress on Defense Industry Conversion," August 1990; Murray Weidenbaum, "The Future of the U.S. Defense Industry," unpublished paper prepared for the annual meeting of the Western Economic Association, Seattle, Wash., July 1, 1991; Steven Pearlstein, "Trying to Give Peace a Chance," *Washington Post*, May 24, 1992; Richard T. Minnich, "Defense Downsizing and Economic Conversion: An Industry Perspective," in *Downsizing Defense*, ed. Ethan B. Kapstein (Washington, D.C.: Congressional Quarterly, 1993); and C. R. Neu and Michael Kennedy, "Do We Need Special Federal Programs to Aid Defense Conversion?" Rand Issue Paper, Santa Monica, Calif., Feb. 1993. For a dissenting view, see Jurgen Brauer and John Tepper Marlin, "Converting Resources from Military to Non-Military Uses," *Journal of Economic Perspectives* 6, no. 4 (fall 1992): 145–64.

3. Minnich, "Defense Downsizing and Economic Conversion," pp. 125, 128.

4. See Kenneth L. Adelman and Norman R. Augustine, "Defense Conversion: Bulldozing the Management," *Foreign Affairs* 71 (spring 1992): 26–47.

5. David Bernstein, "Spin-offs and Start-ups in Russia: A Key Element of Industrial Restructuring," in *Privatization, Conversion, and Enterprise Reform in Russia*, ed. Michael McFaul and Tova Perlmutter (Stanford, Calif.: Stanford University Center for International Security and Arms Control, 1994).

6. Arkadii Sosnov, interview with Il'ia Klebanov, "Nash investor stoit u poroga" (Our investor stands at a threshold), *Nevskoe Vremia* (St. Petersburg), Jan. 10, 1995.

7. Here are some examples. The Moscow Aviation Production Association (MAPO-MiG) in 1995 still employed 20,000 people, produced eighteen MiG-29 jet fighters for sale to Malaysia and was continuing MiG production for sales to India and possibly the Philippines. See "Swords to Ploughshares—MiGs to Microlights," Reuters, Dec. 15, 1994; and "Russia MiG Maker Completes $550 Million

Malaysia Deal," *Reuters*, June 6, 1995. The Il'iushin Design Bureau, using Pratt and Whitney engines, Rockwell International avionics, and a variety of other Western parts, began manufacturing low-cost passenger airplanes that caused even the Boeing Corporation to fear it as a competitor. See "Boeing Objects to Russia Deal," *Associated Press*, Mar. 7, 1995. The Baltiiskii Zavod shipbuilding plant in St. Petersburg began building chemical tankers for a German company, making up for the losses it suffered when two Russian state orders were fulfilled but not paid for. See L. Rakhmanov, " 'Iberia' plyvet na mezhdunarodnyi rynok" (The 'Iberia' is sailing into the international market), *Sankt-Peterburgskie Vedomosti*, Aug. 2, 1994; and O. Steshenko, "Odin iz poslednikh rossiiskikh zakazov" (One of the Last Russian Orders), *Sankt-Peterburgskie Vedomosti*, Oct. 21, 1994. And the Izhorskie Zavody complex in a suburb of St. Petersburg (which made nuclear submarine reactors, among other items) won a reactor contract from the Perm' Oil Refining Factory, which promised to keep twelve Izhorskie shops operating at capacity for at least a year. See "Zakaz s Urale snial ugrozu bankrotstva" (An order from the Urals prevented the threat of bankruptcy), *Sankt-Peterburgskie Vedomosti*, Dec. 20, 1994.

8. See Kevin O'Prey, *The Arms Export Challenge: Cooperative Approaches to Export Management and Defense Conversion*, Brookings Institution Occasional Papers, Washington, D.C., 1995, pp. 5–15.

9. Vitalii Vitebskii, "The Military-Industrial Complex in the First Quarter of 1995," *Krasnaia Zvezda*, Apr. 29, 1995, as reported in *Foreign Broadcast Information Service Daily Report—Central Eurasia* (FBIS-SOV), May 2, 1995, pp. 22–23.

10. A defense enterprise whose workers successfully sought to have the firm declared bankrupt, in hopes the enterprise might survive under new management appointed by the regional Arbitrage Court, is the Lazur' plant in Nizhnii Novgorod. See V. Seryi, "Eshche odno miagkoe bankrotstvo" (One more gentle bankruptcy), *Nizhegorodskie Novosti*, Feb. 8, 1994. Another enterprise that followed suit is the Samara Aviation Works; see "Avis Aviation Works Declares Bankruptcy," Moscow Mayak Radio Network, Sept. 15, 1994, as reported in *FBIS-SOV*, Sept. 15, 1994, p. 25. The ELION defense electronics factory in Zelenograd, as of September 1994, was in the midst of a similar process. See I. Makhovskaia, summarizing a report of Aleksandr Ivanovich Lebedev, the first deputy prefect of Zelenograd, "Novye avansy, starye dolgi . . ." (New advances, old debts . . .), *Sorok Odin* (Zelenograd), no. 36 (May 13, 1994); and "Poteriavshii doverie A. Vetchinkin" (A. Vetchinkin has lost trust), *Sorok Odin* (Zelenograd), no. 68 (Sept. 2, 1994).

11. In fact, to my knowledge there is only one report of a Russian defense enterprise ending its existence: the Teleradio Factory in the city of Cheremkhovo, in the Siberian region of Irkutsk. Apparently only 98 of its 5,400 workers remained at the plant, and its director disappeared without a trace. The Irkutsk Electric Company was therefore allowed to take over its premises. See Natal'ia Gotova,

"Voennyi radiozavod budet remontirovat' eletrooborudovanie" (Electrical equipment will overhaul a military radio factory), *Kommersant-Daily*, Oct. 21, 1994.

12. See Tatiana Kirshina, "Vzroslye ushli na kanikuly. Deti nachali rabotat' " (The grown-ups are going on summer vacation. The children have begun to work), *Sibirskaia Gazeta*, no. 28 (July 1993).

13. For example, see an untitled item from *Rossiiskaia Gazeta*, June 22, 1993, as reported in *Foreign Broadcast Information Service Daily Report—Central Eurasia (FBIS-SOV)*, June 24, 1993, pp. 39–40. The general director of the Vladivostok Dalpribor Production Association, Viktor Paulo, said he was resigning "because the Russian government was no longer committed to military production."

14. By October 1994, 40 percent of Russian defense enterprises had been sold to private owners, and an additional 40 percent had restructured as state-controlled joint-stock companies, signaling the start of privatization (A. N. Shulunov, as quoted by Leonid Kosals and Rozalina Ryvkina, "Gosudarstvennoi politiki v sfere VPK net" [There is no state policy in the sphere of the military-industrial complex], *Segodnia*, Oct. 18, 1994).

15. Michael McFaul, "State Power, Institutional Change, and the Politics of Privatization in Russia," *World Politics* 47 (January 1995): 210–43, esp. 233.

16. Anders Aslund, *How Russia Became a Market Economy* (Washington, D.C.: Brookings, 1995), pp. 233–34; and McFaul, "State Power," pp. 230–31.

17. Aslund, *How Russia Became a Market Economy*, p. 234.

18. Ibid. Also see McFaul, "State Power," p. 230.

19. Aslund argues that Russian voters in 1990 paid insufficient attention to who the candidates were and what they stood for (*How Russia Became a Market Economy*, pp. 54–5, 61). McFaul, "State Power," p. 230, has gone so far as to claim that the legislature that resulted was not part of a truly pluralistic, parliamentary system but instead a herald of sectoral corporatism, against which the interests of individual citizens had little chance.

20. For examples, see Michael McFaul, "Agency Problems in the Privatization of Large Enterprises in Russia," in *Privatization, Conversion, and Enterprise Reform in Russia*, p. 45; and "Dinamika kursov obyknovennnykh aktsii privatizirovannykh predpriiatii S. Peterburga s 01.12.94 po 10.1.95" (The exchange action of common stock of privatized enterprises in St. Petersburg, Dec. 1, 1994 to Jan. 10, 1995), *Sankt-Peterburgskie Vedomosti*, Jan. 19, 1995. This finding is seconded by Kevin O'Prey, *A Farewell to Arms? Russia's Struggle with Defense Conversion* (New York: Twentieth Century Fund Press, 1995), p. 58. For the argument that this is common throughout all sectors in Russia, see Igor Gurkov and Gary Asselbregs, "Ownership and Control in Russian Privatized Companies: Evidence from a Survey," *Communist Economies and Economic Transformation* 7, no. 2 (June 1995): 208.

21. O'Prey, *Farewell to Arms?* p. 58.

22. From an interview conducted by members of the CISAC team, including the author, Sept. 1994.

23. This is apparently a common occurrence when banks buy shares at auction; they sell them back to the enterprise either on credit or at a higher price. See Larisa Gorbatova, "Formation of Connections Between Finance and Industry in Russia: Basic Stages and Forms," *Communist Economies and Economic Transformation* 7, no. 1 (Mar. 1995): 24.

24. Andrei Nikolaev, "Vooruzhennyi direktor zakhvatil vlast' v NII" (An armed director seized power at a scientific institute), *Segodnia*, Aug. 17, 1994, reports this of the Central Scientific Institute of Experimental Engineering Equipment in Moscow.

25. Scott Gerber, "The Financial Revolution," *Bisnis Bulletin* (U.S. Department of Commerce), Jan./Feb. 1995, p. 4.

26. Pavel Kuznetsov, "Fondovye reguliatory nadeiutsia na uskorenie oborota direktorov" (Bond regulators hope for an acceleration of director turnover), *Segodnia*, Jan. 31, 1995.

27. The Russian government maintains a list of defense enterprises that are forbidden to privatize because of the necessity of maintaining their current output profile or because of the dangerous nature of their products. The size of this list has varied over time, and enterprises have lobbied both to be stricken from and added to it. *Goskomoboronprom* figures from August 1995 put the size of the "not-for-privatization" list at 350 enterprises; see Vladimir Belov, "Fond Konversii ne konkurirovat' s bankami" (Conversion fund not to compete with banks), *Kommersant-Daily*, Aug. 30, 1995.

28. An interesting example is that of the Polet aerospace enterprise in Omsk. According to a newspaper report, General Director Valentin Zaitsev was unseated by a "coup" based on a vote by forty-two of his forty-eight enterprise shops while he was on a business trip in Moscow. See "Director 'Poleta' 'sletel' po vole trudiashchikhsia" (The director of Polet "flew away" by the will of the laborers), *Kommersant-Daily*, Apr. 15, 1995.

29. See, for example, Andrei Garavskii, "Kupite zavod v zelenograde, nedorogo" (You can buy a factory in Zelenograd, cheap), *Krasnaia Zvezda*, Sept. 17, 1994, which states that four STKs in Zelenograd have tried without success to unseat their directors; and Irina Vladykina, "Ob'edinenie 'Avtomatika' dobilos' vyplaty zarplaty" (The Avtomatika Association obtained wage payments), *Segodnia*, Nov. 29, 1994, which says the same thing about the Avtomatika plant in Yekaterinburg.

30. An example was the leadership change made at the Izmash artillery plant in Udmurtiia. The former leaders had decided to pay dividends to investors despite having been declared insolvent by the federal courts. The Izmash Council of Directors replaced the president with the factory's chief engineer and named the factory's former general director as its new chairman. See Yevgenii Ostapov,

"Predpriiatie—bankrot vuplachievaet dividendy" (Enterprises—A bankrupt one pays dividends), *Kommersant-Daily*, May 25, 1995.

31. Interview conducted by the author during a plant visit with a team from Stanford CISAC, Sept. 1994.

32. Paul R. Lawrence and Charalambo A. Vlachoutsicos, eds., *Behind the Factory Walls: Decision Making in Soviet and U.S. Enterprises* (Boston: Harvard Business School Press, 1990), p. 167.

33. David J. Denis and Diane K. Denis, "Performance Changes Following Top Management Dismissals," *Journal of Finance* 50, no. 4 (Sept. 1995): 1029. This study of 908 management changes unrelated to takeovers that were reported in the Wall Street Journal between 1985 and 1988 found the external appointment pattern in 52 percent of the cases of forced resignations.

34. Interview by the author with the deputy general director for personnel, during a plant visit with the Stanford CISAC team, Sept. 1994.

35. Brenda Horrigan, "How Many People Worked in the Soviet Defense Industry?" *Radio Free Europe/Radio Liberty Research Report* 1, no. 33 (Aug. 21, 1992): 35.

36. Gherman Lomanov, "Military-Industrial Complex Losing Personnel," *Moscow News*, Mar. 13, 1993.

37. A. N. Shulunov, chairman of the League for Assistance to Defense Enterprises, as quoted in Leonid Kosals and Rozalina Ryvkina, "Gosudarstvennoi politiki v sfere VPK net" (There is no state policy in the sphere of the military-industrial complex), *Segodnia*, Oct. 18, 1994.

38. While such "voluntary" departures may have occurred under extreme economic pressure, given the fact of low and unpaid wages, this does represent a separate activity from the involuntary firing of employees or downsizing of workforces. O'Prey states that around 50 percent of the workforce may have left voluntarily (*Farewell to Arms*, p. 45). A Russian report from February 1995, apparently sponsored by defense industrial interests, claims, however, that the defense industrial workforce has only shrunk by 23 percent since 1991. See I. V. Prostakova and A. M. Folometov, "Intellektual'naia sobstvennost' i privatizatsiia v VPK" (Intellectual property and privatization in the military-industrial complex), *EKO*, no. 2 (Feb. 1995): 120.

39. In 1993 only 5.8 percent of Russian defense enterprises employed fewer than 1,000 people per enterprise; 49.8 percent employed from 1,001 to 5,000 people, and 44.4 percent employed more than 5,000. These figures are according to Alexander Ozhegov, "Conversion and Russia's Regions," in *The Post-Soviet Military Industrial Complex: Proceedings of a Symposium*, ed. Lars B. Wallin (Stockholm: Swedish National Defense Research Establishment, 1994), p. 59.

40. See Doug Clarke, "Hard Times in Defense Industry," *Radio Free Europe/Radio Liberty Daily Report*, Nov. 22, 1994, and idem, "Defense Workers Want Yeltsin Out," *Omri Daily Digest*, no. 10 (Jan. 13, 1995).

41. See *Kodeks Zakonov o Trude Rossiiskoi Federatsii* (Codex of labor law of the Russian Federation) (Moscow: Firma Spark, 1994), article 92, p. 39.

42. Some newspapers have columns giving legal advice to the public, and a frequent complaint is that managers are not following the rules of the codex. For example, see A. Vorob'ev, "Za chei schet—v otpusk?" (Who has to pay for the leave?), *Sankt-Peterburgskie Vedomosti*, Oct. 5, 1994.

43. Shulunov, as quoted by Kosals and Ryvkina, "Gosudarstvennoi politike v sfere VPK net."

44. From an interview conducted by the CISAC team, including the author, Sept. 1994.

45. Reported by George Nikides, "Millions Work on the Side," *Moscow Times*, Oct. 1, 1994.

46. Jerry F. Hough, "Russia—On the Road to Thermidor," *Problems of Post-Communism* 41, special (unnumbered) issue (fall 1994): 28.

47. Alessandra Stanley, "In Russia, a Breakdown on the Road to Capitalism," *International Herald Tribune*, Aug. 25, 1994. Also see Pavel Felgenhauer (*sic*), "Nuclear Cities' Secrets Revealed," *Moscow Times*, Aug. 25, 1994, which claims that the potatoes grown by residents of the closed nuclear cities at their dachas "are now becoming an increasingly important part of their diet."

48. This example is cited in Sonni Efron, "Russians Doff Lab Coats for Suits," *Los Angeles Times*, as reported in the *Minneapolis Star-Tribune*, Dec. 27, 1994.

49. This point is made by V. I. Zhil'tsov, general director of the Submikron Scientific Production Association, as quoted by Kosals and Ryvkina, "Gosudarstvennoi politike v sfere VPK net." Also see Aleksandr Yakushev, "Chto imel—ne sbereg. Chto nashel—poterial" (What it had is not retained. What it found is lost), *Vechernyi Barnaul*, Feb. 7, 1995, who says that workers leaving the large Sibenergomash enterprise in Barnaul are "disqualifying" themselves by working elsewhere. A similar point was raised by a senior official of the Russian government's Interdepartmental Analytic Center who works as a consultant on defense industrial economic policy, interviewed by the author in Moscow, Oct. 1994.

50. For examples, see a report on the ELMA factory in Zelenograd, with complaints about sewage treatment, ventilation systems, and unsafe density and spacing of equipment, in I. Korenev, "Deputaty trebuiut otseleneiia zhitelei vos'mogo mikroraiona" (Deputies demand the outward settling of inhabitants of a potential microregion), *Sorok Odin*, no. 31 (Oct. 1991); and a roundtable discussion on the danger of radioactive dispersion from accidental conventional explosion in the dismantling of nuclear warheads at the Avangard factory, reported by Petr Khven', "Liubimyi gorod mozhet spat' spokoino?" (Can the favorite city sleep peacefully?), *Gorodskoi Kur'er* (Arzamas-16), Nov. 4, 1992.

51. "Life Expectancies in Russia to Fall Further," Jamestown Foundation *Monitor* 1, no. 23 (June 1, 1995).

52. Quoted by Thomas Sigel, "Unemployment Gradually Increasing," *OMRI Daily Digest*, no. 141 (July 21, 1995).

53. For an example, see the description of the Uralmash factory's microcity in Sverdlovsk (now Yekaterinburg), in Bill Keller, "In Urals City, the Communist Apparatus Ends but Not the Communist Power," *New York Times*, Dec. 13, 1990.

54. See, for example, Alfred John DiMaio Jr., *Soviet Urban Housing: Problems and Policies* (New York: Praeger, 1974), p. 102. I have also experienced this firsthand.

55. Ibid., pp. 167–70.

56. Andrei Sakharov, *Memoirs*, trans. Richard Lourie (New York: Knopf, 1990), p. 114.

57. See Mikhail Agursky, *The Soviet Military-Industrial Complex*, Jerusalem Papers on Peace Problems 31 (Jerusalem: Hebrew University Leonard Davis Institute for International Relations, 1980). Also see Matthew Evangelista, *Innovation and the Arms Race: How the United States and the Soviet Union Develop New Military Technologies* (Ithaca, N.Y.: Cornell University Press, 1988), pp. 33–35.

58. Author's interview with the deputy general director for social services at the Mashinostroenie plant in Reutov, with the CISAC group, Sept. 1994.

59. Nikolai Anishchenkov, *A Soviet Factory: Past, Present, and Future*, Soviet Booklet no. 59 (London: Soviet Booklets, 1959), p. 18.

60. Author's interview with the deputy general director for social services at the Mashinostroenie plant in Reutov.

61. Lawrence et al., *Behind Factory Walls*, p. 275.

62. Information from a 1970s internal "multiple-page newspaper" article, from a defense enterprise in the Moscow region.

63. Ibid.

64. Author's interview with the deputy general director for personnel.

65. Blair A. Ruble, *Leningrad: Shaping a Soviet City* (Berkeley: University of California Press, 1990), p. 144.

66. V. M. Yurasov, *Admiralteitsy: Istoriia Leningradskogo Admiralteiskogo Ob'edineniia* (The admiralty workers: A history of the Leningrad Admiralty Association) (Leningrad: Lenizdat, 1976), pp. 26–27.

67. For another example, see Stanley, "In Russia, a Breakdown."

68. See, for example, Nikolai A. Kaniskin (general director of the Sibelektrotiazmash enterprise in Novosibirsk), "The Western Executive and the Soviet Executive," trans. Arlo Shultz (of "Zapadnyi menedzher i Sovetskii direktor," *EKO* no. 5 [1990]), in *The Russian Management Revolution: Preparing Managers for the Market Economy*, ed. Sheila M. Puffer (Armonk, N.Y.: Sharpe, 1992), p. 45.

69. Lawrence and Vlachoutsicos, *Behind the Factory Walls*, p. 79.

70. For one manager's lament about how this ate up his time, see Kaniskin, "The Western Executive and the Soviet Executive."

71. Dmitrii Sladkov, "Otkrytie zakrytogo goroda: O problemakh Arzamasa-16 (Sarova)" (Opening a closed city: On the problems of Arzamas-16 [Sarov]), *Moskva*, no. 10 (1993): 134–38.

72. Clifford Gaddy, "Brief History of a Soviet Defense Enterprise and the Development of its Social Assets," appendix D of "Notes for a Theory of the Paternalistic Russian Enterprise," unpublished paper prepared for the annual convention of the American Association for the Advancement of Slavic Studies, Philadelphia, Pa., Nov. 1994, p. 35.

73. Keller, "In Urals City, the Communist Apparatus Ends."

74. Peter Almquist, *Red Forge: Soviet Military Industry since 1965* (New York: Columbia University Press, 1990), p. 100.

75. Ibid.

76. McFaul, "State Power."

77. Janos Kornai, *The Socialist System: The Political Economy of Communism* (Princeton: Princeton University Press, 1992), esp. pp. 122–23, 140–42, 150.

78. Joseph S. Berliner, *Factory and Manager in the USSR* (Cambridge: Harvard University Press, 1957), esp. pp. 64, 111–12, 120; and Lawrence and Vlachoutsicos, *Behind the Factory Walls*, p. 279.

79. Almquist, *Red Forge*, p. 46. For examples of careers that followed this path, see Valerii A. Radchenko (general director of the Zvezda factory in St. Petersburg), "Pochem banany v Afrike?" (How much are bananas in Africa?), *Nevskoe Vremia*, Oct. 5, 1994; Alevtina Gorelova, interview with Vladimir S. Sandovich, chief engineer of the Sokol fighter-jet design bureau in Nizhnii Novgorod, " 'Sokol' obiazan byt' sokolom" (Sokol must be a hawk), *Birzha* (Nizhnii Novgorod), no. 42 (Oct. 22, 1993); and Vladislav Tarasov, interview with Boris A. Konstantinov (general director of NPO Zenit), "My vyzhivem pri liubom pravitel'stve" (We will survive under any government), *Sorok Odin*, no. 10 (Mar. 1992). When interviewed by the author during a visit from the Stanford CISAC group in September 1994, the deputy general director for personnel at the Mashinostroenie plant in Reutov said that he was appointed as an engineer at the plant immediately after he graduated from the Kharkov Aviation Institute and that he had been at his current post since 1976.

80. Oleg Kharkhordin and Theodore P. Gerber, "Russian Directors' Business Ethic: A Study of Industrial Enterprises in St. Petersburg, 1993," *Europe-Asia Studies* 46, no. 7 (1994): 1075–1107.

81. In 1996 this committee was renamed the Ministry of Defense Industry.

82. Kathryn Hendley, "The Spillover Effects of Privatization on Russian Legal Culture," *Transnational Law and Contemporary Problems* 4, no. 1 (spring 1995). For another example of a defense industrial firm facing problems with monopoly suppliers, see "Enterprise Profiles: Energia," *Conversion: Report on Russia's Defense Industry* (Stanford University CISAC), no. 5 (April 1995): 8, 10.

83. For an example of power shifts over time in a defense-heavy city, see Vladimir Gel'man and Mary McAuley, "The Politics of City Government: Leningrad/St. Petersburg, 1990–1992," in *Local Power and Post-Soviet Politics*, ed. Theodore H. Friedgut and Jeffrey W. Hahn (Armonk, N.Y.: Sharpe, 1994).

84. The best report on this activity is Simon Johnson and Heidi Kroll, "Managerial Strategies for Spontaneous Privatization," *Soviet Economy* 7, no. 4 (1991): 281–316. Also see McFaul, "State Power," pp. 222–23. For Russian analyses of the situation, see V. Vladimirov, "Neplatezhni: yesli oni narastaiut, znachit, eto komu-nibud't nuzhno?" (Insolvent companies: If they are growing, does this mean someone needs it?), *Sankt-Peterburgskie Vedomosti*, Sept. 2, 1994; and, most strikingly, Arkadii Vol'skii, "Tendentsii" (Tendencies), *Moskovskie Novosti*, no. 14 (April 3–10, 1994).

85. Petr Khven', "Zakon surov . . . A surov li?" (The law is strict—or is it?), *Gorodskoi Kur'er*, Jan. 29, 1994.

86. For a hint of this, see "Oboronka ne pogibnet, yesli budet vypuskat' . . . inkubatory" (The defense complex will not perish, if they issue . . . incubators)," *Sibirskaia Gazeta*, no. 24 (June 1994). In addition, observers of a large Moscow trade union demonstration in late October 1994 overheard right-wing political party participants in the demonstration say that trade union representatives were participating only because their directors had paid them to do so (personal communication from Sharon Shible, Oct. 1994).

87. Gregory D. Andrusz, *Housing and Urban Development in the USSR* (London: Macmillan, 1984), pp. 71–72.

88. Ibid., p. 66.

89. For a discussion of the laws and a set of examples, see Tova Perlmutter, "Reorganization of Social Services," in *Defense Industry Restructuring in Russia: Case Studies and Analysis*, ed. David Bernstein (Stanford, Calif.: Stanford University Center for International Security and Arms Control, 1994). See also Yelena Tregubova, "Viktor Chernomyrdin obeshchaet podderzhat' promyshlennikov" (Viktor Chernomyrdin promises to support industrialists), *Segodnia*, Nov. 10, 1994, who cites the example of the Kirovo-Chepetskii military chemical factory gladly transferring its social assets to the local government.

90. T. Belkina, "Housing Statistics and the Condition of the Housing Sector," *Voprosy Ekonomiki*, no. 7 (1993): 60–69, as trans. and reprinted in *Problems of Economic Transition* 37, no. 1 (May 1994): 56–71.

91. Perlmutter, "Reorganization of Social Services," p. 189.

92. Yevgenii Maifet (chairman of the trade union committee of NIIME and Mikron), interviewed by Tatiana Kutyreva, in "Stanet li profkom zashchitnikom?" (Will the trade union become the defender?), *Sorok Odin*, no. 4 (Feb. 1992).

93. Blair A. Ruble, "From Khrushcheby to Korobki," in *Russian Housing and the Modern Age: Design and Social History*, ed. William Craft Brumfield and Blair A. Ruble (New York: Cambridge University Press, 1993), pp. 234, 263.

94. Reported by Aleksandr Vysokovskii, "Will Domesticity Return?" trans. Carl Sandstrom, in *Russian Housing and the Modern Age*, p. 279.

95. Interview by the author, Sept. 1994, with a Nizhnii Novgorod official who did not wish to be named.

96. Affordable, reliable moving companies were not listed in the yellow pages to call for estimates. Even if one managed to obtain access to a truck for long-distance hauling, navigating the heavy load over poor roads, often gravel or stone at best and thus subject to flooding and mud-slicked during spring thaws, remained a formidable challenge.

97. Kevin O'Prey notes that the city and region of Perm' have been able to absorb those leaving the defense complex into other work (*Farewell to Arms*, p. 56). Perm' has a major oil refinery (see Isabel Gorst, "Russian Companies Reorganize," *Petroleum Economist* 62 (Sept. 1995): S66), as well as enough diamonds to warrant its governor visiting the United States to pursue a sorting and cutting joint venture (see "Rossiisko-amerikanskoe SP dlia ogranki permskikh almazov" [Russian American JV for evaluating Perm' diamonds], *Segodnia*, Nov. 10, 1994).

98. For example, see "Novosibirsk khochet poluchit' status 'zony natsional'nogo bedstviia' " (Novosibirsk wants to receive the status of a "zone of national poverty"), *Kommersant-Daily*, Apr. 1, 1995.

99. "World Bank OKs $400 mln Loan for Russian Housing," Reuters, Mar. 7, 1995; and Michael Mihalka, "World Bank Approves $400 Million Loan to Russia," *OMRI Daily Digest*, no. 48 (Mar. 8, 1995).

100. According to page 5 of "Impuls 1994," an advertising brochure put out by the Impuls' enterprise in Moscow, "company-owned medical service and voluntary medical insurance for all employees" are major employee attractions. The Mashinostroenie plant in Reutov still owns a polyclinic that can serve 1,200 people; it provides free medical treatment and doctor visits for employees, including at hospitals in Moscow with which it has agreements, and pays for half the cost of employee medicines (interview by the author with the deputy general director for social services of the Mashinostroenie plant). Perlmutter, "Reorganization of Social Services," confirms these two examples and adds that of TsAGI.

101. Perlmutter, "Reorganization of Social Services."

102. See Murray Feshbach, "A Disease Crisis Strikes Russia," *Eurasian Reports* 4, no. 1 (winter 1994/95): 51–54; and Rita von Luelsdorff, interviewed by Gerard J. Janco, in "Lending a 'Helping Hand,' " *Eurasian Reports* 4, no. 1 (winter 1994/95): 54–58.

103. Advertisement, *Priglashaem: ezhenedel'naia reklamno-informatsionnaia gazeta*, no. 38 (Oct. 1994).

104. "Uchitelam, ekonomistam . . . akteram" (For teachers, economists . . . actors), *Nevskoe Vremia*, Jan. 5, 1995.

105. V. Luk'ianov, "Kollektivnye dogovora i soglasheniia: zashchita ot bezrabotitsy" (The collective contract and agreement: Defense from unemployment), *EKO*, no. 1 (Jan. 1995): 206.
106. "Russia Berated on Women's Rights," Associated Press, Mar. 8, 1995.
107. Efron, "Russians Doff Lab Coats for Suits."
108. Galina N. Vladimirova (chief legal counsel for the St. Petersburg Mayor's Committee on Labor and Employment), "Bezrabotitsa: Pravovye aspekty" (Unemployment: Legal aspects), *Nevskoe Vremia*, June 1, 1993.
109. Author's interview with the deputy general director for personnel.
110. Mikhail Zelenkov, "Da zdravstvuet 'uravnilovka'? . . ." (Long live "leveling"? . . .), *Nevskoe Vremia*, Sept. 29, 1993.
111. Kornai, *The Socialist System*, esp. p. 223.
112. Vladimir E. Gimpel'son, "From Labour Shortage to Unemployment: Soviet Workers' Attitudes About Possible Changes in Labour Relations," *Labour* 5, no. 3 (1991): 71.
113. For examples, see Vsevolod Mikhelev's interview with Dmitrii Sobolev, chief of the Conversion Department for the Mayor's Committee on Economics and Finance in St. Petersburg, " 'Oboronka' zhdet kreditov, kotorykh na vsekh ne khvatit" (The defense complex awaits credits, which will not be sufficient for all), *Nevskoe Vremia*, Apr. 19, 1994; and Elena Denezhkina, *Is There a Future for Russia's Defence Industry? Conversion in the Context of Current Economic Reforms*, Lectures and Contribution to East European Studies at FOA, no. 7 (Stockholm: Swedish National Defense Research Establishment, 1994), p. 3.
114. "Provintsial'naia khronika" (Provincial chronicle), *Segodnia*, Nov. 9, 1994.
115. See Yevgenii Kuznetsov, "Enterprise Adjustment and Interest Groups Within the Military Industrial Complex," in *The Post-Soviet Military-Industrial Complex: Proceedings of a Symposium* (Stockholm: Swedish National Defense Research Establishment, 1994), pp. 84–85; Vladimir Gimpel'son, "Politika rossiiskogo menedzhmenta v sfere zaniatosti" (The policy of Russian management in the sphere of employment), *Mirovaia Ekonomika i Mezhdunarodnye Otnosheniia*, no. 6 (1994): 5–20; McFaul, "State Power," p. 233.
116. See Kimberly Marten Zisk, "Arzamas-16: Economics and Security in a Closed Nuclear City," *Post-Soviet Affairs* 11, no.1 (Jan.–Mar. 1995): 72–73, for one example where such concern had important consequences for privatization of pieces of a nuclear weapons enterprise. For other examples, see Mikhail Ul'iashchenko writing on the Malakhit shipbuilding design bureau in St. Petersburg in "Chtoby sokhranit' umy" (To retain minds), *Inzhenernaia Gazeta*, no. 8 (Jan. 1992); Kutyreva, "Stanet li profkom zashchitnikom?"; and Gorelova, " 'Sokol' obiazan byt' sokolom." A similar concern was raised by Anatolii A. Kutumov, head of the labor dept. of the Central Aerohydrodynamics Institute (TsAGI) in Zhukovskii, during interviews by the Stanford CISAC group (including the author) in Sept. 1994. In that regard, also see the speech made by Deputy

Prime Minister Oleg Soskovets at TsAGI's seventy-fifth anniversary jubilee in 1993: "My gordimsia, chto u nas est' takoi institut" (We are proud to have such an institute), *Inzhenernaia Gazeta*, no. 135 (Dec. 1993). Confirmation that this is a generalizable phenomenon across enterprises is found in Gimpel'son, "Politika rossiiskogo menedzhmenta."

117. Vladislav Borodulin, "Trudnee vsego zastavit' ikh rabotat' ne na Rodinu" (The hardest thing of all is to compel them to work not for the motherland), *Kommersant-Daily*, Mar. 2, 1995.

118. David Bernstein and Jeffrey Lehrer, "The Central Aerohydrodynamic Research Institute (TsAGI)," in *Defense Industry Restructuring in Russia*, pp. 11, 15–16.

119. Tova Perlmutter, Michael McFaul, and Jeffrey Lehrer, "The Mashinostroenie Enterprise," in *Defense Industry Restructuring in Russia*, p. 67.

120. See O. Steshenko, reporting on the Elektron Scientific Production Association in St. Petersburg, in "Vremia zimnikh otpuskov" (The time of winter vacations), *Sankt-Peterburgskie Vedomosti*, Sept. 14, 1994; also see Vitalii Zemskov, writing on the Almaz shipbuilding factory in the same city, in "Spasatel'nyi krug dlia 'Almaza'" (A lifesaver for Almaz), *Nevskoe Vremia*, Dec. 6, 1994.

121. This report about A. Vetchinkin, who remained director of the ELION enterprise until Sept. 1994, appears in A. Lavrent'ev, "Otkrovennyi razgovor" (Frank conversation), *Sorok Odin*, no. 38 (May 20, 1994).

122. Valerii Baberdin, "It's Nearly July, but There's Still No Clarity," *Krasnaia Zvezda*, June 23, 1995, as reported in *FBIS-SOV*, June 28, 1995, p. 29. This is confirmed by Tova Perlmutter, Michael McFaul, and Elaine Naugle, "Impuls," in *Defense Industry Restructuring in Russia*, p. 47.

123. For an example, see Pearlstein, "Trying to Give Peace a Chance."

124. An excellent description of this situation is provided in Dorothy S. Zinberg, "Better Off Back Home," *London Times Higher Educational Supplement*, Mar. 4, 1994, and "Russia's Hard Frontier," *London Times Higher Educational Supplement*, Nov. 5, 1993.

125. Interview conducted by the Stanford CISAC group, including the author, Sept. 1994. The director of TsAGI, G. I. Zaiganov, talked about the importance of training new Russian scientific personnel in his remarks before the League for Assistance to Defense Enterprises, as reported in the league's *Informatsionnyi Sbornik*, no. 2 (Apr. 22, 1993): 34. A senior official at the Russian government's Interdepartmental Analytic Center confirmed that TsAGI in particular considers this a pressing concern (author's interview in Moscow, Oct. 1994).

126. Interview conducted by members of the Stanford CISAC team (including the author), Moscow region, Sept. 1994.

127. Bernstein and Lehrer, "The Central Aerohydrodynamic Research Institute," p. 16.

128. G. I. Zagainov, "Griadut ser'eznye izmeneniia" (Serious changes are coming), radio address of Feb. 21, 1994, as reported in *Novosti TsAGI*, no. 33 (1994).

129. For example, at the Mashinostroenie enterprise in Reutov, "each section of the enterprise has drawn up a list of its top people" to receive special benefits, according to Perlmutter, McFaul, and Lehrer, "The Mashinostroenie Enterprise," p. 66; the Impuls' enterprise in Moscow encouraged "growth in real wages for the most active 'core' employees of each division," according to Perlmutter, McFaul, and Naugle, "Impuls," p. 52.
130. Perlmutter, McFaul, and Naugle, "Impuls," p. 52.
131. Aleksandr V. Grigor'ev, interview conducted by the Stanford CISAC group, including the author, Sept. 1994.
132. The rule changing this requirement was Presidential Decree no. 1195 of July 11, 1994, "On Curtailment of the Mobilization Capacity and the Mobilization Reserve," reprinted in *Sobranie Zakonodatel'stva Rossiiskoe Federatsii* 11 (1994): 1655–56.
133. Valerii Lisitsyn (deputy general director for the Krasnoe Sormovo shipbuilding factory in Nizhnii Novgorod), "O politike zastavliaet dumat' ekonomika" (Economics is compelled to think about politics), *Birzha*, no. 49 (Dec. 10, 1993).
134. Radchenko, "Pochem banany v Afrike?"
135. Adi Ignatius, "Russians Resent Array of U.S. Partners Chosen to Convert Defense Industry," *Wall Street Journal*, Sept. 19, 1994.
136. For examples, see Aleksandr Batkov, a department head at the Ministry of Aviation Industry, interviewed by Yurii Kozmin, TASS (in English), July 4, 1990, as reported in *FBIS-SOV*, July 5, 1990, p. 65; V. Shishkovskii and A. Rudakov, *Vremia* television broadcast, Sept. 10, 1990, as reported in *FBIS-SOV*, Sept. 14, 1990, p. 51; Viktor M. Chepkin, general designer of the A. M. Liulka aircraft engine design bureau, interviewed by A. Manushkin, in "Turbines, Onions, Sheepskins . . ." *Krasnaia Zvezda*, Feb. 12, 1991, as reported in *Soviet Press: Selected Translations* (U.S. Air Force Technology Division, FTD-266OP-295–91) 1 (summer 1991): 3–4; Mikhail P. Simonov, director and chief engineer, Sukhoi Design Bureau, interviewed by Laurie Hays, in "Soviet Fighter Maker Takes a Sharp Turn," *Wall Street Journal*, June 12, 1992; and William S. Ritter Jr., "Soviet Defense Conversion: The Votkinsk Machine-Building Plant," *Problems of Communism*, Sept.–Oct. 1991, pp. 45–61.
137. "Goskomoboronprom rassmatrivaet vozmozhnost' perevod 60% predpriiatii VPK v razriad grazhdanskikh" (The state committee for defense industry reviews the possibility of transferring 60% of military-industrial complex enterprises to the rank of civilian), *Segodnia*, Dec. 14, 1994.
138. Tatiana Belova, head of the trade union committee at the ELMA Scientific-Production Association in Zelenograd, which specializes in microcircuitry pastes and photographic template equipment, interviewed in "Na 'ELME'—ideal'nyi koldogovor" (At ELMA—An ideal labor contract), *Sorok Odin*, no. 52 (July 8, 1994); and a report on the Angstrem microchip and crystal factory, by

Aleksei Lavrent'ev, "Vse budet Chip-top" (All will be chip-top), *Sorok Odin*, no. 5 (Feb. 1–7, 1993).

139. A good example of this is the success found by the Izhorskie Zavody enterprise in St. Petersburg. It appeared to be surviving because of a single order for a reactor from a Perm' oil refinery; the Izhorskie director said in December 1994 that if it hadn't been for this order, the company would have been forced to declare bankruptcy. He hoped that the successful fulfillment of the order would be good advertising for the enterprise in the future, but the order itself was scheduled to end on September 15, 1995. See M. Matrenin, "Izhortsy vyigrali konkurs na krupnyi zakaz" (The Izhorskie employees won a competition for a huge order), *Sankt-Peterburgskie Vedomosti*, Dec. 12, 1994.

140. For an example of such reasoning, see Perlmutter, McFaul, and Lehrer, "Mashinostroenie Enterprise," p. 68.

141. Robert S. Pindyck and Daniel L. Rubinfeld, *Microeconomics*, 2d ed. (New York: Macmillan, 1992), p. 199.

142. Perlmutter, "Reorganization of Social Services," pp. 189–90.

143. "O naloge na soderzhanie zhilishchnogo fonda i ob'ektov sotsial'no-kul'turnoi sfery" (About taxes on the upkeep of the housing fund and objects of the social-cultural sphere), *Altaiskaia Pravda*, July 12, 1994; "Nalogovaia sistema v Sankt-Peterburge izmenitsia" (The tax system in St. Petersburg will change), *Segodnia*, Dec. 29, 1994.

144. For example, the Raduga laser design bureau in the Vladimirskaia oblast reportedly saved 3 billion rubles per year in taxes by giving its farmland and social facilities to county (*raion*) authorities. See "Administratsiia Vladimirskoi oblasti predostavliaet nalogovye l'goty KB 'Raduga' " (The Vladimirskaia oblast administration offers tax benefits to the Raduga Design Bureau), *Segodnia*, Nov. 1, 1994.

145. The case is described in Zisk, "Arzamas-16," pp. 70–71.

146. See Radchenko, "Pochem banany v Afrike?"; and N. Figurovskii, interview with Irina Mikhailova Rukina, head of the Moscow Duma Committee on Economic Reform and Property and coordinator on industrial questions, in "Otechestvennaia promyshlennost' ne mozhet ne vozrodit'sia" (Domestic industry must be reborn), *Ekonomika i Zhizn'—Vash Partner (Moskovskii Vypusk)*, no. 12 (June 1994). Rukina makes the argument in regard to the Moscow Aviation Production Association (MAPO).

147. Interview conducted by the author.

148. N. Sinitsyna, "Teplo nelaskovogo leta" (The warmth of an unfriendly summer), *Sovremennik* (Zhukovskii), Aug. 3, 1994.

149. Belova, "Na 'ELME.' "

150. Stanley, "In Russia, a Breakdown."

151. Andrusz, *Housing and Urban Development*, p. 71.

152. Radchenko, "Pochem banany v Afrike?"

153. Perlmutter, "Reorganization of Social Services," p. 196.

154. Zisk, "Arzamas-16," p. 71.

155. Anishchenkov, A Soviet Factory, p. 9.

156. Interview conducted by the author.

157. A 1992 psychological survey of Russian managers in the defense-heavy region of Cheliabinsk found that Russian managers placed a higher intrinsic value on the goal of having power over other people's lives than did a sample of U.S. managers in similar positions (David N. Holt, David A. Ralston, and Robert H. Terpstra, "Constraints on Capitalism in Russia: The Management Psyche, Social Infrastructure, and Ideology," California Management Review 36, no. 3 [Mar. 22, 1994]: 124).

158. Berliner, Factory and Manager in the USSR, p. 68.

159. Kutyreva, "Stanet li profkom zashchitnikom?"

160. Jeffry A. Frieden, Debt, Development, and Democracy: Modern Political Economy and Latin America, 1955–1985 (Princeton: Princeton University Press, 1991); and Eduardo Silva, "Capitalist Coalitions, the State, and Neoliberal Economic Restructuring: Chile, 1973–88," World Politics 45 (July 1993): 526–59.

161. Bernstein and Lehrer, "The Central Aerohydrodynamic Research Institute."

162. For an expansion of this argument, see Kimberly Marten Zisk, "The Foreign Policy Preferences of Russian Defense Industrialists: Integration or Isolation?" in The Sources of Russian Foreign Policy After the Cold War, ed. Celeste Wallander (Boulder, Colo.: Westview, 1996).

163. See Helen Milner, Resisting Protectionism: Global Industries and the Politics of International Trade (Princeton: Princeton University Press, 1988).

164. For examples, see Pavel Fel'gengauer, "Sudnyi den' VPK" (Judgment day for the military-industrial complex), Segodnia, Mar. 15, 1994; and Mikhail Malei, "VPK mozhet stat' detonatorom sotsial'nykh bur' " (The military-industrial complex may become the detonator of a social storm), Sankt-Peterburgskie Vedomosti, Aug. 30, 1994.

165. Mikhail Leont'ev, "Yurii Skokov pokazhet tovar litsom" (Yurii Skokov will show to good effect), Segodnia, July 30, 1993.

166. A. N. Shulunov (president of the league), "Otchet o rabote prezidiuma Ligi za period mart 1992 g.–mart 1993 g. i osnovnye napravleniia dal'neishei deiatel'nosti ligi" (Report on the work of the league's presidium from Mar. 1992–Mar. 1993 and the basic direction of further activities of the league), Informatsionnyi Sbornik (of the league), no. 2 (1993): 5.

167. For examples, see "Ekstrennoe zasedanie rabotnikov VPK" (Extraordinary conference of military-industrial complex workers), Segodnia, Mar. 12, 1994; and "MO RF rassmotrelo voprosy struktornoi perestroiki oboronno-promysh-lennogo potentsiala" (The Russian Defense Ministry considers the question of restructuring military-industrial potential), Segodnia, Nov. 3, 1994.

168. Shulunov, "Otchet o rabote," pp. 16–17.

169. Off-the-record comment.

170. Off-the-record comment.

171. Shulunov, "Otchet o rabote," pp. 15–16.

172. Aleksei Sokovnin, " 'Voennyi parad' ob'iavil voinu pravitel'stvennoi gazete" ("Military Parade" has proclaimed war against a government newspaper), *Kommersant-Daily*, Feb. 8, 1995.

173. For an argument that lobbying by individual directors rather than interest groups has been the norm across Russia, see Borodulin, "Trudnee vsego."

174. See Jack Snyder, *Myths of Empire: Domestic Politics and International Ambition* (Ithaca, N.Y.: Cornell University Press, 1991).

175. *Trud*, July 25, 1995, as reported in "Withholding of Pay Sparks More Strikes," (Jamestown Foundation) *Monitor* 1, no. 61 (July 27, 1995).

176. This was confirmed to the author by two knowledgeable sources, one associated with the Nizhnii Novgorod regional administration and the other a Muscovite with close connections to the Defense Ministry. The workers were said to have been drunk. For press reports of these events (which do not directly mention the threat of violence against the authorities but do say that authorities were frightened by the events), see V. Seryi, "Kogda vydadut zarplatu?!" (When will they give us our pay?!), *Nizhegorodskie Novosti*, July 28, 1994; "Grom grianul—kto perekrestilsia?" (The thunder clapped: Who crossed himself?), *Nizhegorodskie Novosti*, Aug. 3, 1994; and Ye. Starichenkova, "Verkhom i bez vozhzhei" (On horseback without reins), *Nizhegorodskie Novosti*, Aug. 5, 1994.

177. The summary here is from Yelena Ovchinnikova and Viktor Smirnov, "Ispytatel' ugnal tank ot otchaianiia" (A drunk stole a tank in despair), *Kommersant-Daily*, June 17, 1995. A similar report was made by Valentina Nikiforova, "I stal tank oruzhiem proletariata" (And the tank became a weapon of the proletariat)," *Pravda*, June 12, 1995.

178. Ovchinnikova and Smirnov, "Ispytatel' ugnal tank ot otchaianiia."

179. Penny Morvant, "OMON Breaks up Shipyard Workers' Protest," *OMRI Daily Digest*, no. 111 (June 7, 1996).

180. Aleksandr Tsvetkov, "Direktor zavoda nachal bor'bu s rossiiskim rukovodstvom" (A factory director has begun a struggle with the Russian leadership), *Kommersant-Daily*, Feb. 1, 1995.

181. Yevgenii Ostapov, "Valeriia Anikina uvolili pod grokhot vzryvov" (Valerii Anikin is fired under the crash of explosions), *Kommersant-Daily*, Apr. 18, 1995.

3. Conglomerates, Lobbies, and Soviet Connections

1. See Ol'ga Romanova, "Finansovo-promyshlennye gruppy: Net zakona, net problemy" (Financial-industrial groups: No laws, no problem), *Segodnia*, June 6, 1995.

2. Anna Ostapchuk, "Deputaty chetyrekh respublik sozdali 'ekonomicheskii souiz' " (Deputies of four republics have created an "economic union"), *Nezavisimaia Gazeta*, Oct. 7, 1994.

3. In these official groups, the founders cannot own shares in each other's separate companies; banks are limited to ownership of 10 percent of the FIG stock; and monopoly enterprises, or those with more than 25,000 employees, cannot belong. See "Chto takoe finansovo-promyshlennye gruppy?" (What are financial-industrial groups?), *Ekonomicheskie Novosti*, no. 15 (Aug. 1994): 6; and "Proekt Programmy: Finansovo-promyshlennye Gruppy" (Draft program: Financial-industrial groups), *Rossiiskaia Gazeta*, Oct. 29, 1994.

4. Aleksandr Bekker, interview with Andrei Kokoshin, "Andrei Kokoshin: Yesli promyshlennost' umret segodnia, banki skonchaiutsia zavtra" (Andrei Kokoshin: If industry dies today, banks will die tomorrow), *Segodnia*, Sept. 14, 1993.

5. Oleg Soskovets, "Rozhdaetsia promyshlennaia politika Rossia" (An industrial policy for Russia is born), *Inzhenernaia Gazeta*, no. 131 (Nov. 1993).

6. A September 1994 estimate claimed that there were eleven FIGs planned in Russian defense industry (Mikhail Kuprianov, "VPK sozdaet mezhgosudarstvennye korporatsii" [The military-industrial complex is creating interstate corporations], *Segodnia*, Sept. 15, 1994), but an August 1994 estimate claimed that forty had already been created in the defense industry (Yulii Lebedev, "Finansovo-promyshlennye gruppy kak novyi instrument integratsii" [Financial-industrial groups as a new instrument of integration], *Nezavisimaia Gazeta*, Aug. 27, 1994). This is undoubtedly due to the lack of precision used in defining the term.

7. Jane E. Prokop provides the example of the PAKT FIG in Primorskii Krai. See her "Industrial Conglomerates, Risk Spreading and the Transition in Russia," *Communist Economies and Economic Transformation* 7, no. 1 (Mar. 1995): 35–50.

8. A. B. Voiakina, "Sozdanie novykh krupnykh organizatsionnykh form osnovnykh khoziastvennykh zven'ev oboronnogo kompleksa" (Creation of new large organizational forms from the basic economic links of the defense complex), *Voprosy Ekonomiki i Konversii*, 1992, no. 4: 110; and Kuprianov, "VPK sozdaet mezhgosudarstvennye korporatsii."

9. G. Bruce Knecht, "From Soviet Minister to Corporate Chief," *New York Times Sunday Magazine*, Jan. 26, 1992.

10. Kevin O'Prey, "Coping with Crisis: Enterprise Adaptation in the Russian Defense Sector," *Soviet Defense Notes* (MIT) 5, no. 2 (June 1993): 5–6. One example in this category is the Russian Aviation Corporation, which unites the Aeroflot airline company with the manufacturers of its Tu-204 planes and their suppliers of engines and parts; see Yevgenii Ostapov and Leonid Zavarskii, "Aviazalozhniki ob'edinilis' v proforganizatsiiu" (Avia-hostages have united into a union), *Kommersant-Daily*, June 8, 1995. Another example is the Volzhsko-Kamskaia FIG, which unites the military truck maker KamAZ, the AvtoVAZ auto production factory, and many of their suppliers. See Lev Ambinder, "Finansovo-promyshlennaia gruppa obrastaet postavshchikami" (Financial-industrial group surrounds itself with suppliers), *Kommersant-Daily*, Mar. 14, 1995. This FIG is

headed by Vitalii Poliakov, former Soviet minister of the automobile industry; like the Aviaprom case mentioned above, the creation of this FIG suggests that those who held state authority in the past are now being granted financial authority by the enterprises they supervised. See Konstantin Lange and Yevgenii Ostapov, "AvtoVAZ i KamAZ okonchatel'no oformili svoi souiz" (AvtoVAZ and KamAZ finally formalize their union), Kommersant-Daily, Jan. 12, 1995.

11. Examples include the Russian Association of Conversion Enterprises and Manufacturers of Gas Weapons ("Entrepreneurs Dispute Weapons for Civilian Use," Moscow News, Sept. 10, 1993) and the Light Aviation of Russia Interbranch Association (Leonid Kostrov and Valentina Kulakova, "Maloi aviatsii pora na bol'shuiu dorogu" [It is time for small aviation to set out on the big road], Segodnia, Dec. 17, 1994).

12. As the Soviet state began to collapse and Russian authorities assumed control over the economy, the seven defense industrial ministries in existence at that time went into limbo; for a few months, it was unclear exactly who was in charge of supervising defense industrial orders. See Peter Almquist, "Arms Producers Struggle to Survive as Defense Orders Shrink," RFE/RL Research Report 2, no. 25 (June 18, 1993): 34. When the Russian state took over Soviet administrative functions, those seven former ministries were first designated departments of the Russian Ministry of Industry. For an example of this, see "Naval Equipment Manufacturers Reorganize," Ekonomika i Zhizn, Dec. 14, 1991, as reported by Reuter Textline. Later, that ministry itself was abolished, and all the remaining former defense industrial ministries became departments of the newly formed Goskomoboronprom. See Adam N. Stulberg, "The High Politics of Arming Russia," RFE/RL Research Report 2, no. 49 (Dec. 10, 1993): 3. Viktor Glukhikh served initially as the first deputy minister of industry in charge of defense industry and later as the founding chairman of Goskomoboronprom. See A. Dolgikh, "Russian Federation Committee for Defense Sectors of Industry Created," Krasnaia Zvezda, Nov. 26, 1992, as reported in BBC Summary of World Broadcasts, SU/1551/C3/1, Nov. 30, 1992.

13. Almquist, "Arms Producers Struggle," p. 37; Laure Després, "Financing the Conversion of the Military-Industrial Complex in Russia: Problems of Data," Communist Economies and Economic Transformation 7, no. 3 (1995): 333.

14. Peter Almquist, Red Forge: Soviet Military Industry since 1965 (New York: Columbia University Press, 1990), pp. 23–24.

15. In 1996 a new version of this ministry was re-created.

16. For an example, see Voiakina, "Sozdanie novykh krupnykh organizatsionnykh form," p. 110.

17. Knecht, "From Soviet Minister to Corporate Chief."

18. The Committee on the Defense Branches drew up the original "not-for-privatization" list that Goskomoboronprom later enforced; see Anna Shcherbakova, "Sud'ba sudostroitel'nogo zavoda poka ne reshena" (The fate of the shipbuild-

ing factory is still not decided), *Kommersant-Daily*, Jan. 28, 1993. Furthermore, many articles published by the Scientific Research Institute of Economics and Conversion, which was associated first with the VPK and later with Goskomoboronprom, indicate a continuing desire by former central planners to map out the "correct" future paths for Russian defense enterprise activity, even as privatization was well under way. For example, an article sent to press in November 1993 used mathematical models to analyze production by enterprises in market conditions with disparities between supply and demand, in order to "predict the dynamic of enterprise development [and] its economic indicators, [and] to choose the most rational path for development in the presence of alternative variants for both civilian and defense enterprises," particularly as it related to government agencies providing "measures for economic stimulation . . . of the given enterprise" (B. M. Bogdanov and A. P. Kotov, "Modelirovanie razvitiia predpriiatiia v usloviizkh neravnoveshogo rynka" [Modeling of enterprise development in conditions of market disequilibrium], *Voprosy Ekonomiki i Konversii*, 1993, no. 4: 48). The format and content of the article parallel the structure of those appearing in state planning journals during Soviet times.

19. For examples, see Aleksandr Bekker, "The Government Is Putting Everything on the Altar of the Fatherland," *Segodnia*, May 12, 1993, as reported in *Current Digest of the Post-Soviet Press* 45, no. 19 (June 9, 1993): 7; and "Usloviia formirovaniia promyshlennoi politiki (obzor)" (Conditions for the formation of industrial policy [Review]), *Ekonomist*, no. 2 (Feb. 1994): 11.

20. George Lysenko, "Market Manages the Ball," *Military Parade* (Moscow), Nov./Dec. 1994, 62; and Almquist, *Red Forge*, p. 153.

21. Author's interview, Aug. 1994, with a Moscow sociologist who himself interviewed many defense complex representatives between 1990 and 1994.

22. See Sergei Oslikovsky, "On the Way to Increasing Effectiveness of Military-Technical Cooperation," *Military Parade*, Nov./Dec. 1994, 13; and Victor Samoilov, "Russian Arms Trading," *Military Parade*, May/June 1994: 14–17.

23. "USSR: Aviation Ministry Abolished," *Izvestiia*, Oct. 19, 1991, as reported in Reuter Textline.

24. Kuprianov, "VPK sozdaet mezhgosudarstvennye korporatsii."

25. "Bankirskii dom—otkryt" (The banking house is open), *Nizhegorodskie Novosti*, Aug. 6, 1992.

26. Aleksandr Blagov, "Milliony na konversiiu" (Millions for conversion), *Gorod i Gorozhane* (Nizhnii Novgorod), no. 33 (Aug. 22–28, 1992).

27. Ibid.

28. Aleksandr Fedotov (procurator for the Nizhnii Novgorod oblast), "Prokuror oblasti kommentiruet . . ." (The oblast procurator comments . . .), *Birzha* (Nizhnii Novgorod), no. 7 (Feb. 1993).

29. Vladimir Ulyanov, "Tax Credits to Munitions Factories," *Delovoi Mir/Business World Weekly*, Aug. 29, 1994.

30. U.S. Department of Commerce, *Russian Defense Business Directory*, 3d installment (Washington, D.C.: National Technical Information Services, 1993), p. 8-1.

31. Rustam Arifdzhanov and Anatolii Yershov, "Nizhnii Reform: A Less 'Liberal' Alternative?" *Izvestiia*, Mar. 29, 1994, as reported in *Current Digest of the Post-Soviet Press* 46, no. 13 (Apr. 27, 1994): 2.

32. Vladimir Bessarabov, speech delivered at the Vooruzhenie, Voennaia Tekhnika, Konversiia (Armaments, military technology, conversion) Fair, Nizhnii Novgorod Fairgrounds, Sept. 13, 1994, as observed and noted by the author.

33. Irina Vladykina, "Profkom '333' golodaet bessrochno" (Trade union committee 333 is quickly starving), *Segodnia*, Nov. 17, 1994; and idem, "Golodovka na 'Spetstekhnike' priostanovlena" (The hunger strike at the Spetstekhnia plant has been halted), *Segodnia*, Dec. 15, 1994.

34. Doug Clarke, "Far Eastern Military Shipyard Workers Get Some Back Pay," *OMRI Daily Digest*, no. 143 (July 25, 1995).

35. V. Seryi, "Kogda vydadut zarplatu?!" (When will you give out our pay?!), *Nizhegorodskie Novosti*, July 28, 1994.

36. Tatarstan has paid defense workers back wages out of its own tax money earmarked for the federal government. I say more about this below. See Robert Orttung, "Tatarstan Stops Payments to Federal Budget," *OMRI Daily Digest*, no. 152 (Aug. 7, 1995).

37. "V Moskve provoditsia programma 'Konversiia-gorod' " (In Moscow the "City Conversion" program is implemented), *Segodnia*, Dec. 1, 1994.

38. S. Fastov, "Zhizn'—kak zebra—polosata" (Life is like a zebra—striped), *Sorok Odin* (Zelenograd), no. 47 (Nov. 23–30, 1992).

39. N. Figurovskii, interview with Irina M. Rukina, chairman of the Moscow City Duma Committee on Economic Reform and Property, "Otechestvennaia promyshlennost' ne mozhet ne vozrodit'sia" (Domestic industry must be revived), *Ekonomika i Zhizn'—Vash Partner* (Moscow Edition), no. 12 (June 1994).

40. The contribution of V. A. Teleshov (deputy director of the Moscow City Administration Department of Industry) in "Sila FPG—V ob'edinenii struktur, raznykh po knarakhteru deiatel'nosti" (The strength of the FIG—In a unified structure, different activities), *Ekonomika i Zhizn'—Vash Partner* (Moscow Edition), no. 18 (Sept. 1994).

41. Kathryn Brown, "Nizhnii Novgorod: A Regional Solution to National Problems?" *Radio Free Europe/Radio Liberty Research Report* 2, no. 5 (Jan. 19, 1993): 22; Boris Nemtsov, "Initsiativnykh podderzhivaem" (We Will Support Those with Initiative), *Predprinimatel'*, no. 3 (Sept. 1994).

42. Interview conducted by the author in the Nizhnii Novgorod Kremlin, Sept. 1994.

43. For example, Anatolii Andreev, chief of the Main Administration for Electronics Industry in Goskomoboronprom, has been a vocal and successful advocate for state debt relief and subsidies to electronics enterprises in Zelenograd. See

"Gosudarstvo zadolzhalo predpriiatiam elektronnoi promyshlennosti 150 mlrd rublei" (The state owes electronics industry enterprises 150 billion rubles), *Segodnia*, Nov. 11, 1994.

44. See George Breslauer, "Soviet Economic Reforms Since Stalin: Ideology, Politics, and Learning," *Soviet Economy* 6 (July–Sept. 1990): 252–80; and Peter Rutland, "The Dynamics of the Soviet Economic Mechanism: Insights from Reform Debates, 1977–1987," in *Political Implications of Economic Reform in Communist Systems: Communist Dialectic*, ed. Donna L. Bahry and Joel C. Moses (New York: New York University Press, 1990).

45. David Holloway, *The Soviet Union and the Arms Race* (New Haven: Yale University Press, 1983), p. 118; also idem, "Soviet Military R&D: Managing the 'Research-Production Cycle,' " in *Soviet Science and Technology: Domestic and Foreign Perspectives*, ed. John R. Thomas and Ursula M. Kruse-Vaucienne, National Science Foundation Report NSF-GWU-77-1 (Washington, D.C.: George Washington University, 1977), pp. 195–97.

46. This list is drawn from Julian Cooper, "The Defense Industry and Civil-Military Relations," in *Soldiers and the Soviet State: Civil-Military Relations from Brezhnev to Gorbachev*, ed. Timothy J. Colton and Thane Gustafson (Princeton: Princeton University Press, 1990), p. 164; idem, "The Civilian Production of the Soviet Defence Industry," in *Technical Progress and Soviet Economic Development*, ed. Ronald Amann and Julian Cooper (New York: Basil Blackwell, 1986), p. 32; and Holloway, *Soviet Union and Arms Race*, p. 120.

47. Julian Cooper, *The Soviet Defence Industry: Conversion and Economic Reform*, Chatham House Papers (New York: Council on Foreign Relations Press, 1991), p. 10.

48. Arthur J. Alexander, *Decision-Making in Soviet Weapons Procurement*, Adelphi Papers 147/8 (London: International Institute for Strategic Studies, 1978), p. 26.

49. Ibid., p. 23; Holloway, *Soviet Union and Arms Race*, pp. 140–41; Matthew Evangelista, *Innovation and the Arms Race: How the United States and the Soviet Union Develop New Military Technologies* (Ithaca, N.Y.: Cornell University Press, 1988), p. 42.

50. For examples of complaints about this separation, see Bekker, "Andrei Kokoshin"; Valentin Pashin (director of the Krylov Central Scientific Research Institute), "Ostanetsia li Rossiia velikoi morskoi derzhvoi?" (Will Russia remain a great naval power?), *Nezavisimaia Gazeta*, Oct. 13, 1994; Anatolii Ladin, "When the Locomotive Grinds to a Halt, the Cars Stop Too," *Krasnaia Zvezda*, Mar. 4, 1995, as reported in *Foreign Broadcast Information Service Daily Report—Central Eurasia* (FBIS-SOV), Mar. 7, 1995, p. 74; and Tamara Ivanova and Viacheslav Anichkov, "Russian, Ukrainian Defense Officials Meet at Arms Fair," ITAR-TASS in English, Mar. 20, 1995, as reported in *FBIS-SOV*, Mar. 21, 1995, p. 13.

51. Janos Kornai dubs this process "vertical bargaining." See *The Socialist System: The Political Economy of Communism* (Princeton: Princeton University Press, 1992), pp. 122–24.

52. This is also noted in Almquist, *Red Forge*, p. 33.

53. Ed A. Hewett, *Reforming the Soviet Economy: Equality Versus Efficiency* (Washington, D.C.: Brookings, 1988), pp. 176–78.

54. Alexander notes that the Military-Industrial Commission of the Soviet Council of Ministers was the one place where interchange among ministries would have occurred; the issues considered at this level were probably limited to those not involving day-to-day operations of the enterprises and may not even have included questions regarding trade-offs in weapons purchase decisions; see *Decision-Making in Soviet Weapons Procurement*, p. 26.

55. In *Red Forge*, p. 101, Almquist notes that a common career path for enterprise managers was promotion to a position in the ministry that supervised their enterprises.

56. For a useful explanation of this system, see Hewett, *Reforming the Soviet Economy*, pp. 104–51.

57. P. Bol'shakov, "Khozraschet ob'edineniia" (Cost-accounting of the association), *Plannovoe Khoziastvo*, no. 5 (1969): 21–28.

58. Ruben Lamdany, *Russia: The Banking System During Transition* (country study) (Washington, D.C.: World Bank, 1993), p. 16.

59. Andrei Grigor'ev, "Promyshlennost' i banki: Integratsiia na kommercheski vygodnykh usloviiakh" (Industry and banks: Integration in commercially profitable conditions), *Segodnia*, Nov. 22, 1994.

60. See, for example, Joseph S. Berliner, *Factory and Manager in the USSR* (Cambridge: Harvard University Press, 1957), p. 260.

61. Almquist, *Red Forge*, p. 101.

62. For useful reviews of these policies, see Jan Ake Dellenbrant, "Reformists and Traditionalists: A Study of Soviet Discussions About Economic Reform, 1960–1965," *Publications of the Political Science Association in Uppsala*, no. 63 (Stockholm: Raben and Sjogren, 1972); and Sergei Freidzon, *Patterns of Soviet Economic Decision-Making: An Inside View of the 1965 Reform* (Falls Church, Va.: Delphic Associations, 1987).

63. Freidzon, *Patterns of Soviet Economic Decision-Making*, pp. 30–31.

64. For examples, see M. Alekseev (director of the Red October Machine-building Factory in Odessa), "Khozraschet, priamye sviazi, effektivnost' proizvodstvennykh fondov" (Cost-accounting, direct ties, and effectiveness of the production funds), *Plannovoe Khoziaistvo* no. 4 (1965): 55–58; I. Kurtynin (director of the Moscow Factory of Thermal Automatics), "Podgotovka predpriiatiia k rabote po-novomu" (Preparation of enterprises to work in the new style), *Plannovoe Khoziaistvo*, no. 5 (1966): 70–74; Bol'shakov, "Khozraschet ob'edineniia"; and P. F. Derunov (director of the Rybinskii Engine Construction Plant), with A. A.

Baklankin and V. A. Mazal'son, *Nauchnaia Organizatsiia Proizvodstva Truda i Upravleniia* (Scientific organization of labor productivity and management) (Moscow: Izdatel'stvo Ekonomika, 1968), pp. 220–27.

65. Stulberg, "High Politics of Arming Russia," pp. 1, 3. Also see Mikhail D. Malei, "VPK mozhet stat' detonatorom sotsial'nykh bur' " (The military-industrial complex may become the detonator of a social storm), *Sankt-Peterburgskie Vedomosti*, Aug. 30, 1994.

66. Ye. Zubatov, "Direktora neispravimy; polozhenie nado ispravliat!" (The directors are incorrigible; they must correct the situation!), *Sorok Odin*, no. 29 (Aug. 1992): 4.

67. Yu. A. Filimonov, "Kooperativy v mashinostroenii" (The cooperatives in the machine-building sector), *Mashinostroitel'*, no. 11 (Nov. 1990).

68. Sergei Markov, "Reform of Property Rights: The History, the Players, the Issues," *Conversion: Report on Russia's Defense Industry* (Stanford Center for International Security and Arms Control), no. 2 (Aug. 3, 1993): 3.

69. See "Firme otkazano v privatizatsii" (A firm is refused privatization), *Kommersant-Daily*, Nov. 4, 1992; Steven Erlanger, "Capitalists Short of Capital, Russian Managers Privatize at a Time of Scarcity," *New York Times*, Aug. 19, 1992; Shcherbakova, "Sud'ba sudostroitel'nogo zavoda"; and Yekaterina Zapodinskaia, "Soskovets ne razreshil Chubaisu privatizirovat' aviazavod" (Soskovets did not allow Chubais to privatize an aviation factory), *Kommersant-Daily*, Jan. 14, 1995.

70. For a statement indicating that Goskomoboronprom is the primary authority on this issue, see Irina Vladykina, "Ob'edinenie 'Avtomatika' dobilos' vyplaty zarplaty" (The Avtomatika Association obtained wage payments), *Segodnia*, Nov. 29, 1994.

71. Andrei Serov, " 'Rybinskie Motory' kak dvigatel' privatizatsii VPK" (Rybinskie Motors as an engine for privatization of the defense sector), *Kommersant-Daily*, Aug. 19, 1995.

72. Aleksandr Tsvetkov and Yevgenii Ostapov, "Polet v budushchee planiruetsia na ustarevshikh dvigateliakh" (Flight into the future is planned on obsolete engines), *Kommersant-Daily*, June 23, 1995; Aleksandr Volzhskii, "Rybinskie Motory chuvstvuiut sebia ne kak ryba v vode" (Rybinskie Motors feels like a fish out of water), *Kommersant-Daily*, July 26, 1995; and Serov, " 'Rybinskie Motory' kak dvigatel.'"

73. Aleksandr Tsvetkov and Yevgenii Ostapov, "Valerii Anikin ukhodit s ringa" (Valerii Anikin exits the ring), *Kommersant-Daily*, Apr. 11, 1995.

74. Volzhskii, "Rybinskie Motory chuvstvuiut sebia."

75. "Dosrochno prodaetsia gosudarstvennyi paket aktsii AO 'Rybinskie Motory' " (The state packet of Rybinskie Motors stock will be sold early), *Kommersant-Daily*, Aug. 8, 1995.

76. Serov, " 'Rybinskie Motory' kak dvigatel.'"

77. Ibid.

78. While by late 1994 it was unclear to what extent the Defense Ministry contin-
    ued to consult with Goskomoboronprom before placing armaments orders,
    Defense Ministry and Goskomoboronprom personnel did continue to work
    together through a variety of interdepartmental bureaucratic councils, includ-
    ing one that supervised arms exports. The Interdepartmental Commission on
    Military-Technical Cooperation with Foreign Countries, which was responsi-
    ble for approving all arms exports, included representatives from both the
    Defense Ministry and Goskomoboronprom. See Colonel General Vladimir
    Zhurbenko, first deputy chief of the General Staff, interviewed by Valentin
    Rudenko, in "Interesy gosudarstvo prevyshe vsego" (The interests of the state
    above all else), *Krasnaia Zvezda*, Aug. 27, 1994.

79. Viktor Ivanov, "Minoborony mogut' osvobodit' ot platy za vooruzhenie" (The
    Defense Ministry may be freed from paying for weapons), *Kommersant-Daily*,
    Feb. 15, 1995.

80. L. Ivaniutin, B. Sedunov, and V. Sokolov, "Na oblomkakh mikroelektronnoi
    imperii" (In the clouds of the microelectronics empire), *Sorok Odin*, no. 32
    (Nov. 1991): 1.

81. Aleksandr Voinov, director of the Russian section of the Aviaeksport joint-stock
    company, pointed out in 1993 that this "company" "has over thirty-five years'
    experience of supplying aviation equipment abroad and has assumed all orga-
    nizational work to form the Russian section and ensure the participation of
    Russia's aircraft builders in the [United Arab Emirates air] show" (interviewed
    with Valentin Rudenko, "Russian Aircraft Builders Leaving for Dubai not for
    Sensations but for Contracts," *Krasnaia Zvezda*, Oct. 19, 1993, as reported in
    FBIS-SOV, Oct. 20, 1993, pp. 15–16).

82. "Nizhny's Trade Fair Holds Russia's Largest Armaments Show," *Nizhny
    Novgorod Times*, Sept. 28, 1994.

83. S. Tselibeev, "Vozlagaiutsia bol'shie nadezhdy" (Many hopes are being raised),
    Kapital Nizhnii Novgorod, Sept. 5–12, 1994.

84. From an advertisement in *Tekhnika i Vooruzhenie*, no. 1–2 (Jan. 1994), inside
    front cover.

85. Vladimir Klimov, "Byli by sekrety, a prodavets naidetsia" (These had been
    secrets, but the salesman is hopeful), *Rossiiskaia Gazeta*, Oct. 29, 1994.

86. Anatolii Andreev, as cited in "Gosudarstvo zadolzhalo predpriiatiam elektron-
    noi promyshlennosti 150 mlrd rublei" (The state is indebted to electronics
    industry enterprises for 150 billion rubles), *Segodnia*, Nov. 11, 1994.

87. Leonid Kostrov and Valentina Kulakova, "Maloi aviatsii pora na bol'hsuiu
    dorogu" (It is time for small aviation to set out on the big road), *Segodnia*, Dec.
    17, 1994.

88. Leonid Zavarskii, "Stroiteli aviadvigatelei reshili zakliuchit' 'semeinyi soiuz' "
    (Aviation engine builders have decided to create a "family union"), *Kommersant-
    Daily*, Sept. 28, 1994.

89. "Entrepreneurs Dispute Weapons for Civilian Use," *Moscow News*, Sept. 10, 1993.

90. Kostrov and Kulakova, "Maloi aviatsii."

91. "Russia Needs $550 Million to Rescue Airlines," Reuters, Apr. 27, 1995.

92. Andrei Viktorov, "Malaia aviatsiia poluchila sobstvennuiu programmu razvitiia" (Small aviation received its own development program), *Segodnia*, June 7, 1995.

93. Victor Anoshkin, "Russian Planemakers Seek New Markets in West," Reuters, July 16, 1995.

94. Ibid. For useful discussions of the nontransparent nature of Russian extra-budgetary financing in general, see Christine I. Wallich, "Intergovernmental Finances: Stabilization, Privatization, and Growth," in *Russia and the Challenge of Fiscal Federalism*, ed. Christine I. Wallich (Washington, D.C.: World Bank, 1994), pp. 85–87; and Natal'ia Olenich, "Vnebiudzhetnye fondy riskuiut popast' pod gosudarstvennyi kontrol' " (Extrabudgetary funds risk falling under state control), *Segodnia*, June 7, 1995.

95. A. V. Grigor'ev, as cited by Leonid Kosals and Rozalina Ryvkina, in "Gosudarstvennoi politiki v sfere VPK net" (There is no state policy in the sphere of the military-industrial complex), *Segodnia*, Oct. 18, 1994.

96. Interview conducted by the author with members of the CISAC group at Impuls', Sept. 1994.

97. Oleg Kharkhordin and Theodore P. Gerber, "Russian Directors' Business Ethic: A Study of Industrial Enterprises in St. Petersburg, 1993," *Europe-Asia Studies* 46, no. 7 (1994): 1077.

98. Elena Denezhkina, "Is There a Future for Russia's Defence Industry? Conversion in the Context of Current Economic Reforms," *Lectures and Contributions to East European Studies at the Swedish National Defense Research Establishment*, no. 7 (Aug. 30, 1994): pp. 30–31.

99. Kathryn Hendley, "The Spillover Effects of Privatization on Russian Legal Culture," *Transnational Law and Contemporary Problems* 4, no. 1 (spring 1995).

100. Kharkhordin and Gerber, "Russian Directors' Business Ethic," pp. 1078, 1080, 1081.

101. Lamdany, *Russia: The Banking System*, p. 13.

102. Aleksandr Kuznetsov, "Torgovyi kapital perekhodit v promyshlennost' " (Trading capital is moving into industry), *Finansovye Izvestiia*, no. 42 (Sept. 22–28, 1994).

103. L. V. Gorbatova (of the Institute of the Economic Problems of the Transition Era), "Banki i promyshlennost': Nekotorye aspekty vzaimodeistviia" (Banks and industry: Some aspects of their cooperation), *EKO*, no. 11 (1994): 77.

104. Maksim Zarezin, "Telega dlia lapy" (A cart for the hand), *Rossiiskaia Gazeta*, Oct. 29, 1994; Kuznetsov, "Torgovyi kapital."

105. Interview with Filippov, "Promstroibank Sankt-Peterburg nameren usiilit' svoe vliianie v evrope" (Promstroibank St. Petersburg intends to strengthen its influence in Europe), *Sankt-Peterburgskie Vedomosti*, June 7, 1994.

106. Valerii V. Filippov, "The Managers' Perspective: Star Wars to High-Tech Consumer Goods," in *After the Cold War: Russian-American Defense Conversion for Economic Renewal* (New York: New York University Press, 1993).

107. Konstantin Zbarovskii, "Zavod khochet podruzhit'sia s moskovskimi bankirami" (A factory wants to make friends with Moscow bankers), *Kommersant-Daily*, May 3, 1995.

108. Romanova, "Finansovo-promyshlennye gruppy."

109. Jerry F. Hough, *The Soviet Prefects: The Local Party Organs in Industrial Decision-Making* (Cambridge: Harvard University Press, 1969), esp. pp. 257–65; and Hewett, *Reforming the Soviet Economy*, pp. 165–68.

110. Hough, *Soviet Prefects*, pp. 235–242; Blair A. Ruble, *Leningrad: Shaping a Soviet City* (Berkeley: University of California Press, 1990), p. 10; and Markov, "Reform of Property Rights," p. 2.

111. Julian Cooper discovered through demographic analysis that in terms of employment levels, the top ten defense areas in the USSR were all located on Russian territory: the cities of Leningrad (now St. Petersburg) and Moscow; the oblasts of Gor'kii (now Nizhnii Novgorod), Moscow, Novosibirsk, Perm', Samara (now Kuibyshev), and Sverdlovsk; and the republics of Tatarstan and Udmurtiia. See Cooper, *Soviet Defence Industry*, p. 22.

112. These included, among others, the cities of Cheliabinsk, Izhevsk, Nizhnii Novgorod, Novosibirsk, Perm', Sverdlovsk (now Yekaterinburg), and Tula. See Cooper, *Soviet Defence Industry*, pp. 22–24.

113. These included towns such as Zelenograd, the electronics industry satellite city outside of Moscow.

114. See, for example, Roy A. Medvedev and Zhores A. Medvedev, *Khrushchev: The Years in Power*, trans. Andrew R. Durkin (New York: Columbia University Press, 1976), p. 104; Almquist, *Red Forge*, p. 190 n. 23; and Bruce Parrott, *Politics and Technology in the Soviet Union* (Cambridge, Mass.: MIT Press, 1983), pp. 174–75.

115. While the actual documents of the Defense Industry Department of the Central Committee remain classified and closed, the *opisi* (finding aids) of the department from 1954 through 1974 are open to foreign scholars, or at least were in fall 1992. Each item in the finding aids is a paragraph summarizing approximately 50 to 150 pages of documents.

116. Fond 5, opis' 39, Otdel Oboronnoi Promyshlennosti TsK KPSS, 1954–1966, p. iv.

117. Ibid., podriadkovyi 56, p. 18.

118. Ibid., podriadkovyi 61, p. 19; podriadkovyi 67, p. 21; podriadkovyi 71, p. 23; and podriadkovyi 72, p. 23.

119. Ibid., podriadkovyi 317, p. 102; and podriadkovyi 332, p. 108.

120. Nikolai Anishchenkov, *A Soviet Factory: Past, Present and Future*, Soviet Booklet no. 59 (London: Soviet Booklets, 1959), p. 12.

121. Yu. G. Belenko, et al., *Gor'kovskii Dizel'nyi: Ocherki Istorii Zavod 'Dvigatel' Revoliutsii* (The Gorkii diesel workers: Historical notes on the Dvigatel' Revoliutsii factory) (Moscow: Mysl', 1985), p. 117.

122. A. Polukhin, "Struktura i organizatsiia raboty Sovetov narodnogo khoziaistva" (Structure and organization of work of the *sovnarkhozy*), *Plannovoe Khoziaistvo*, no. 8 (1957): 34–42, esp. p. 39.

123. Elena Denezhkina argues that military and civilian enterprises throughout the Soviet era "would be neighbors in the same street and yet have no contact." See Denezhkina, "Is There a Future for Russia's Defence Industry?" p. 20.

124. B. Khomiakov, "Opyt raboty Sverdlovskogo sovnarkhoza" (Work experience of the Sverdlovsk *sovnarkhoz*), *Plannovoe Khoziaistvo*, no. 11 (1957): 65–73, esp. p. 69.

125. Markov, "Reform of Property Rights," p. 2; Paul R. Lawrence and Charalambo A. Vlachoutsicos, eds., *Behind the Factory Walls: Decision Making in Soviet and U.S. Enterprises* (Boston: Harvard Business School Press, 1990), p. 104.

126. Anishchenkov, *A Soviet Factory*, p. 9.

127. Kharkhordin and Gerber, "Russian Directors' Business Ethic," p. 1085.

128. Vladislav Tarasov, "Assotsiatsiia 'ELANG'—Novoe ob'edinenie starykh pred-priiatii" (The ELANG Association—A new association of old enterprises), *Sorok Odin*, no. 35/36 (1991).

129. Kathryn Elizabeth Stoner-Weiss, "Local Heroes: Political Exchange and Government Performance in Provincial Russia," doctoral dissertation, Dept. of Government, Harvard University, Nov. 1994, p. 251.

130. Yu. E. Solodovnikov, "Osnovye printsipy raboty Komissii Lensoveta pri Vzaimo-destvii s Konversiruemymi Predpriiatiiami Oboronnogo Kompleksa Leningrada" (Basic working principles of the Lensovet Commission on Cooperation with Converting Enterprises of the Defense Complex in Leningrad), in *Dostizheniia Nauchno-Tekhnicheskogo Progressa—Leningradskim Predpriiatiiam* (Achievements of scientific-technological progress by Leningrad enterprises), seminar of chief engineers of the Leningrad House of Scientific-Technical Propaganda (St. Petersburg: "Znanie" Society of the RSFSR, 1991), pp. 4–5.

131. Stoner-Weiss, "Local Heroes," p. 255.

132. Ibid., p. 256.

133. Vladimir Ionov, "Personalities: Boris Nemtsov," *Moscow News*, July 30, 1992; and May McGrory, "Dollars for Democracy," *Washington Post*, May 27, 1993.

134. This continued through 1995. See Vladislav Borodulin, "Pravitel'stvo prodemon-stirovalo sposobnost' k novatsiiam" (The government demonstrated its capacity for innovations), *Kommersant-Daily*, Jan. 13, 1995.

135. Ruble, *Leningrad*, p. 10.

136. Christine I. Wallich, *Fiscal Decentralization: Intergovernmental Relations in Russia*, Studies of Economies in Transition Paper 6 (Washington, D.C.: World Bank, 1992), p. 5; and Wallich, *Russia and the Challenge of Fiscal Federalism*, p. 76.

137. It has been reported by the Institute of Economic Analysis that federal subsidization of "unprofitable enterprises" totaled 3 percent of the Russian gross domestic product (GDP) in 1994, while similar subnational government subsidization totaled 8 percent. See Aleksandr Bekker, "Eksperty schitaiut, chto biudzhetnyi defitsit mozhno svesti k nuliu v budushchem godu" (Experts believe that the budget deficit may approach zero next year), *Segodnia*, May 19, 1995.

138. Yelena Viktorova, "V Rossii snova poiavutsia 'zakrytye goroda' " (In Russia, "closed cities" are reappearing), *Segodnia*, Nov. 12, 1994.

139. "Mer Izhevska izbit piketshikami" (The mayor of Izhevsk is beaten up by picketers), *Kommersant-Daily*, June 28, 1995.

140. There have been numerous complaints that defense orders have not been subject to contract law and that the Defense Ministry can thus place orders without paying for them without suffering any consequences. See Colonel Yu. Chirkov (senior officer of the Center of Operational-Rear Services Research of the Rear Services of the Armed Forces), "Obespechenie vooruzhennykh sil i ekonomika Rossii" (Providing for the armed forces and the Russian economy), *Voenno-ekonomicheskii Zhurnal*, no. 6 (June 1994): 12–16; and Yu. Kolbakov and O. N. Dmitriev, "Kontseptsiia gosudarstvennogo regulairovaniia kontraktatsii na postavku voennoi produktsii" (The concept of state regulation of contracting for procurement of military products), *Voennaia Mysl'*, no. 8 (Sept./Oct. 1994): 71–75.

141. Valerii Baberdin, "It's Nearly July, but There's Still No Clarity," *Krasnaia Zvezda*, June 23, 1995, as reported in *FBIS-SOV*, June 28, 1995, pp. 27–30.

142. Author's interviews with advisers to a member of the Duma and a member of the Federation Council, Oct. 1994, Moscow. Also see Yefim Ya. Liuboshits (a retired officer from the Scientific Institute of the Rocket Forces), "Kak udalit' zhir iz oboronnogo buidzheta?" (How can the fat be removed from the defense budget?), *Segodnia*, Oct. 16, 1993; John W. R. Lepingwell, "A Sudden Fall from Grace," *Transition* (OMRI), Feb. 15, 1995, 26; and Doug Clarke, "Expert Calls for Reform of Military Budget System," *OMRI Daily Digest*, no. 154 (Aug. 9, 1995).

143. Wallich, *Russia and the Challenge of Fiscal Federalism*, p. 27.

144. T. Boiko and A. Lavrov, "Biudzhetnye otnosheniia v Rossii" (Budget relations in Russia), *EKO*, no. 1 (1995): 162–78; for a specific example, see the discussion of the Perm' oblast legislature's actions in "Protest prodolzhaetsia" (The protest continues), *Sankt-Peterburgskie Vedomosti*, Oct. 21, 1994.

145. Wallich, *Fiscal Decentralization*, p. 7.

146. Wallich, *Russia and the Challenge of Fiscal Federalism*, p. 57.

147. See V. Fedorov, V. Shirshov, and S. Boiko, "Struktura i mekhanizm nalogovoi sistemy" (Structure and mechanism of the tax system), *Ekonomist*, no. 11 (Nov. 1994): 25–37; and "Front 'budzhetnoi voiny' protianulsia ot Omska do

Vladivostoka" (The budget war front extends from Omsk to Vladivostok), *Sibirskaia Gazeta*, no. 36 (Sept. 1993).

148. Roy Bahl, "Revenues and Revenue Assignment: Intergovernmental Fiscal Relations in the Russian Federation," in *Russia and the Challenge of Fiscal Federalism*, p. 143.

149. I am grateful to Roy Allison for having suggested to me that Tatarstan might be a case where defense industry played a role in federal bargaining.

150. See Radik Batyrshin, "Tatarstan Has 'United' with Russia," *Nezavisimaia Gazeta*, Feb. 16, 1994, as reported in *Current Digest of the Post-Soviet Press 46*, no. 7 (1994): 11.

151. R. Rashitov, "Defense Industry Problems at the Center of Attention," *Respublika Tatarstan*, June 2, 1994, as reported in *FBIS-SOV*, June 6, 1994, p. 31; Tamara Zamiatina, "Russia-Tatarstan Treaty: Key to Political Stabilization," *Rossiiskaia Gazeta*, June 3, 1994, as reported in *FBIS-SOV*, June 6, 1994, pp. 20–21; Moscow Interfax, Sept. 27, 1994, as reported in *FBIS-SOV*, Sept. 18, 1994, p. 38; Yevgenii Ostapov, "Committee on the Defense Industry Collegium in Kazan," *Kommersant-Daily*, Sept. 28, 1994, as reported in *FBIS-SOV*, Sept. 29, 1994, p. 42; and Dmitrii Lukashov, "Prem'er-ministr Tatarii posle sta dnei u vlasti" (The prime minister of Tatarstan after 100 days in power), *Segodnia*, May 6, 1995.

152. Anatolii Yershov, "V nizhnem snova oruzheinaia yarmarka" (A weapons fair once more in Nizhnii), *Izvestiia*, Sept. 10, 1994.

153. Robert Orttung, "Tatarstan Has Stopped Making Payments to the Russian Budget," *OMRI Daily Digest*, no. 135 (July 13, 1995); and Orttung, "Tatarstan Stops Payments to Federal Budget."

154. Fedorov, Shirshov, and Boiko, "Struktura i mekhanizm nalogovoi systemy."

155. Wallich, *Russia and the Challenge of Fisal Federalism*, pp. 30, 38, 82, 85.

156. Peter Kirkow, "Regional Politics and Market Reform in Russia: The Case of Altai," *Europe-Asia Studies* 46, no. 7 (1994): 1176, notes that in the defense-heavy region of Altai, the item on the regional budget labeled "credits" was in fact loans from enterprises.

157. "Profsoiuzy sozdaiut stachkom" (The trade unions are creating a strike committee), *Sankt-Peterburgskie Vedomosti*, Mar. 17, 1994.

158. Denezhkina, "Is There a Future for Russia's Defence Industry?" p. 32.

159. Kharkhordin and Gerber, "Russian Directors' Business Ethic," p. 1086.

160. Aleksei Vorob'ev, "Sobchak obeshchal, chto 'izbieniia' direktorov ne budet" (Sobchak promised that there would not be a "slaughter" of directors), *Nevskoe Vremia*, June 18, 1994.

161. "Kto vy, doktor Sobchak?" (Who are you, Dr. Sobchak?), *Kommersant-Daily*, Mar. 17, 1995.

162. Valentina Shestakova, "Vlasti ne ostaviat 'oboronku' v bede" (The authorities have not left the defense complex in a calamity), *Nevskoe Vremia*, Jan. 14, 1995.

163. Dmitrii Gromadin, "Indiiskaia partiia peterburgskogo VPK" (The Indian Party of the St. Petersburg military-industrial complex), *Nevskoe Vremia*, Jan. 30, 1993.

164. Dmitrii Gromadin, "Kreditnye stradaniia" (Credit suffering), *Nevskoe Vremia*, Feb. 5, 1993.

165. Vadim Nesvizhskii, "V Peterburge prodolzhaetsia spad proizvodstva" (In St. Petersburg, the production fall continues), *Segodnia*, Feb. 26, 1994. This is higher than the 25 percent cited in Cooper, *The Soviet Defence Industry*, p. 24, based on information he found in a 1990 *Leningradskaia Pravda* article.

166. Gromadin, "Kreditnye stradaniia."

167. "Kredit 'razmorozhen' " (The credit is unfrozen), *Nevskoe Vremia*, Feb. 16, 1993.

168. Dmitrii Gromadin, "Novye igry pravitel'stva" (New games of the government), *Nevskoe Vremia*, Feb. 23, 1993.

169. Vadim Tiagniriadno, "Segodnia my perezhivaem finansovniui katastrofu" (Today we are living through a financial catastrophe), *Nevskoe Vremia*, Feb. 27, 1993.

170. Vadim Tiagniriadno, "Ne po obshchim zakonam" (Not by general law), *Nevskoe Vremia*, Apr. 2, 1993.

171. Ibid.

172. "Mer ne teriaet optimizma" (The mayor hasn't lost his optimism), *Nevskoe Vremia*, Apr. 21, 1993.

173. Kharkhordin and Gerber, "Russian Directors' Business Ethic," p. 1085.

174. Radio Rossii, May 22, 1992, as reported in *FBIS-SOV*, May 27, 1992, pp. 26–27.

175. Sergei Kraiukhin, "Georgii Khizha: 'I Represent Major Industrial Interests,' " *Izvestiia*, May 25, 1992, as reported in *FBIS-SOV*, May 27, 1992, p. 27.

176. ITAR-TASS World Service in Russian, May 19, 1993, as reported in *FBIS-SOV*, May 20, 1993, p. 24.

177. Almquist, "Arms Producers Struggle," p. 37; and Anders Aslund, *How Russia Became a Market Economy* (Washington, D.C.: Brookings, 1995), pp. 305–6. For some reason, Aslund reports that Khizha was sacked in December 1992, which does not accord with press reports about his career.

178. Aleksandr Bekker, "Krupneishee predpriiatie VPK vykhodit iz gossobstven-nosti" (The largest military-industrial enterprises are leaving state ownership), *Segodnia*, Nov. 2, 1993; and Nesvizhskii, "V Peterburge prodolzhaetsia spad proizvodstva."

179. Vadim Stasov, " 'Oboronka' narushaet obet molchanii" (The defense complex is violating the vow of silence), *Nevskoe Vremia*, Feb. 23, 1994.

180. "Profsoiuzy sozdaiut stachkom."

181. Andrei Vermishev, "Profsoiuzy vnov' piketiruiut smol'nyi" (The trade unions are picketing the Smol'nyi anew), *Nevskoe Vremia*, June 8, 1994.

182. A. Vorob'ev, "Vlasti dolzhnyi vypolnit' obeshchannoe" (The authorities should fulfill what has been promised), *Sankt-Peterburgskie Vedomosti*, Oct. 20, 1994.

183. Ibid.

184. The higher figure was provided by the trade union; the lower one by the police. See "Takogo Dvortsovaia davno ne videla," (Palace Square hasn't seen such a thing for a long time), *Sankt-Peterburgskie Vedomosti*, Oct. 28, 1994.

185. "Lozungi na Teatral'noi" (Slogans on Theater Square), *Sankt-Peterburgskie Vedomosti*, Oct. 28, 1994.

186. O. Steshenko, interview with Makarov, "K partnerstvu—cherez piketu" (Toward partnership through picketing), *Sankt-Peterburgskie Vedomosti*, Nov. 4, 1994.

187. "Ofitsilan'no" (Officially), *Sankt-Peterburgskie Vedomosti*, Jan. 6, 1995.

188. Shestakova, "Vlasti ne ostaviat 'oboronku' v bede."

189. "Kirovskii zavod gotovitsia k proizvodstvu avtobusov" (Kirovskii Factory prepares for production of buses), *Kommersant-Daily*, Mar. 15, 1995.

190. "VPK prodolzhaet gibnut' " (The military-industrial complex continues to perish), *Segodnia*, Jan. 18, 1995.

191. Robert W. Orttung, "A Government Divided Against Itself," *Transition* (OMRI), May 12, 1995, pp. 48–51.

192. See ITAR-TASS World Service in Russian, Mar. 24, 1994, as reported in *FBIS-SOV*, Mar. 24, 1994, p. 2021; State Duma Decree no. 99-1, "On Elections to the St. Petersburg City Assembly," *Rossiiskaia Gazeta*, Apr. 30, 1994, as reported in *FBIS-SOV*, May 4, 1994, pp. 17–18; and "City Assembly Finally Complete," *Sankt-Peterburgskie Vedomosti*, Nov. 1, 1994, as reported in *FBIS-SOV*, Nov. 8, 1994, pp. 29–30.

193. O. Steshenko, "Liudi razuverili' vo vsem" (People have lost faith in everything), *Sankt-Peterburgskie Vedomosti*, Apr. 27, 1994; idem, "Poka . . . nedoverie direktoru" (Still . . . no confidence in the director), *Sankt-Peterburgskie Vedomosti*, June 1, 1994.

194. Igor' Arkhipov, "Na kreslo Sobchaka t'ma pretendentov" (The ignorance of candidates to Sobchak's seat), *Kommersant-Daily*, July 8, 1995; and idem, "Democrats Prepare to Take Smolny," *Kommersant-Daily*, Feb. 15, 1996, as reported in *Current Digest of the Post-Soviet Press* 48, no. 7 (Mar. 13, 1996): 12.

195. Anna Paretskaya, "St. Petersburg Governor Appoints Deputy," *OMRI Daily Digest*, no. 111 (June 7, 1996).

196. Mark Granovetter, "The Social Construction of Economic Institutions," in *Socio-Economics: Toward a New Synthesis*, ed. Amitai Etzioni and Paul R. Lawrence (Armonk, N.Y.: Sharpe, 1991), p. 78.

197. Peter Rutland, "Defense Conversion Hopes in Sverdlovsk," *OMRI Daily Digest*, no. 27 (Feb. 27, 1996).

198. "Provintsial'naia khronika" (Provincial chronicle), *Segodnia*, June 29, 1995.

199. Galina Pechilina, ". . . i milost' k padshim prizyval" (. . . and called for mercy to the fallen), *Kommersant-Daily*, June 29, 1995.

200. See John M. Goshko and George C. Wilson, "U.S. Escalates Countermoves to Afghan Invasion," *Washington Post*, Jan. 22, 1980; and Serge Schmemann,

"Brezhnev Souvenir: Vast, Limping Truck Factory," *New York Times*, Feb. 4, 1983.

201. General Sergei Oslikovskii, first deputy director of Rosvooruzhenie, has made this argument; see Pavel Fel'gengaeur, "Yeltsin obeshchaet ne prodavat' oruzhie Iranu" (Yeltsin promises not to sell weapons to Iran), *Segodnia*, Sept. 29, 1994.

202. Author's interview with representative of the Russian Foreign Ministry Directorate on Conversion and Export Control, Sept. 1994, Moscow.

203. Leonid Zavarskii, " 'Rosvooruzhenie' Company Press Conference," *Kommersant-Daily*, May 21, 1994, as reported in *FBIS-SOV*, May 23, 1994, pp. 37–38.

204. Yurii Golotiuk, "Izgotoviteli MiGov proryvaiutsia na mirovoi oruzheinyi rynok" (The builders of MiGs breach the world weapons market)," *Segodnia*, Oct. 29, 1994.

205. Leonid Zavarskii, "Proizvoditeli oruzhiia pritselilis' v trekh zaitsev" (Weapons producers have aimed at three rabbits)," *Kommersant-Daily*, Sept. 24, 1994.

206. Pavel Fel'gengauer, "Rossiiskie 'stvoly' ishchut investerov" (Russian "gun barrels" are looking for investors), *Segodnia*, Sept. 24, 1994.

207. Doug Clarke, "Legal Problems of Arms Company Delays [*sic*] Exports," *OMRI Daily Digest*, no. 104 (May 30, 1995).

208. Viacheslav Chebanov, "Pavlu Grachevu trebuetsia 80 trillionov rublei v god, no on soglasen i na 60" (Pavel Grachev demands 80 trillion rubles a year but has agreed to 60), *Segodnia*, Sept. 15, 1994.

209. Aleksandr Temerko, interviewed by Valentin Rudenko, in "Finansovyi tupik" (Financial dead-end), *Krasnaia Zvezda*, Aug. 17, 1994.

210. See " 'Separatist' Regions Support Chernomyrdin Bloc," *Monitor* (Jamestown Foundation) 1, no. 66 (Aug. 3, 1995).

211. Mikhail Lantsman, "Predpriiatiia VPK stroiat kapitalizm s chelovecheskom litsom" (Enterprises of the military-industrial complex build capitalism with a human face), *Segodnia*, Oct. 16, 1993; and Konstantin Cheremnykh, "Nizhegorodskii balans" (The Nizhnii Novgorod balance sheet), *Sankt-Peterburgskie Vedomosti*, Aug. 10, 1994.

212. Boris Bronshtein, "KamAZ: One Year after the Fire," *Izvestiia*, Apr. 13, 1994, as reported in *Current Digest of the Post-Soviet Press* 46, no. 15 (1994): 23; and "Provintsial'naia Khronika" (Provincial chronicle), *Segodnia*, June 14, 1995.

4. Spin-offs and Start-ups

1. U.S. business literature defines the term *spin-off* as a divestiture having a particular ownership structure, distinct from equity carve-outs, split-offs, and split-ups; see J. Fred Weston, Kwang S. Chung, and Susan E. Hoag, *Mergers, Restructuring, and Corporate Control* (Englewood Cliffs, N.J.: Prentice Hall, 1990), pp. 224–25. The ownership structures of the small Russian enterprises I am analyzing here vary. The terms *spin-off* and *start-up* are accessible to a wide audience, and I use them to identify any small company arising out of a Russian defense industrial

enterprise, not to imply that all these firms are controlled subsidiaries with pro rata share distributions matching that of the mother enterprise.

2. Russian defense industrial managers themselves have recognized the necessity to spin off subdivisions to attract foreign investment. See "Aleksandrovskii radiozavod stanovitsia kholdingom" (The Aleksandrovskii Radio Factory is becoming a holding company), *Segodnia*, Nov. 11, 1994; " 'Permskie motory' preobrazuiutsia v kholding" (The Perm' Engine enterprise is transforming itself into a holding company), *Segodnia*, Dec. 15, 1994; and Arkadii Sosnov, interview with Il'ia Klebanov, general director of the LOMO enterprise, "Nash investor stoit u poroga" (Our investor is standing at the threshold), *Nevskoe Vremia* (St. Petersburg), Jan. 10, 1994. The point was also raised by Aleksandr Grigor'ev in an interview with the Stanford CISAC group, including the author, in September 1994.

3. For examples, see Nikolai Labutin, "Elektronnye igry Aleksandra Yemil'evicha—na blago komu?" (The electronic games of Aleksandr Yemil'evich—who benefits?), *Sorok Odin* (Zelenograd), no. 35/36 (1991); P. Alekseev, "Otpochkovalis' ot 'Angstrema' " (Propagated from Angstrem), *Sorok Odin*, no. 46 (Oct. 11–17, 1993); Mikhail Ul'iashchenko, "Chtoby sokhranit' umy" (In order to retain minds), *Inzhenernaia Gazeta*, no. 8 (Jan. 1992); and Sosnov, "Nash investor stoit u poroga."

4. Interview conducted by the CISAC group, including the author, at TsAGI, Sept. 1994.

5. For a thorough discussion of the history of consumer goods production by Soviet defense industries, see Julian Cooper, "The Civilian Production of the Soviet Defence Industry," in *Technical Progress and Soviet Economic Development*, ed. Ronald Amann and Julian Cooper (New York: Basil Blackwell, 1986). An example is the Arton joint-stock company in St. Petersburg; as a shop in its mother enterprise, the Arsenal Factory, Arton produced toy copies of Arsenal's military weapons. That line proved unprofitable, but Arton is now using the same equipment to produce gas pistols for civilian use. See Dmitrii Satsenko, interview with V. A. Sychev, director of AO Arton, "Gazovyi revol'ver: Rodom iz Peterburga" (The gas revolver: Born in St. Petersburg), *Nevskoe Vremia*, Feb. 13, 1993.

6. The Binar firm in Arzamas-16 reportedly makes an essential component for natural gas extraction that is based on technology developed by its mother enterprise, the nuclear weapons institute. See S. Mikhailova, "Formula Binara: Liudi + Tekhnika = Tovar Litsom" (The binar formula: People + technology = an advantage), *Gorodskoi Kur'er*, Dec. 2, 1993.

7. An example here is the Almaz Foreign Trade Company, which sells the satellite images it obtains using the equipment of its mother enterprise, Mashinostroenie, in Reutov. See Tova Perlmutter, Michael McFaul, and Jeffrey Lehrer, "The Mashinostroenie Enterprise," in *Defense Industry Restructuring in Russia: Case Studies and Analysis*, ed. David Bernstein (Stanford, Calif.:

Stanford University Center for International Security and Arms Control, 1994), p. 70.

8. For example, the local newspaper reported that in Arzamas-16, ten of the new small enterprises are "secret," which prevents authorities from the State Property Committee from examining the points of their founding agreements; another issue of the newspaper reports that two of the small enterprises are engaged in competitions to produce weapons for foreign customers. See "S gosudarstvennym imushchestvom, kak so svoim" (Treating state property as if it were their own), *Gorodskoi Kur'er*, Aug. 5, 1993; and Dmitrii Sladkov, "V teni bol'shogo utesa: O rabote malykh predpriiatii VNIIEF" (In the shadow of a great cliff: On the work of the small enterprises of VNIIEF), *Gorodskoi Kur'er*, Sept. 4, 1993. The manager of the ELVIS+ spin-off in Zelenograd, whose own firm is completely civilian, noted that a couple of the other spin-offs from the ELAS enterprise are engaged in defense orders for the Russian state (interview conducted by the Stanford CISAC group, including the author, Sept. 1994).

9. See Anders Aslund, *Gorbachev's Struggle for Economic Reform* (Ithaca, N.Y.: Cornell University Press, 1989).

10. Paul R. Lawrence and Charalambo A. Vlachoutsicos, eds., *Behind the Factory Walls: Decision Making in U.S. and Soviet Enterprises* (Boston: Harvard Business School Press, 1990), pp. 131–33.

11. For a detailed description of these incentives, see Simon Johnson and Heidi Kroll, "Managerial Strategies for Spontaneous Privatization," *Soviet Economy* 7, no. 4 (Oct.–Dec. 1991): 281–316.

12. Yu. A. Filimonov, "Kooperativy v mashinostroenii" (Cooperatives in machine building), *Mashinostroitel'*, no. 11 (Nov. 1990).

13. Johnson and Kroll, "Managerial Strategies," p. 287.

14. For an excellent on-site description of how this worked in a nondefense Russian enterprise in 1991, see Michael Burawoy and Kathryn Hendley, "Between Perestroika and Privatisation: Divided Strategies and Political Crisis in a Soviet Enterprise," *Soviet Studies* 44, no. 3 (1992): 371–402.

15. Johnson and Kroll, "Managerial Strategies," pp. 288–89.

16. See Maxim Boycko, Andrei Shleifer, and Robert W. Vishny, "Privatizing Russia," *Brookings Papers on Economic Activity* 2 (1993): 148–49.

17. For an example, see A. Vaganov, interview with Nikolai Vasil'evich Mikhailov, president of the Vympel interstate corporation, "Shans dlia novoi ekonomiki" (Chance for a new economy), *Inzhenernaia Gazeta*, no. 132/133 (Nov. 1992).

18. Arkadii Vol'skii, "Tendentsii" (Tendencies), *Moskovskie Novosti*, no. 14 (April 3–10, 1994). B. Sedunov commented on this article in "Proryv v direktorskom korpuse" (A breach in the directors' corps), *Sorok Odin*, Apr. 12, 1994.

19. See Aleksandr Privalov, interview with Sergei Beliaev, general director of the Federal Bankruptcy Administration, "Na to i federal'naia shchuka v more" (For

that, and a federal pickerel in the sea), *Kommersant*, no. 36 (Sept. 6, 1994): 6–9; and Peter Graff, reporting on economic adviser Peter Oppenheimer, in "Non-Payments Crisis Caused by 'Lawlessness,'" *Moscow Tribune*, Oct. 5, 1994.

20. V. Vladimirov, "Neplatezhni: Yesli oni narastaiut, znachit, eto komu-nibud' nuzhno?" (Insolvency: If it is growing, does this mean that someone needs it?), *Sankt-Peterburgskie Vedomosti*, Sept. 2, 1994.

21. These newspapers (*Sorok Odin* and *Gorodskoi Kur'er*) are now available at the Russian State Library Newspaper Reading Room in Khimki, just outside of Moscow.

22. Aleksandr Maliutin, "Ob'edinenie mozhet stat' kholdingom ili tekhnoparkom" (The association may become a holding company or a technopark), *Kommersant-Daily*, Sept. 21, 1994.

23. Alekseev, "Otpochkovalis' ot 'Angstrema.'"

24. V. Shishkin, "Budet li tret'em direktor Kvanta?" (Will there be a third director of Kvant?), *Sorok Odin*, no. 47 (Oct. 18–24, 1993).

25. I. Kataeva, "Krytoe pastbishche dlia kommersantov" (Sheltered pasture for businessmen), *Gorodskoi Kur'er*, Mar. 12, 1994.

26. David Bernstein and Elaine Naugle, "ELVIS+ and the Moscow Center for SPARC Technology (MCST)," in *Defense Industry Restructuring in Russia*, pp. 29–44.

27. O. Steshenko, "Poka . . . nedoverie direktoru" (Still . . . they have no confidence in the director), *Sankt-Peterburgskie Vedomosti*, June 1, 1994.

28. Mikhail Vasil'ev, "Investor ne vydast—Inflatsiia ne s'est" (The investor will not pay out—The inflation rate is not known), *Nevskoe Vremia*, Sept. 10, 1993.

29. "Griadut ser'eznye izmeneniia" (Serious changes are coming), *Novosti TsAGI*, no. 33 (1994). Zagainov's radio address on this theme took place on February 21, 1994.

30. See Tova Perlmutter, "Reorganization of Social Services," in *Defense Industry Restructuring in Russia*, p. 189.

31. Ye. Perekalin, "Bezrabotitsa, kotoroi ne dolzhno byt'" (Unemployment that shouldn't exist)," *Sorok Odin*, no. 15 (Mar. 29–Apr. 4, 1993).

32. Ye. Zubatov, "Direktora neispravimy; polozhenie nado ispravliat!" (The directors are irredeemable; the situation must be redeemed!), *Sorok Odin*, no. 29 (Aug. 1992).

33. Interview conducted by the Stanford CISAC group, including the author, Sept. 1994.

34. David Bernstein, "Organizational Restructuring," in *Defense Industry Restructuring in Russia*, p. 159.

35. Interview conducted by the Stanford CISAC group, including the author, Sept. 1994.

36. This was pointed out during one interview conducted by the Stanford CISAC group, including the author, Sept. 1994.

37. Interview conducted by the Stanford CISAC group, including the author, Sept. 1994.

38. Interview conducted by the Stanford CISAC group, including the author, Sept. 1994.

39. Alekseev, "Otpochkovalis' ot 'Angstrema.' "

40. Petra Opitz, "Institutional Aspects of Conversion—A Look at St. Petersburg," in *The Post-Soviet Military-Industrial Complex: Proceedings of a Symposium*, ed. Lars B. Wallin (Stockholm: Swedish National Defense Research Establishment, 1994), p. 93.

41. Some examples: The Permskie Motory aircraft engine plant turned itself into a holding company for fifteen independent enterprises, where it will hold 100 percent of the capital; see " 'Permskie motory' preobrazuiutsia v kholding" (Permskie Motory is transforming itself into a holding company), *Segodnia*, Dec. 15, 1994. TsAGI has split thirty subsidiaries into three categories; in the two most closely related to its core technology, it retains controlling ownership. See David Bernstein and Jeffrey Lehrer, "The Central Aerohydrodynamic Research Institute (TsAGI)," in *Defense Industry Restructuring in Russia*, pp. 9–28. The Mashinostroenie enterprise in Reutov owns between 45 and 100 percent of the shares of each of its privatized spinoffs (interview conducted by the Stanford CISAC group, including the author, Sept. 1994). The Arsenal company in St. Petersburg owns 20 percent of the stocks of each of its nine privatized divisions; see Sergei Tachaev, "Chto dast nam trast" (What will give us a trust), *Nevskoe Vremia*, Oct. 2, 1993.

42. Bernstein and Naugle, "ELVIS+ and the Moscow Center," p. 34.

43. "NIIMP ili NII Malykh Predpriiatii?" (NIIMP or the Scientific Institute of Small Enterprises?), *Sorok Odin*, no. 3 (Jan. 1993); and Maliutin, "Ob'edinenie mozhet stat' kholdingom ili tekhnoparkom."

44. Aleksandr Galitskii, interviewed by the Stanford CISAC group including the author, Sept. 1994.

45. Sladkov, "V teni bol'shogo utesa."

46. For examples, see Alekseev, "Otpochkovalis' ot 'Angstrema,' "; and Mikhailova, "Formula Binara."

47. Lynne Bennett, "Kings of Know-How: Transferring Technology from Research Laboratories to Business," *California Business* 28, no. 3 (Apr. 1993): 33.

48. Ibid.

49. Daniel J. McConville, "Intellectual Property Gains Respect," *Industry Week*, Mar. 7, 1994.

50. Bennett, "Kings of Know-How."

51. William B. Scott, "Tech Transfer Impact Remains Elusive," *Aviation Week and Space Technology* 141, no. 19 (Nov. 7, 1994): 42.

52. For example, see Michael A. Dornheim, "Public, Private Interests Vie in Cooperative Research," *Aviation Week and Space Technology* 139, no. 19 (Nov.

8, 1993): 49; and Christopher Anderson, "Rocky Road for Federal Research Inc.," *Science* 262, no. 5133 (Oct. 22, 1993): 496.

53. Sladkov, "V teni bol'shogo utesa."

54. Private communication, June 1995.

55. Bernstein and Lehrer, "The Central Aerohydrodynamic Research Institute," p. 20.

56. Interview conducted by the Stanford CISAC group, including the author, Sept. 1994.

57. Maliutin, "Ob'edinenie mozhet stat' kholdingom."

58. Labutin, "Elektronnye igry Aleksandra Yemil'evicha."

59. Ibid.

60. Ye. Perekalin, "Bezrabotitsa, kotoroi ne dolzhno byt' " (Unemployment that should not exist), *Sorok Odin*, no. 15 (Mar. 29–Apr. 4, 1993).

61. Ibid.

62. Ibid.

63. From an interview conducted by the Stanford CISAC group, including the author, Sept. 1994.

64. See Vladimirov, "Neplatezhni"; and Vadim Nesvizhskii, "Nalogovaia politsiia trebuet povysheniia statusa i polnomochii" (The tax police demand higher status and more authority), *Segodnia*, Nov. 26, 1994.

65. A. Lavrent'ev, "Ser'eznykh konfliktov s administratsei u nas net" (Serious conflicts with the administration are something we don't have)," *Sorok Odin*, no. 37 (May 17, 1994).

66. Dmitrii Sladkov, "Zadacha na delenie s neizvestnym otvetom: VNIIEF ÷ 3 =?" (A division problem with an unknown answer: VNIIEF ÷ 3 =?)," *Gorodskoi Kur'er*, June 12, 1993.

67. P. Gal'chenko, "Dogovor dorozhe deneg" (The contract is dearer than money), *Gorodskoi Kur'er*, Mar. 19, 1994. The front page of this issue is incorrectly dated November 11, 1993, apparently a printing error. The content of articles makes it clear that the events described took place in March 1994, not November 1993, and the correct date is printed on the inside pages of the issue.

68. S. Kholin, "Mnenie predsedatelia STKI" (The opinion of the STKI chairman), *Gorodskoi Kur'er*, Mar. 10, 1994.

69. Kataeva, "Krytoe pastbishche dlia kommersantov."

70. Sladkov, "V teni bol'shogo utesa."

71. "S gosudarstvennym imushchestvom, kak so svoim."

72. S. Kholin, "Kommertsiia—Privarok dlia rukovoditelei?" (Commerce—A food ration for the leaders?), *Gorodskoi Kur'er*, Mar. 12, 1994.

73. Petr Gal'chenko, "Zakliuchen kollektivnyi dogovor" (The collective contract is concluded), *Gorodskoi Kur'er*, Apr. 21, 1994.

74. V. Belugin, "VNIIEF finansiruetsia na 69%" (VNIIEF is 69% financed), *Gorodskoi Kur'er*, Apr. 21, 1994.

75. Interview conducted by the author in 1996.

76. "Printsipal'nye zamechaniia" (Principal remarks), a memo that apparently received the unanimous approval of the STK on June 29, reprinted in *Gorodskoi Kur'er*, July 31, 1993.

77. See the précis of a presentation by V. Belugin, in Dmitrii Sladkov, "VNIIEF ozhidaet perekhod na tematicheskoe finansirovanie" (VNIIEF awaits the switch to thematic financing), *Gorodskoi Kur'er*, Dec. 23, 1993; idem, interview with V. Belugin, "My budem rabotat' nesmotria na trudnosti" (We will work despite difficulties), *Gorodskoi Kur'er*, Jan. 13, 1994.

78. P. Khven', "Komandovat' paradom budu ya" (I will command the parade), *Gorodskoi Kur'er*, May 20, 1993.

79. Paul Milgrom and John Roberts, "Bargaining Costs, Influence Costs, and the Organization of Economic Activity," in *Perspectives on Positive Political Economy*, ed. James E. Alt and Kenneth A. Shepsle (New York: Cambridge University Press, 1990), esp. pp. 79–83.

80. For a discussion of the problems the closed cities face at present, including monopoly retail trade outlets, see Kimberly Marten Zisk, "Arzamas-16: Economics and Security in a Closed Nuclear City," *Post-Soviet Affairs* 11 (Jan.–Mar. 1995): 57–79.

81. See David N. Holt, David A. Ralston, and Robert H. Terpstra, "Constraints on Capitalism in Russia: The Management Psyche, Social Infrastructure, and Ideology," *California Management Review* 36, no. 3 (Mar. 22, 1994): 124.

82. Joseph S. Berliner, *Factory and Manager in the USSR* (Cambridge: Harvard University Press, 1957), pp. 40, 43.

83. Paul R. Laurence and Charalambo A. Vlachoutsicos, eds., *Behind the Factory Walls: Decision Making in Soviet and U.S. Enterprises* (Boston: Harvard Business School Press, 1990), pp. 70, 72.

84. Ibid., p. 72.

85. See, for example, Emily S. Plishner, "1993 Brings Bigger, Bolder Financial Moves," *Chemical Week*, Oct. 6, 1993, which focuses on divestiture by chemical manufacturers; and Evelyn Heitman and Shaker A. Zahra, "Examining the U.S. Experience to Discover Successful Corporate Restructuring," *Industrial Management* 35, no. 1 (Jan. 1993): 7, which cites the example of divestiture by the Burlington Industries textile company.

86. Arnoud W. A. Boot, "Why Hang on to Losers? Divestitures and Takeovers," *Journal of Finance* 47, no. 4 (Sept. 1992): 1401.

87. J. Fred Watson, Kwang S. Chung, and Susan E. Hoag, *Mergers, Restructuring, and Corporate Control* (Englewood Cliffs, N.J.: Prentice Hall, 1990), pp. 224–39.

88. An example of this is the policy followed by the Hyatt Hotel Corporation, which encourages its employees to pursue new business lines, such as catering, that

are outside its own core business. Employees receive start-up capital and advisory assistance but no equity. See D. Keith Denton, "Entrepreneurial Spirit: Employee Empowerment," *Business Horizons* 36, no. 3 (May 1993): 79.

89. An example is the Eastman Chemical Co. spin-off from Eastman-Kodak, where a new board of directors from outside was appointed. See Joe D. Goodwin, "Building an All-New Board," *Corporate Board* 15, no. 89 (Nov. 1994): 15.

90. Richard M. White Jr., *The Entrepreneur's Manual: Business Start-ups, Spin-offs, and Innovative Management* (Radnor, Pa.: Chilton Book Co., 1977), p. 84.

91. For example, according to Aleksandr V. Sokolov, executive vice president of ELVIS+, one-third of the firm's current employees were not part of the work group in the past (interview conducted by the Stanford CISAC group, including the author, Sept. 1994).

92. Interview conducted by the Stanford CISAC group.

93. Mikhailova, "Formula Binara."

94. I. Kataeva, interview with Stanislav S. Bochkanov and Tat'iana A. Fadeeva, "TOFIS: Ot zhvachki k supermarkety" (TOFIS: From chewing gum to a supermarket), *Gorodskoi Kur'er*, June 3, 1993.

95. Interview conducted by the Stanford CISAC group, including the author, Sept. 1994.

96. Tova Perlmutter, "Reorganization of Social Services," in *Defense Industry Restructuring in Russia*, p. 192.

97. Bernstein and Naugle, "ELVIS+ and the Moscow Center," p. 40.

98. Richard D. Harroch, *Start-up Companies: Planning, Financing, and Operating the Successful Business* (New York: Law Journal Seminars-Press, 1990), II-10.

99. Ibid.

100. Bernstein and Naugle, "ELVIS+ and the Moscow Center," p. 35.

101. Clifford G. Gaddy, "Notes for a Theory of the Paternalistic Russian Enterprise," unpublished paper prepared for the annual conference of the American Association for the Advancement of Slavic Studies, Nov. 1994, Philadelphia, Pa.

102. For example, when workers at the Polet aerospace enterprise in Omsk discovered that their director was making huge personal profit from the daughter companies he had created, with a salary level exceeding that of many of the workers by a factor of a thousand, they staged a "coup" against him while he was on a business trip to Moscow and convinced both Goskomoboronprom and the Omsk oblast administration to support his firing. See "Direktor 'Poleta' 'sletel' po vole trudiashchikhsia" (The director of Polet "flew away" by will of the workers), *Kommersant-Daily*, Apr. 15, 1995.

103. David Ellerman, "Spin-offs as a Restructuring Strategy for Post-Socialist Enterprises," in *Commercializing High Technology: East and West*, ed. Judith B. Sedaitis (Stanford, Calif.: Stanford University Center for International Security and Arms Control, 1996), p. 253.

104. Norman D. Williams, reporting data from the National Federation of Independent Businesses, in "Experts Offer Tips for New Ventures," *Sacramento Bee*, June 6, 1994.

105. Peter Rutland, "U.S. Computer Maker Halts Russian Production," *OMRI Daily Digest*, no. 42 (Feb. 28, 1996).

106. Interview with Mashinostroenie's deputy general director for personnel, Vitalii M. Chekh, conducted by the author, with the Stanford CISAC group, Sept. 1994.

107. Interview conducted by the Stanford CISAC group, including the author, Sept. 1994.

108. "S gosudarstvennym imushchestvom, kak so svoim."

109. Petr Khven', "Zakon surov . . . A surov li?" (The law is strict . . . Or is it?), *Gorodskoi Kur'er*, Jan. 29, 1994.

110. Author's interview, 1996.

111. Sladkov, "V teni bol'shogo utesa."

112. Veronika Romanenkova, "Uchenye Arzamasa-16 i Los Alamosa sozdali 'nedremliushchee oko' " (Scientists from Arzamas-16 and Los Alamos have created a "sleepless eye"), *Segodnia*, May 11, 1995.

113. Pavel Felgengauer, "To Live and Die in a Special Zone—Closed Russia," *Megapolis-Express*, July 22, 1992, as reported in *Current Digest of the Soviet Press* 44, no. 30 (1992): 12–13.

114. Zisk, "Arzamas-16."

115. A. Pokhil'ko, interview with Aleksandr K. Borodin, chief of the local bureau of the Russian Federal Counterintelligence Service, "Unikal'nost' ob'ekta i obilie sekretov opredeliaiut nashu rabotu" (The uniqueness of the installation and the abundance of secrets defines our work), *Gorodskoi Kur'er*, Apr. 21, 1994.

116. "Uchenye-atomshchiki navorovali izotopov na 48 milliardov rublei" (Nuclear scientists have stolen isotopes worth 48 billion rubles), *Moskovskii Komsomolets*, June 6, 1995.

117. See, for example, Vasilii Fatigarov and Aleksandr Mukomolov, "Submachine Guns Made by Crooks," *Krasnaia Zvezda*, June 22, 1994, as reported in *Foreign Broadcast Information Service Daily Reports—Central Eurasia* [FBIS-SOV], June 23, 1994, pp. 26–27; and Interfax, "Arms Manufacturing Ring Uncovered in Kazan," July 30, 1994, as reported in *FBIS-SOV*, Aug. 1, 1994, p. 31.

118. The report comes from Russian television investigative journalist Yurii Shchekochikhin, as reported in "Journalist: Russian Generals Sold Guns to Dudaev," Jamestown Foundation *Monitor* 1, no. 50 (July 12, 1995).

119. Anatolii Yershov and Igor Andreev, " 'Caspian Monster' Has Appealed to Spies for a Long Time," *Izvestiia*, Aug. 16, 1994, as reported in *FBIS-SOV*, Aug. 16, 1994, pp. 26–27.

120. Interview with a member of VNIIEF's financial management team, conducted by the author in 1996.

121. Sergei Serafimov, "Terrorist podorvalsia na sobstvennoi bombe" (A terrorist blows up with his own bomb), *Kommersant-Daily*, Mar. 28, 1995.

122. Quoted in Penny Morvant, "Leading Arms Designer Murdered," *OMRI Daily Digest* 2, no. 58 (Mar. 21, 1996).

123. Sergei A. Kholin, interviewed by ITAR-TASS, "Priostanovit' osobo opasnye raboty" (Especially dangerous work will be stopped), *Gorodskoi Kur'er*, July 29, 1993.

124. "Provintsial'naia khronika [Provincial Chronicle]," *Segodnia*, June 16, 1995.

5. Conclusions and Implications

1. James R. Millar writes, for example, that reformers and their Western advisers were "led astray" because of their belief in the efficacy of rational choice, among other things; see "From Utopian Socialism to Utopian Capitalism: The Failure of Revolution and Reform in Post-Soviet Russia," *Problems of Post-Communism* 42, no. 3 (May–June 1995): 7–14. He states, "To one steeped in the rationality of the marketplace it is difficult to imagine why a transactor would not maximize profits if presented with the opportunity, but there is plenty of evidence that Russian managers have not done so" (p. 9). The rest of his article, however, completely supports the analysis presented here and stresses the importance of holdover Soviet political institutions that structure managerial behavior. It appears that Millar has simply defined "rational choice" more narrowly than has the literature on positive political economy.

2. See the essays by W. Carl Kester, "American and Japanese Corporate Governance: Convergence to Best Practice?" Yutaka Kosai, "Competition and Competition Policy in Japan: Foreign Pressures and Domestic Institutions," and Wolfgang Streek, "Lean Production in the German Automobile Industry: A Test Case for Convergence Theory," in *National Diversity and Global Capitalism*, ed. Suzanne Berger and Ronald Dore (Ithaca, N.Y.: Cornell University Press, 1996).

3. David M. Kreps, "Corporate Culture and Economic Theory," in *Perspectives on Positive Political Economy*, ed. James E. Alt and Kenneth A. Shepsle (New York: Cambridge University Press, 1990).

4. See the discussion and literature review on this point by Friedrich V. Kratochwil, *Rules, Norms, and Decisions* (New York: Cambridge University Press, 1989), pp. 21–94.

5. For an interesting discussion about how the real human thought process affects the assumptions of the neoclassical economics model, see Robin M. Hogarth and Melvin W. Reder, eds., *Rational Choice: The Contrast Between Economics and Psychology* (Chicago: University of Chicago Press, 1986).

6. The scholars who have most contrasted prospect theory with pure rational choice are Amos Tversky and Daniel Kahneman; see their "Rational Choice and the Framing of Decisions," in *Rational Choice*. For an example of econom-

ics scholarship that is compatible with prospect theory (even though it does not speak in terms of framing), see Raquel Fernandez and Dani Rodrik, "Resistance to Reform: Status Quo Bias in the Presence of Individual-Specific Uncertainty," *American Economic Review* 81 (Dec. 1991): 1146–55.

7. See William H. Riker, "Political Science and Rational Choice," in *Perspectives on Positive Political Economy*, p. 172, who gets around the problem nicely by saying that the assumed set of choices includes all the choices that the actor believes are relevant.

8. Terry M. Moe, "Political Institutions: The Neglected Side of the Story," *Journal of Law, Economics, and Organization* 6, special issue (1990): 213.

9. See Michael McFaul, "State Power, Institutional Change, and the Politics of Privatization in Russia," *World Politics* 47 (Jan. 1995): 242; and Michael D. Intriligator, with Robert McIntyre, Marshall Pomer, Dorothy J. Rosenberg, and Lance Taylor, "Letters to the Editor: Checklist for Action in the Russian Economy," *Transition* (World Bank newsletter) 6, no. 9–10 (Sept.–Oct. 1995): 11.

10. The arguments of these paragraphs are explored in more depth in Kimberly Marten Zisk, "The Foreign Policy Preferences of Russian Defense Industrialists: Integration or Isolation?" in *The Sources of Russian Foreign Policy after the Cold War*, ed. Celeste A. Wallander (Boulder, Colo.: Westview, 1996).

Index